920
HYA   Hyatt, Richard.
         The Carters of Plains.

	DATE DUE		

1990

This Book presented to the

CHURCH LIBRARY IN MEMORY OF

Tom P. Bell

BY

Nora and Wayne Stovall

Code 4386-23, No. 3, Broadman Supplies, Nashville, Tenn. Printed in USA

BELL

Tom Bell, Tomball, Texas passed away Sunday, Aug. 19, 1990. Preceded in death by his only son Richard "Gridiron" Bell in 1981. Survived by loving wife, Doris; two daughters, Tommie Maynard and husband Phil, Doris Merrifield and husband Earl. Seven grandchildren, Tammy Miller and husband Mark, David Rudel and wife Deanna, Rich Rudel and wife Cindi, Elisa, Jim and Melanie Gayle, Jamie Howard. Five great grandchildren, Joshua Miller, Sara and Aaron Provost, Chris and Ashley Rudel; two sisters and one brother, mother-in-law, Oris Capps. Interment Klein Memorial Park. Klein Funeral Home & Cemetery.

THE
CARTERS
OF
PLAINS

PLAINS, GA.
Jimmy Carter
PRESIDENTIAL
CAMPAIGN HEADQUARTERS
Carter Country Tour

THE CARTERS OF PLAINS

By

Richard Hyatt

THE STRODE PUBLISHERS, INC.
HUNTSVILLE, ALABAMA 35802

Photographs courtesy of Al Alexander (pages 199 and 256); Roger Grigg (pages 97, 98, 118, 148, 159, 280, 282, and 283); Allen Horne (pages 67, 69, 71, 75, 77, 78, 81, 83, 91, 148, 191, 200, 204, 220, 234, 255, and 261); Joe Maher (pages 100, 134, 143, 157, 166, 179, 230, 245, 247, and 298); Lawrence Smith (pages 2, 14, 23, 49, 61, 68, 79, 81, 87, 92, 120, 121, 124, 126, 131, 132, 135, 136, 137, 139, 141, 145, 146, 149, 151, 154, 155, 156, 161, 163, 165, 169, 172, 174, 175, 176, 180, 181, 183, 184, 185, 190, 203, 207, 213, 218, 225, 226, 228, 237, 238, 240, 246, 258, 259, 263, 264, 268, 272, 273, 278, 281, 285, 286, 289, 291, 292, 294, 295, 296, 297, 303, 305, 306, 308, 311, 313, 314, 315, and 317); Richard Thomason (page 210); the Columbus *(Georgia)* Ledger-Enquirer *(pages 18, 20, 21, 24, 25, 26, 28, 31, 32, 33, 35, 36, 40, 44, 46, 48, 49, 50, 51, 52, 54, 56, 57, 58, 59, 64, 80, 83, 194, 196, 198, 201, 209, 215, 222, 223, 227, 235, 241, 251, and 253); WSB-TV, Atlanta, Georgia (pages 64 and 72); and by the author (pages 104-107, 109, and 112-116).*

Copyright 1977
By Richard Hyatt
All Rights In This Book
Reserved Including The Right
To Reproduce This Book Or Parts
Thereof In Any Form—Printed In U.S.A.
Library of Congress Catalog Number 76-58240
Standard Book Number 87397-117-5

To Peggy...whose encouragement is between every line

Acknowledgments

If space would permit listing the 683-person population of Plains, it would be appropriate to thank them all, for they opened their doors and were gracious hosts. To a reporter who sometimes felt he would be added to the voting list in Plains, they became familiar faces.

It is difficult to overlook the helpfulness of Maxine and Buford Reese, C. L. and Sandra Walters, all of those named Carter who live in Plains, and the sharp-witted fellows who spend their evenings at Billy's service station. The counsel and support of John and Betty Pope of Americus and Bo and Billie Cosby of Preston, Georgia, will not be forgotten either. Special thanks should go to Milton Jones of Columbus, the first true believer in Jimmy Carter I heard saying he might really become President.

Acknowledgment also should be made to Executive Editor Carrol Dadisman of the *Columbus* (Georgia) *Ledger-Enquirer* who gave permission to use "Miss Lillian at the Convention," on which he collaborated with the President's mother. Thanks are also due to Ralph Morris, formerly of the *Columbus Ledger*, who seven years ago wrote the definitive newspaper biography of Jimmy Carter, and to Jack Swift, Mrs. Beverly Greer, and Mrs. Nita Massey, who donated their watchful eyes to the editing.

Finally, there is Lawrence Smith, chief photographer of the *Columbus Ledger-Enquirer*. His photos are evident throughout, and he served as photo consultant for this book. But he did more than open and close his shutter. His advice, prodding, and interest will not be forgotten.

Contents

Introduction

Part I: JIMMY CARTER

1. "It's A Boy" For Earl 17
2. A Carter Shall Not Lie 27
3. Suddenly He Became "Mr. Jimmy" 37
4. The Unforgettable Miss Julia 45
5. A Homecoming In Plains 62
6. Progress For A Georgia Turtle 73
7. Jimmy's Running For What? 90
8. Peanuts Can Grow In New Hampshire 103
9. Clearing One More Hurdle 111
10. The Coronation Of Jimmy Carter 123
11. Politics In Their Own Back Yard 142
12. The End And The Beginning 153
13. "Don't It Make You Proud?" 160
14. The Greening Of Plains 171

Part II: THE CARTER CLAN

15. Miss Lillian: She's Everybody's Mother 189
16. Billy Carter: Baron Of The Beer Cooler 212
17. Amy Carter: Lemonade And Freckles 233
18. Rosalynn Carter: A Wife And A Partner 249

19. Gloria Carter Spann: At Home In Plains 266
20. Cousin Hugh And Uncle Buddy: Worms And Antiques 270

    Part III: A TIME FOR "AMAZING GRACE"

21. A High-Priced Cameraman 277
22. The Impossible Dream Comes True 287
23. Returning To Reality 307
24. There's Even A Red Light 312

    A Quick Glance At The Carters Of Plains .319

Introduction

Into every Southern babe is born a trace of paranoia, a paranoia that warns you that folks outside the South—you know, those Damn Yankees—are out to fleece you.

From the cradle we've been taught that Yankees are to be mistrusted. Our mamas pointed to 100 years of history; to that most famous of firebugs, Bill Sherman; to those who came bearing carpetbags; to that rascal Earl Warren who had the nerve to tell us to open up our schools to black children. And if we didn't believe mama, just look at what those Yankees did to Scarlett O'Hara.

It's not uncommon to find this disease outside of Dixie, although the symptoms are somewhat different. Many Northerners picture a massive plantation south of Richmond. The living is easy and the cotton is high. Living on their plantation are a few Ladies and Gentlemen, sipping mint juleps out on the veranda.

But they're outnumbered by a strange breed of slow-talking, slow-thinking, slow-moving folks commonly referred to as "Red Necks," also known as "Crackers" or "Good Ole Boys." This quirk of nature travels by pickup truck, a rifle balanced on the rack in its back window. He smokes Camels, wears white socks, drinks Blue Ribbon beer, and the roof of his barn urges one and all to "See Rock City First."

These are the overdone extremes, the stereotypes. But a century after the final curtain was drawn on the Civil War, every battle is being replayed over and over again in the minds of many. Ferget, Hell! North's still North. South's still South. And never the twain shall meet. Not even time has been able to fully erase the Mason-Dixon Line.

Politically, the South rejoined the Union over 100 years ago. Our Senators sat next to their Northern neighbors, and because of Congress' seniority system a few of them grew into well-known figures around Washington.

Many were like Lil Abner's comical but real Senator Phogbound. With buttons popping over an overgrown belly, they would shut their eyes to certain things as long as somebody threw their district an occasional bone. Getting reelected was no problem. If they could go home around election time and holler "Nigger" louder than their opponent, they could take out a lifetime lease in Congress.

Georgia had some notable exceptions to this stereotype, namely the late Sen. Richard B. Russell and former Rep. Carl Vinson. They were gentlemen first and politicians second. But back home, the state was under the spell of leaders like suspender-popping Gene Talmadge. A four-time governor, he called himself the best friend the people had—next to Sears and Roebuck and Jesus Christ.

Ole Gene would take to the stump, pop his red galluses, and prey on the people's natural fear of their black neighbors. Since the state had an all-white primary system, this was the thing to say. With the antiquated mode of politics known as the County Unit System (a ploy to give rural Georgia a louder voice than the urban areas) controlling the outcome, folks like Ole Gene held control for decades.

It is this history that leads you to believe that the stately old columns of the gold-domed state capitol shook when a newly inaugurated governor spoke these words seven years ago: "I say to you quite frankly, that the time for racial discrimination is over. Our people already have made this major and difficult decision. No poor, rural, weak or black person should ever have to bear the additional burden of being deprived of the opportunity of an education, a job, or simple justice."

The speaker was James Earl Carter, Jr., known to the folks back home simply as Jimmy. His voice was calm and controlled, seeming to take no special note of his executive proclamation to end segregation and to end a tradition as old as the new governor's own 200-year-old Georgia roots. But the rest of the country did take note. Jimmy Carter became a cover boy on Time *magazine and a frequent spokesman for what was being called still another rebirth of a New South.*

But one thing was not so new about this South. Though they sometimes were able to pull a few strings, Southerners were still out of the political mainstream. They were a little like Cinderella—appreciated while they were doing the work but told to stay home when it came time for the ball. Sometime during his four years in Georgia's governor's mansion, Jimmy Carter decided to see if his foot wouldn't fit the Glass Slipper.

Jimmy Carter wanted to be President.

A few of his lieutenants were told of his plans, but Carter's desire was a well-kept secret. Not even his mother, Mrs. Lillian Carter, was told until after the strategy was set. Her reaction was typical of most of his Georgia neigh-

bors.

"I'm going to run for President," he told her.

"President of what?" she wanted to know.

When the formal announcement came on December 12, 1974, no newspaper presses were stopped and no TV stations interrupted another "I Love Lucy" rerun to inform viewers that Jimmy Carter was going to run for President. Why should they? Who was this Carter? Or as the Atlanta Constitution—largest daily newspaper in Georgia—headlined an editorial page column: "Jimmy Carter's Running for What?" No one took him seriously, figuring he would gladly settle for a shot at Vice President or, at the least, a run for the Senate.

People back home found it difficult to think of one of their own in the White House. It was that paranoia again, that feeling that the rest of the country was looking down their dignified noses at Dixie. Presidents were names in history books, faces on the six o'clock news. Until recent years, we had seen those who would be President only in election years, and often times not even then.

A President was a cut above the rest, a politician from some faraway place, from a town we have never visited. For a man from Plains, Georgia, to say he wanted to be President seemed a futile dream. After all, wasn't this the same guy who had fussed and fought with Lester Maddox all over the state capitol? Wasn't this the fellow who promised us that four-lane highway to Atlanta and didn't deliver? And he wants to be President?

It was hard for those of us back home to realize that we were looking at him through the same kind of eyes that neighbors in Michigan might look at a Gerald Ford. This was a new game. And we were playing without a rule book.

Sure, Jimmy Carter had opened a string of campaign offices. He even had a slogan. He was traveling around the country making speeches whenever anybody would listen, though only a few would. He called himself a candidate. But did this make us offer to help him pack his bags for Washington? Hardly.

For me the realization that my neighbor was indeed a candidate came on a wintry, snowy day in New Hampshire in January 1976. Covering an enthusiastic band of Georgians—later to be known as the "Peanut Brigade"— on their maiden invasion of a foreign state for their man Carter, I was shocked to see an equally enthusiastic group of New Hampshire Democrats waiting at the Manchester Airport.

During the next four days, that invasion force of 100 Georgians— bundled up with layers of long Johns, sweaters, scarves, and anything else they could find—personally contacted over 18,000 Democratic households, reaching in the process some 40,000 potential Carter voters.

Back home the only sign that Carter was even running came from out-of-town reports. But walking down an icy, snow-banked street in Nashua, New Hampshire, I saw Jimmy Carter's smiling face looking at me from a sign in somebody's front yard. It was an eerie emotion. These people seemed to know something those of us so close had overlooked.

It was a hospitality you don't find often in this supposedly hospitable South to hear a voice scream out the kitchen window: "You fellows from Georgia?" She could probably tell that by the way Columbus, Georgia, attorney Milton Jones negotiated the next doorsteps.

"You working for Jimmy Carter?" she asked.

In a few moments we were sharing the warmth of her kitchen and her steaming coffee. She turned out to be a Carter supporter, and the vote the following month showed she was not alone. The former Georgia governor carried faraway New Hampshire.

But the visitors that week learned as much about themselves as they did about politics. Sitting on the plane returning to Georgia, Dean Fowler, a nursing home executive from tiny Montezuma, summed up the attitude.

"You know, if those people didn't talk so funny, I'd think they were from Georgia," Fowler drawled in his best South Georgia accent. And so they were. So were the people of other faraway villages. Dixie was opening up its eyes and finding that despite the fact that a New Hampshire store owner talks differently than a Georgia shop owner, they think alike in many ways; that despite the snow on the ground, a dairy farmer in Wisconsin is interested in much the same things as a peach grower in Alabama. It had taken 100 years, but at last we were opening our eyes and looking at one another.

This attitude continued as Carter methodically moved toward his goal. His winning streak in the primaries carried him to the Democratic nomination in July. In November, 51 percent of the voters said they wanted Jimmy Carter to be their President.

For the first time in over a century, the South—which knew so little about birthing a president—had borne one. Not some harborer of hate, holding on to a set of decaying ideals. Not some favorite son folks hoped would send a message. This was no message. This time the South was sending a President.

It was a victory earned not only by the white Southerner but by his black neighbors. Old feelings, though not completely erased, can be shelved. George Wallace and Martin Luther King, Sr., could indeed support the same candidate. It made us proud, damn it, made us proud.

What will it mean in the future? Hopefully, the immediate result will be a laying aside of that old resentment, that old paranoia. A century of mutual mistrust has been overcome. Maybe we will now be able to accept one *another for what we are, not for what we think we are.*

Early in Jimmy Carter's meteoric rise to the presidency, his hometown neighbors were lining the streets of Plains to welcome him back from a primary victory. Mrs. Maxine Reese, the mother hen of Carter politics back home, stood on a flat-bed truck that had been turned into a speaker's stand and told one and all that "Plains is willing to share Jimmy Carter with the rest of the country."

This is what those 24 months of wearying work were all about. Sharing. Sharing of ideas. Sharing of needs. Sharing of goals. Sharing of dreams. Sharing of compassion. This book traces Carter's steps through those two years of campaigning and looks at the region that spawned him. It is not told through the eyes of a visitor or a tourist. It is told by those who know best the Carters of Plains.

A year ago in New Hampshire, an eight-year-old boy in the Nashua campaign office took advantage of a question-and-answer session to ask candidate Carter a question. It drew laughter, but it may have been the most serious question of the campaign.

"Mr. Carter, when did all of this stuff begin?" inquisitive David Desnoyers wanted to know.

Carter knelt to talk to this future voter.

"David, it all began about 200 years ago when Americans decided to elect their leaders instead of taking orders from a king. Every four years they look over the candidates and decide who they want to lead them," he answered.

In 1976 Jimmy Carter, a peanut farmer from Georgia, was the man America chose. Hopefully this book will explain to David Desnoyers where all of this stuff began.

Richard Hyatt
Columbus, Georgia

The man of Plains who went for the big one and caught it.

Jimmy Carter

"It's A Boy" For Earl

The pace is slow and leisurely. When the clock strikes Wednesday afternoon, the doors in most of the stores are locked, and folks head for home. Family trees grow tall. Roots run deep. There are no strangers living here. When you want to talk, you visit—not phone. A sleepy railroad crisscrosses the town, only occasionally waking from its slumber for a lonely freight train to whistle through.

To 683 people this is home. This is Plains, Georgia.

Nestled along U.S. Highway 280—55 miles from Columbus and nine miles from Americus, if that will help—downtown Plains is a row of stores, single file, across the railroad tracks from the main highway. There is a grocery store, a dry goods store, an antique store, and the office for what has to be one of the country's few worm farms. The buildings date back to the early days of this century when Plains was still a toddling infant.

Down the street is another grocery and a drug store, along with two of the newer buildings—a branch office of an Americus bank and the post office. On the other side of the street is a fresh-faced old train depot. When Jimmy Carter began his campaign for President, his neighbors turned the depot into his hometown headquarters.

Around town you can see the results of this campaign. Most of the stores offer a complete line of Carter souvenirs: T-shirts, pictures, jewelry, buttons of all descriptions, anything anybody around town can find that has the Carter name on it, anything that resembles a peanut.

One tourist even offered Randy Coleman, an employee of the Carter Peanut Warehouse—the town's chief industry—$5 if he'd cut the Carter patch off his shirt. Laughing, Coleman ended up selling the woman the shirt off his back.

While tourism has become a new source of income, the town's business—its only business—is agriculture. And the primary crop is peanuts.

Narrow, straight rows of peanuts collide with the horizon when you ride the roads around town. The countryside is untouched by the tourist invasion, although some of the farmers take sadistic pleasure in educating "cityfied" visitors to the fact that peanuts don't grow on trees or bushes but are found at the plant's root.

The heart and soul of the area is its churches. Five minister to the 683 people who call Plains home—three of them are white, two are black. There was a Baptist church here 42 years before the depot was raised as the town's first building. This is the Bible Belt, and the town itself got its name from the Old Testament. Daniel called the place where the Babylonian king Nebuchadnezzar raised a golden image of himself Plains of Dura. Through the years, people here shortened it to Plains.

In the beginning there were Carters. The first of the flock, James, Sr., emigrated from Ireland to North Carolina, moving to Georgia in the 18th century, fighting for the state militia in the Revolutionary War. McDuffie County, near the South Carolina border, was then the Carters' home but following the Creek Indians they moved South.

This was Main Street in Plains as Earl Carter saw it in 1904.

By the turn of the century, the Carters were in Cuthbert, Georgia. William Alton Carter, Sr., had bought up acres of raw timber land and was doing a brisk business in railroad ties. William and Nina Carter had five children—Alton, Jr., Ethel, Lulu, Earl, and Janette. They might have stayed in Cuthbert except for a night in 1903 when William Carter argued with Will Tolliver, a business partner, over who owned a desk. Tolliver shot Carter dead in the streets of tiny Arlington, Georgia. Though barely 16, Alton Carter—who witnessed the shooting—overnight became head of a family of five.

Alton didn't know where to turn. He was too young to work the crew of blacks who leveled the family timber, and the land was spread out over most of the surrounding counties. Finally he decided to sell the business and, moving by mule train, the family headed for Sumter County where their late father owned land. They first moved to Americus, but by 1904 they had settled in Plains, nine miles away.

Young Alton Carter showed an eye for the dollar sign and began buying up land around his new home. Paying $2.50 to $5 an acre, he soon owned over a thousand acres. By 1909 he also had opened a general store. Later he would be mayor. Six decades later he still tends shop with his son Hugh at their antique store on Main Street.

"I tried retirement. It wouldn't work," he says, so at 88 Alton Carter still drives into the hard-clay driveway behind their spacious old store every morning, reporting for work. He describes work as a family trait.

"That's the way I tried to raise my brothers and sisters. If they kept busy, they wouldn't get into things. Make 'em mind. Keep 'em busy. All us Carters have a reputation for being hard-headed, too. When we set a stake, we go after it," the white-haired, slightly built Alton Carter says.

And to a young Earl Carter the stake he went after had a dollar sign. After attending Riverside Military Academy in Gainesville, Georgia, and serving in World War I, he came home to open a general store of his own— just like his brother's—right up Main Street. The money he made was put into land which was sharecropper planted and turned into peanuts and other saleable crops.

"Earl was one of those men who turned everything he touched into dollars...nothing shady I mean, he just had a natural streak of finance in him," Alton recalls. Soon he had enough money to think of starting a family of his own.

Walking into a dance at Magnolia Springs, a popular resort near town, Earl met the girl he had been looking for. She was small, with dancing hazel eyes foretelling her personality, the perfect girl to go with his sturdy build and strong will. She wasn't a local girl, being a defector from Richland, 19 miles away. In Plains to study nursing under the Doctors Wise at their clinic,

Everything Earl Carter touched turned to dollars.

her name was Lillian Gordy.

That was 1920. Later Earl mailed an engagement ring to Atlanta, where she was studying at Grady Hospital. Two years later they were married. Half a century later Lillian Gordy Carter says they "kind of drifted together and grew to love one another." They moved their love into an upstairs apartment on Church Street near the Carter store, which by then included any item residents of Plains might need.

Lillian Carter continued her nurses' training at the Wise Clinic, the closest thing to a hospital in the peanut-growing table-top farmland. The Wise doctors—Burr Thaddeus, Samuel Paul, and Burr Thomas—were respected throughout the state. They are now dead, and their clinic later became a nursing home. But in the early 1920s their 25-patient facility on Hospital Street was a center of modern medicine.

It was there, about 7 a.m. on October 1, 1924, that Earl and Lillian's firstborn arrived. "It's a boy," Earl Carter boasted to his friends, the boy he had been wanting so badly. A smile creased his face as he walked through town telling one and all. The fleshy-red baby, all seven pounds, two ounces, of him, was quickly named James Earl Carter, Jr. No one was surprised. Everyone figured the baby would bear his father's name.

This was Earl's day.

Jimmy was a year old when he posed for this.

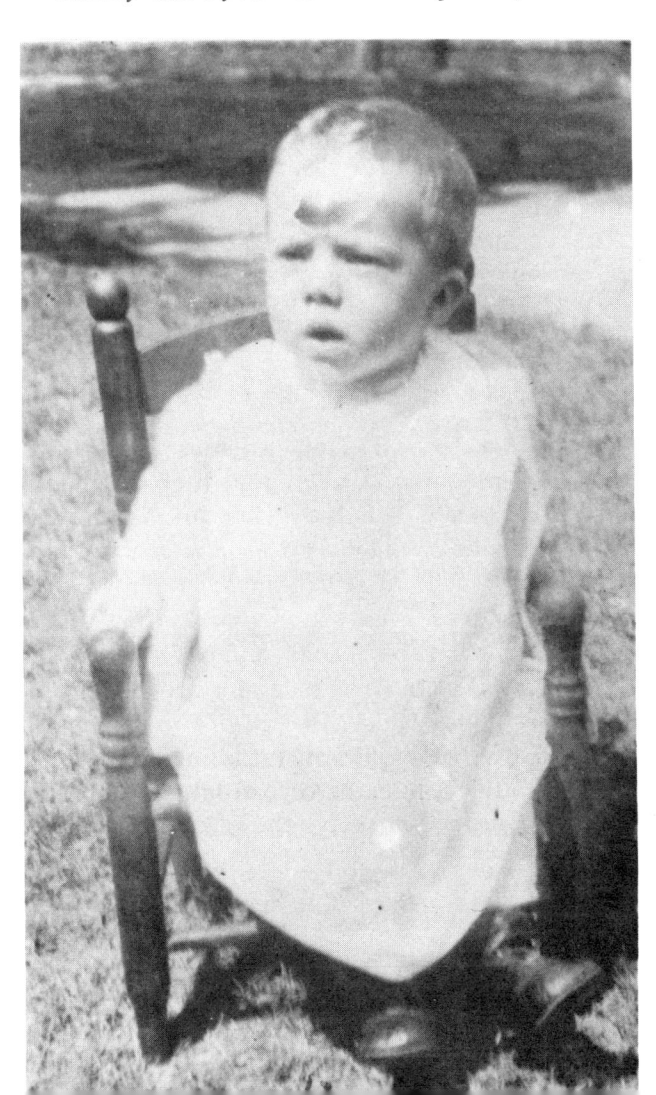

In the next five years the Carter family was to grow by two—Gloria in 1926 and Ruth in 1929. It was to be 13 years after Jimmy's arrival before William Alton—to be called Billy—was born, named after his grandfather and his Uncle Alton. But during that October day in 1924, Earl Carter was thinking only about his new son, already planning all that they would do together.

Lillian's nursing specialty had been childhood diseases, and Jimmy soon gave her an in-the-home test. Jimmy was crying loudly, and his mother knew he was hurting badly. She rushed him to the Wise Clinic, where the doctors determined that the two-year-old was suffering from colitis, an intestinal infection that inflames the colon.

"The doctors couldn't do much for him," his mother now remembers.

Neither could the nurses, although Mrs. Gussie Howell had an idea she could. "What do you want more than anything else?" she asked the freckle-faced patient, tears welling in her eyes.

This, she learned, was not a big decision. He hardly needed to think. "A Billy-goat," Jimmy answered.

Mrs. Howell quickly found one and hurried back to the hospital. Tying up the goat, she put him in a box right in Jimmy's room. His eyes brightened, but not even a new friend could ease that burning inside.

A specialist was called in from Atlanta, a friend of the Wises. Not even the well-trained visitor could help. He agreed with the local doctors that little could be done. Desperate by now, the family called an old country doctor from Oglethorpe, Georgia, remembered now only as Dr. Derrick. One glance brought a diagnosis.

"Give him cornstarch and an enema repeatedly," the old doctor ordered. Improvement came shortly. The family had met its first crisis. Another was soon to come.

This time it was the loss of their home. Everyone tried to help, but the Carter house on Bond Street in Plains was destroyed by fire. Earl Carter had to find them a new home.

Their new home was to be a clapboard house on the old Plains-Preston Road, an unpaved superhighway that at that time was the main road connecting Columbus, Savannah, and the many miles of Georgia which lay between. It was three miles outside of Plains in Archery, a railroading village now as dead as the Americus-Preston & Lumpkin Railroad it once served.

The six-room farmhouse was the perfect setting for an adventurous four-year-old. There were chinaberry, oak, and pecan trees standing guard by the house, perfect for shade, treehouses, and a tire swing. A spacious, open field was next to their home, which, like all of the neighboring houses, had no electricity or indoor plumbing. Franklin Roosevelt had not yet turned the switch on the TVA, so the Carters did their reading by kerosene light. In the yard was a parade of chickens, ducks, geese, and dogs, picking and digging in

The Carter home was three miles from Plains.

the sandy topsoil. Out back was a small barn, and nearby was a blacksmith shed where Earl shod the family's horsepower.

The nearby woods opened new spots to explore. Little Jimmy began to love walking through the peaceful woodland, a habit he still enjoys. On one of these walks his father was along. Coming to a small spring-fed pool, about six feet long, four feet wide, and four feet deep, Earl picked up four-year-old Jimmy, tossed him into the cool water, and simply told him, "Swim, son, swim."

And he did.

The Carters figured their growing son needed someone to play with, so they offered him one of the squirrel dogs Earl raised, but Jimmy had his eye on a Boston bull he called Bozo. His new friend followed his red-haired master everywhere, and soon he became known as the best hunting dog in Sumter County.

"Bozo was a good squirrel dog," Jimmy Carter remembers. "I stayed

When you found Jimmy, you usually found animals.

Fences couldn't keep Jimmy away from Lady.

This friend was as big as eight-year-old Jimmy.

Jimmy and Bozo walked the fields together.

with him so much that when I'd be picking cotton or putting soda on corn, he'd be working around the edge of the field hunting squirrels."

When he was seven, "Baby Dumplin"—he got this nickname from the old "Blondie" comic strip—got a new friend. It was his birthday, and his folks told Jimmy to go out in the yard and see what his present was. It was a small female pony which Jimmy soon named Lady. With Bozo running behind, Jimmy and Lady became a familiar sight along the dusty roads around his house.

However, by this time young Jimmy Carter had already discovered there was more to life than hunting squirrels, swimming in the pond, or riding his pony. Earl Carter worked hard, and he expected his family to be there working with him.

A Carter Shall Not Lie

Before the old clock in the living room could finish striking four, folks in the Carter house would already be scurrying. The echoing of a big bell on the back porch would see to that. A hearty breakfast of eggs from their usually generous chickens, biscuits, ham, and bacon or sausage soon would be on the table. No one was shy about eating his share for everyone knew a day of work was ahead.

Before the sun punched its time clock, Earl and Jimmy—working by lantern light—would have gathered up the mules. They would join the sun in the fields, ready to plow row after row of cotton, corn, or peanuts. If it was harvest time, they might be down on their knees, straining every muscle in their backs, pulling and shaking peanuts.

When he wasn't at work in the soil himself, Jimmy would help the black youngsters who joined them in the fields, sharing the loads of water brought from the well. Sometimes they would turn vines, tote watermelons, or do whatever chore they were told to do. Work was done in streaks—not for the sake of the workers but to offer the mules a needed rest.

One of the jobs Jimmy would often get was poisoning boll weevils. It was a chore no one enjoyed, although Mrs. Carter thinks Jimmy secretly may have for reasons only a boyish mind knew.

Earl and Jimmy would mix molasses with arsenic. Covering the ends of sticks with cloth, then dipping them into the potent, deadly mixture, they would walk the long rows of cotton. The stalks would be covered, letting the crude concoction soak in. The molasses would stick to the plants and carry the poison to the heart of the stalks and the unwanted weevils.

"Jimmy's pants would be stiff from the molasses, so stiff you couldn't even fold them. But every afternoon, when he got home from school and would be heading for the field, he'd put on those same pants. He seemed to enjoy wearing them," his mother says, with a knowing smile.

Mrs. Rachel Clark's husband Jack was the Carters' foreman, and the 88-year-old black woman still remembers those long days in the hot Georgia sun.

As a youngster Jimmy would often study her techniques in the field. After all, he still says, "she picked more cotton than anyone on the farm." He not only wanted to learn. He wanted to compete. "He never did get where he could beat me, though, but he was pretty good," Mrs. Clark says.

"Those days in the field are the most vivid memories I have of growing

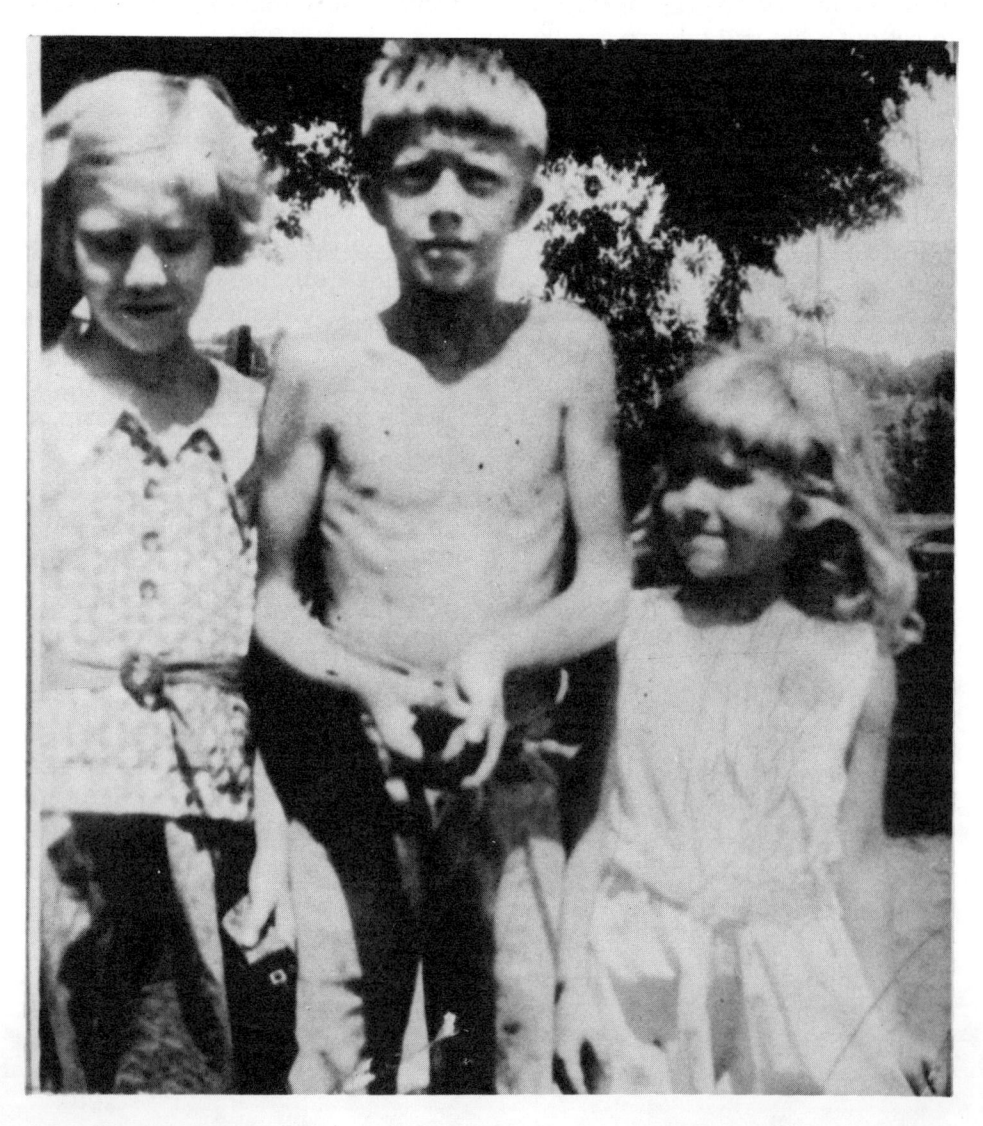

Gloria (left) and Ruth flank brother Jimmy.

up," Carter recalls. "I'd be tired, but I would feel a great satisfaction at the end of the day, knowing I had done all I could that day as a human being."

Earl and Jimmy would return home by wagon, the same way they had gone, turning the mules out to graze before they headed for the house. Riding along they'd talk, like pals, not father and son. Earl, you see, was Jimmy's best friend. Sometimes Earl would push his hat back on his head and hand the reins to his young friend. Around America it was said that a Depression was going on, but that was grownups' business. To a young boy, all he knew was that Earl Carter was his daddy and all was well.

During his presidential campaign Carter would dwell on the poorer side of his childhood. As his mother says, "He makes us sound so poor you want to get out a hat and take up a collection."

But theirs was a life of Sumter County's landed gentry. They had 4,000 acres and 300 blacks who depended on them for their very existence. They weren't rich, not by the world's standards. But they weren't poor, not by Sumter County standards.

It was nevertheless a big day when the lights came on. FDR was president, and the Tennessee Valley Authority was bringing electricity to a section of the country that before had depended on the sun, moon, and kerosene for light. At first it was a novelty. Soon they learned it was to mean much more.

"When we got through working hard in the fields, we had always had to come and pump water for the livestock. When Daddy bought us a pump, it took away a lot of the drudgery from farming," Jimmy remembers.

Not all of it, though.

Poor they were not, but Earl Carter honored a dime as much as he did a dollar, and he intended for his family to learn to respect money, too. So by the time he was five Jimmy was in business for himself. His get-rich scheme involved, naturally, peanuts.

He would go out in the fields in the late afternoon and pull up the peanuts, taking them home to shake and wash. The next morning he and his mother would boil them, then put them in small paper bags. The rest was up to Jimmy. He'd head for Plains to hawk his peanuts on the downtown streets.

"I'd walk to Plains, about two or two and a half miles down the railroad tracks. I'd gross about a dollar a day, which was pretty good money during those Depression days. It didn't take me long to separate the good folks from the bad folks. The good folks would buy peanuts from me. The bad ones wouldn't," he remembers.

A veteran businessman by the time he was nine or ten, he looked for a way to expand. He needed new capital and new help, so he turned to his cousin Hugh, about four years older than he and one of his closest pals. They became partners.

"We did a little bit of everything. We sold old newspapers to the grocery man to wrap mullet in. We sold scrap iron. We helped my daddy with the inventory down at his store.

"You see, our folks didn't know anything about allowances. They expected you to work. I think this is part of the reason for Jimmy's success. He learned right quick the value of work and the value of a dollar," says Hugh Carter, who now holds his cousin's old seat in the Georgia Senate.

Jimmy and Hugh's prime business was in fast foods, Depression-style. For in those years Plains and the rest of the world had not yet been introduced to the neon-cooked food we stand in line for today. They continued to stock peanuts, but diversified into hot dogs, hamburgers, ice cream, and occasionally fruit cakes.

"We'd get up real early on Saturday mornings and start to get things ready," Hugh remembers. "We'd sell ice cream in those old double cones, a nickel a scoop. We sold it from the front of the old bank building my daddy owned. The bank had gone under when they started folding up and wasn't being used for much of anything else.

"We sold hot dogs and hamburgers for a nickel each. Jimmy and I would make our own slaw, too, way back in the back of the bank on a long counter. Jimmy would always sell boiled peanuts. At Christmas time we'd usually sell fruit cakes," says Hugh, now the owner of an antique store in Plains and nationally known himself as the owner of the Carter Worm Farm.

Although the two youngsters occasionally would hitch-hike to Americus to catch a double feature, their fathers kept close tabs on their profits.

"His daddy kept all of the money Jimmy made," Lillian Carter says. "Later Earl bought Jimmy a bale of cotton, and when the price went way up he sold it and bought four houses and rented them for Jimmy."

Years later the money from that cotton and the houses it bought was to be used to buy an engagement ring for pretty, shy Rosalynn Smith.

The boys became crafty businessmen, quickly learning that the "Eagle flew on the third Friday." They discovered that the neighboring farmers, who in the Southern tradition always came to town on Saturdays, would be joined in the marketplace by the wage earners, pockets jingling with money they might want to spend.

"The town would be working alive with folks," Hugh says, the vision of dollar signs still dancing in his eyes. "We could expect that to be our biggest day every month."

Life was not all dollars and cents, however. Despite their business success, Jimmy and Hugh knew their daddies were still in charge.

Take their hair. When it reached a certain prescribed length, Earl or

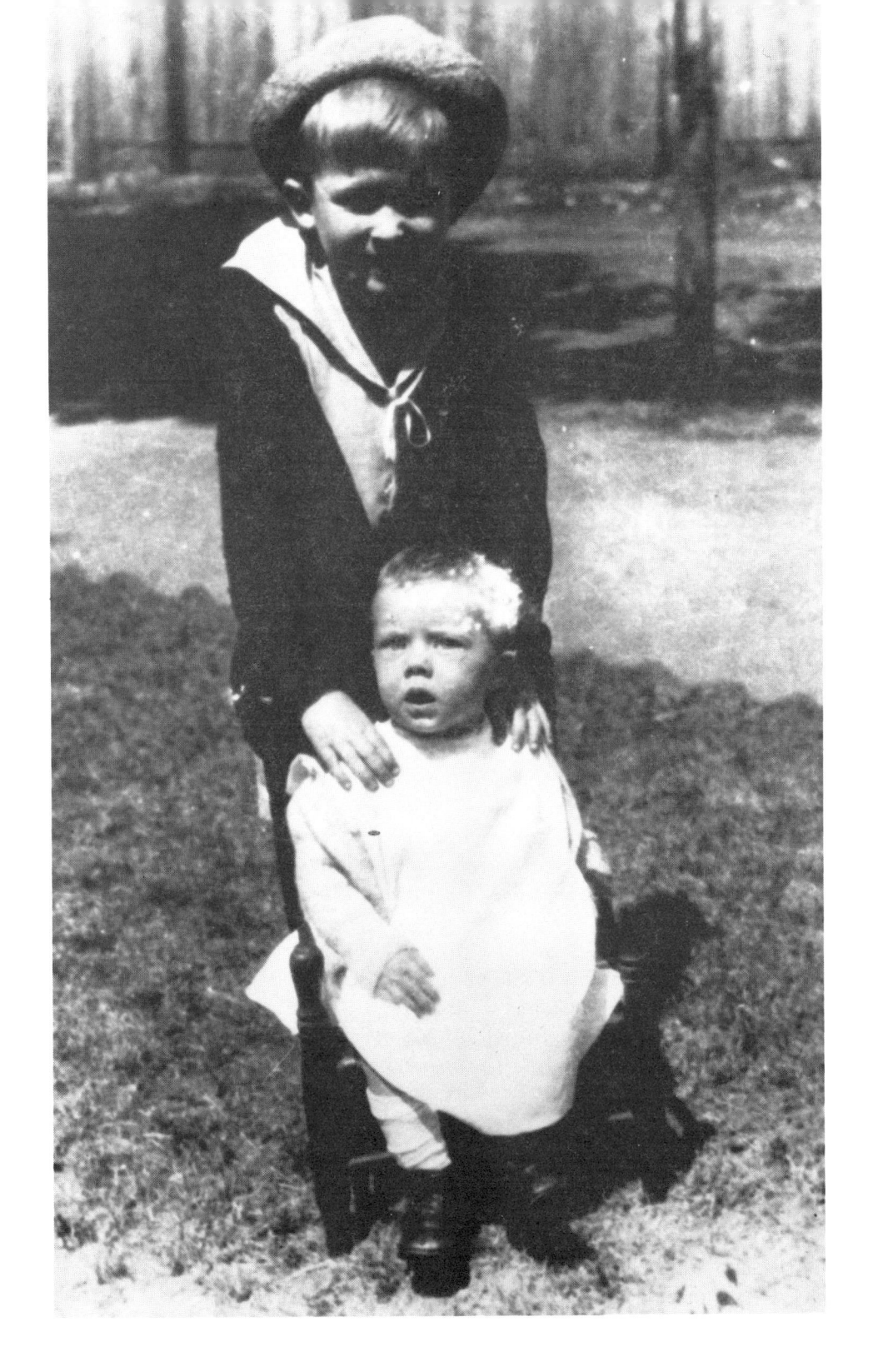

Hugh was a big brother to his younger cousin.

Jimmy already had his famous smile.

Earl Carter made Gloria, Ruth, and Jimmy bashful.

Jimmy, 5, and Gloria, 3, were peaceful here.

Alton would take his son by the arm and lead him not to the barber shop but to the barn. There were no razor cuts or blow dryers in those days, just mule clippers.

One particular Friday, Earl stopped Jimmy to inspect his red hair. This was a special occasion. Jimmy was going to spend the next few days in Columbus visiting his grandparents, and Earl wanted to be proud of him.

So they went out under the chinaberry tree near the barn, and Earl began to cut...and cut...and cut...and cut. There was no way to camouflage the gaps. Even an embarrassed Jimmy agreed that all they could do was cut off the rest of his hair. When the shearing was complete, Earl found Jimmy a hat to wear. The hat and the young bald head became instant companions.

Jimmy stayed with the Gordys for over a week, and when Lillian drove to Columbus to pick him up she asked her mother what she thought about her grandson.

A puzzled Mrs. Gordy answered. "Well, he's a wonderful boy, but there's something kind of strange about him. He stayed up here all this time, and he never has taken off that hat."

There was always time for out-of-doors fun. Earl had always been known as the town's best tennis player. He even built a court near their house so he could keep the edge on that wicked serve of his. He passed on this love of sports to his young namesake.

He taught Jimmy respect for a rifle and how to hunt. He showed him how to fish in the swampy areas around their home. Sometimes they'd even go on overnight and weekend fishing trips to the Little Satilla River, near Hortense in South Georgia.

Try as he might, Jimmy had yet to down his first quail. Finally, he decided he had to try it on his own. Returning to the fields, armed with the .410 shotgun his daddy had given him and a compass he had bought, he bagged his first quail. He had to show his daddy.

"I ran all the way. Daddy looked at it for a long time and finally asked me where my gun was. It took us two days to find it. I had thrown it down out in the woods. I was that excited," Jimmy says.

When he wasn't at school, running his business, working in the fields, or hunting with Bozo, Jimmy's thoughts turned to that favorite pastime of any boy with two younger sisters. Gloria and Ruth became his targets. And one episode with Gloria turned her into a target in the literal sense of the word.

"She threw a wrench at me, so I shot her in the rear end with a BB gun. For the rest of that day, she'd burst into tears every time she'd hear a car. When daddy finally drove up, she turned on her tears and ran to him. Daddy whipped me without further comment," Gloria's older brother says.

There were to be other unscheduled appointments with Earl's peachtree discipline. A plea for matches to burn down the barn caused Earl to cut a switch another time. A threatened runaway caused Jimmy to feel the sting of the peachtree as he got this warning: "Next time you try that, take everything you have with you. And don't come home 'cause you're scared of the dark." But Jimmy's most painful appointment came on a Sunday morning.

As usual Earl had given Jimmy a penny to put in the collection plate when it was passed by. Jimmy still remembers what happened when his daddy looked at the change his son had put on the bedroom dresser.

"I had taken off my Sunday clothes and emptied my pockets out. There were two pennies lying on the dresser. Daddy knew right away what I had done. When the collection plate was passed, I had taken a penny out instead of putting mine in. That was the last money I ever thought about stealing," he says.

Earl handled the discipline, ruling with a heavy but fair hand. And according to Miss Lillian, he stressed that a Carter shall not lie, not if he or she wanted to sit comfortably.

"Daddy would let them get away with just about anything before he'd put up with any one of them telling him a lie. I always told them they should do what they thought was right. Don't worry about what others think—do what you think's best, " Lillian Carter says.

Earl's word stuck with Jimmy Carter. Two decades after his father's death, he was promising America that he'd never tell a lie, never disappoint them. And all the time he may have been feeling the memory of that whistling peachtree switch.

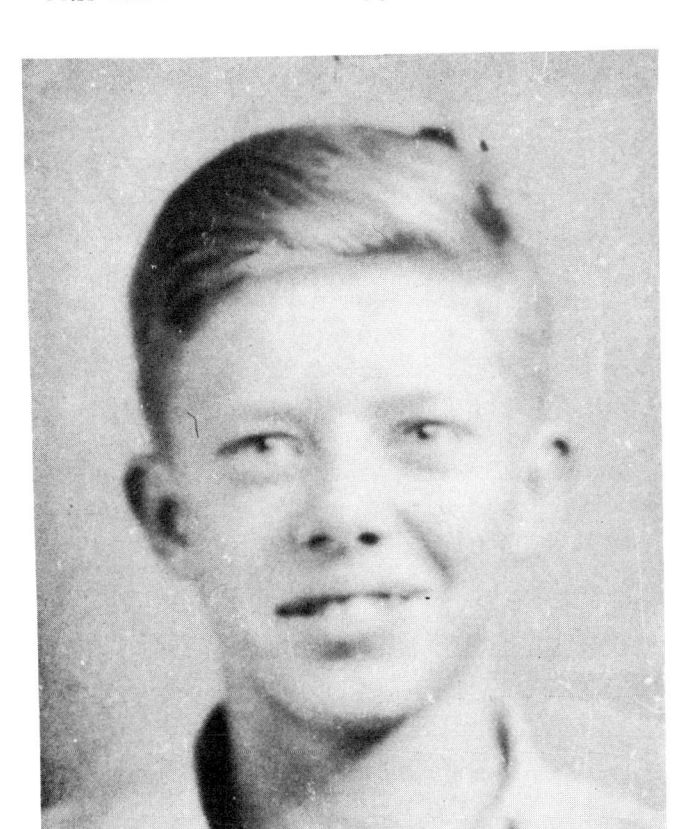

Miss Lillian said he was a typical country boy.

15-year-old Jimmy enjoyed life at summer camp.

Suddenly He Became "Mr. Jimmy"

Sunday morning down South was a quiet, peaceful time, the dewy stillness interrupted only by the ringing of the bell in the church steeple. This was the Sabbath, and folks kept it holy. Work was put aside. Worries were stored away until Monday. The only activity you'd find was mothers trying to convince little boys that ears did need washing.

Their religion and their God played an important part in everyone's life around Plains. Four decades before there was a building in the town there had been a church, the Lebanon Baptist Church. In those days whites and blacks worshipped together, a practice that didn't change until the Civil War. When it did change, the whites left the original church to the blacks and built the Plains Baptist Church, a block away from the railroad tracks on Bond Street. This was the church the Carters called home.

A family's church was more than a place to wear your Sunday-go-to-meeting best on the Sabbath. It was the center of social, even political life, the place a person looked to not only for his solace but for his recreation. It was a place where you heard about Jesus, the place where you heard about next week's picnic, the place where you would meet and court, the place you'd look to in your times of need. When the bell would ring on Sunday morning, the Carters usually would be there.

"Some of our first memories are in Sunday School and church. We were raised as Christians and taught right from wrong, as soon as we were old enough to know it," Hugh Carter says. Today Hugh is the song leader and church clerk, while his cousin Jimmy is a deacon and teaches the men's Sunday School class when he's home, although he's now a member of the First Baptist Church of Washington.

Jimmy Carter was born in faith and reared by the Golden Rule, instilled with that New Testament work ethic that teaches believers that God will bless the toils of their labor. To some this may seem an unusual foundation, but it was the buttress for most of the young people who grew up with him. This was the Bible Belt, and God was at the head of every home.

In Sunday School the youngsters would hear the familiar Bible stories—climbing Jacob's ladder, Jesus and the money changers, about Shadrach, Meshach, and Abednego, that trio who rebelled against the wicked King Nebuchadnezzar—about all of the biblical heroes.

In the eleven o'clock services folks would hear about the wages of sin, the fires of Hell, and the gold-paved streets of Heaven. Between the crackling brimstone and the shiny pavement, there was little choice. That's why no one was surprised when young Jimmy Carter walked down the church aisle, shook hands with the Rev. Royal Callaway, and welcomed Jesus into his heart.

He was born again, 11 years old and born again. When political reporters generations later heard that expression, they were puzzled. But in Plains, the definition is plain. Jimmy Carter had accepted Jesus as his personal Savior and had become a Christian. God had adopted him into His family.

It was a time of love...love of his God in Heaven, of his mother, of his stern father, of his teacher Miss Julia, of his brother and sisters, of his playmates. Jimmy Carter looks back on this time as a period when his world was stable. In an interview with newsman Bill Moyers in May 1976 he explained his feelings.

"I had a stability there. You know, when things started going wrong in my life, my mother and father were there; and my sisters and brother were there; and the church was there; and my community was there—which never did change, never has changed yet—but there was something there around which I built my life.

"In the modern-day world, you don't have that. It's a mobile world, and things to cling to are kind of scarce and few and far between. And which one of those advantages and disadvantages is the greater, I don't know.

"I wouldn't swap the life I had for the new, modern, fast-moving, open, non-structured, minimal family life, but there are advantages now I know— more and earlier traveling, having a tighter interrelationship with your own peer group than I had—but which is best, I don't know.

"But maybe we can go back to some of those old principles that we knew when we went to BYPU (Baptist Young People's Union) on Sunday afternoon...and at the same time keep the advantages of the modern world, but going back to those principles that give stability are things that we're still searching for. We haven't found them yet," Carter told the commentator.

That stability was felt at home, too. His was a Bible-reading family. They asked the Lord to bless their food before eating and said their prayers at night. Jimmy began teaching Sunday School himself in his high school years and continued to teach even after he was a midshipman at the U.S. Naval Academy. This his mother discovered when the family went to Annapolis for his graduation in 1946.

"We were invited to the admiral's house for lunch. I thought this was a tradition, that all of the parents were invited. But when we got there, there was only one other set of parents there. It seems Jimmy had been teaching Admiral Ingersoll's children in Sunday School all the time he was there, and they wanted to tell us how much they appreciated him," Lillian Carter says.

During those days when he was hearing the Bible stories for the first time, young Jimmy discovered things he could understand.

Bible stories taught him to love his neighbor, to help folks who weren't as well off as he was, to treat his neighbor as his brother. Jimmy Carter was sensing something that wasn't taught in Miss Julia's class or talked about in Sunday School. But it was a fact of life, a way of life.

This side of life down South wasn't talked about or instilled in the young, it just happened. If a black person ate food off a white family's table, he ate on the back porch, out of an old, cracked dish, drinking out of an old Bama Jelly jar. If they were riding in a car, the black naturally got in the back seat. At the theater, blacks went to the rear of the balcony. White youngsters just accepted this as fact. As far as they knew, maybe blacks enjoyed eating out back or sitting upstairs at the theater. Nothing was questioned.

In the railroading village of Archery there were more blacks than whites, but though they were outnumbered whites ran the place. Blacks were expected to tip their hats to "Mr. Earl or Miz. Lillian," and when he came of age they were to do the same to "Mr. Jimmy."

To most folks the blacks were simply "niggers," or in the Southern dialect, "nigras." Today the word is demeaning and inhumane, but to many of the whites of the 1930s—and even today—it's just their way of saying Negro. Black has been a difficult word to learn. However, in the Carter household "nigger" was a four-letter word. Lillian Carter forbade it. She taught her children to address their black elders as "uncle" and "aunt."

On the eve of Jimmy Carter's election as President a controversy arose in his home church, and the knife that cut the membership apart was the Reverend Bruce Edwards' contention that the Plains Baptist Church by-laws contained the word "nigger." The question became public when a black activist minister, The Reverend Clennon King, drove 40 miles from Albany and sought to join the church.

In 1965 the church had voted not to admit blacks—a move the Carter family fought bitterly, Jimmy Carter driving all the way from Atlanta to vote again.

Standing outside the church the Reverend Edwards told a crowd of reporters that the 1965 by-law used the term "nigger." Later that week he apologized, correcting his statement.

Mrs. Annie Mae Hollis cared for the Carter children.

"When I said that, I hadn't read the by-laws for myself. I was going by what a deacon told me, and I misunderstood him. The by-law doesn't say 'nigger,' a word I abhor," the Reverend Edwards said.

Carter again spoke out on the question, and this time the church voted to welcome blacks to its services—something it had been doing throughout his presidential campaign—and to refer any membership applications to a watch-care committee. Emotions overflowed during the service that Sunday morning. Tears flowed, and a few tempers overflowed, too. Race is still a delicate question down South, just as it was when Jimmy Carter was a boy. A month after Carter's inauguration, those same tempers exploded, forcing Edwards to resign his pastorate.

The difference in the Carter home was Lillian Carter. She nursed black children just as she would whites. She shared with blacks as she would with her white neighbors. She taught her children to do likewise. These were decisions Earl Carter couldn't understand, but Lillian Carter maintains that had her husband lived he would have put aside his conservative views, too.

This was far from the minds of the youngsters in Archery, however. All Jimmy knew was that A.W. Davis was the best friend he had. That A.W. Davis happened to be black mattered not.

"He was the only white boy who played with us black boys," says Davis, now 50, the father of 14 children, and a mill worker. "See, Jimmy and them were raised up with nothing but colored people. He ain't never acted like he was more than somebody because he was white."

Even for them there were to be stark reminders.

A.W. Davis went along with the Carter children to a movie in Americus, and Mrs. Carter seated the black youngster beside her own children downstairs. Midway through the movie they noticed that A.W. was gone, gone to the darkness of the upper balcony.

"Why did you go back up there?" Miss Lillian wanted to know.

" 'Cause I didn't see nobody in there colored but me, and I decided to go up there where colored folks sit."

Then there was the day Jimmy came of age, the time when all good little black boys were expected to address him as 'Mr. Jimmy." A.W., by then an accepted member of the family, told his friend he didn't know if he could do it.

"I don't blame you. I wouldn't either," Jimmy told him.

As far as Mr. Earl went, however, all was still right in the world, and blacks had best stay in their place. But he would turn his head, even resorting to going out back, when he'd see someone like Alvan Johnson, son of the local African Methodist bishop, coming to visit. Johnson was Boston-educated and would invariably come to the front door, a breach of Southern etiquette that was the talk of the community. But he was always welcomed by Jimmy and his mother. Later as President-elect, Carter shared a pew at the Plains Baptist Church with Johnson.

Jimmy Carter now tells of one particular evening which typifies the type of respect there was between Archery's blacks and whites. It was the night of the second Louis-Schmeling fight. The big German had defeated Alabama-born Joe Louis in their first fight, and the eyes of the world turned to Yankee Stadium for their rematch.

This was more than a championship fight. Max Schmeling was a German, the epitome of Hitler's Aryan elite. The Fuehrer proclaimed him invincible, especially against an American black man.

That was the reason the world was watching; Southern blacks watched for other reasons. Joe Louis was their symbol. He showed what a black man could do with his talents, how he could rise above the resentment and roadblocks. If he lost—they lost.

The fight was being broadcast, and blacks and whites from around town gathered in the Carter yard to listen. The radio was propped up in the window, and folks stood around under the trees outside.

Anyone who arrived late probably missed the fight. Joe Louis destroyed the German in the first round. He was black, and he was champion of the world.

As the visitors started to leave, they sensed the disappointment swelling in Earl Carter. "Thank you, Mr. Earl," were the only words spoken.

But when they were across the tracks, near their own homes, the blacks began to scream and yell. They celebrated Joe Louis's victory as their own. The world had a new champion. They had a hero.

Yet, standing around that old radio, the old courtesies and amenities were not forgotten. Neither the blacks nor Mr. Earl would show disrespect for the other. That was saved for a private moment.

Such was life in Archery and in the South.

At a Law Day address at the University of Georgia in 1974, Jimmy Carter told a childhood story that summed up the bitter inner struggle faced by the South when it considered its generations of dealing with its black neighbors.

"Our home was right across the road from the Seaboard Railroad track. Like all farm boys, I always had a flip or slingshot. I used the little white rocks in the railbed for ammunition. I would frequently go out to the railroad and gather the most perfectly shaped rocks of proper size. There were always a few in my pockets and others cached away around the farm so they would be convenient if I ran out of my pocket supply.

"One day I was leaving the track with my pockets and hands full of rocks, and my mother came out on the front porch and called me. She asked, 'Honey, would you like some cookies?'

"I stood there about 15 or 20 seconds, in honest doubt about whether I should drop those worthless rocks and take the cookies which Mother offered me with a heart full of love," he told the university audience.

Such was the decision Southerners had to make. Whether to put down the worthless old hate and enjoy the fruitful future or to hold on to the stones of the past. In some minds, there is still that honest doubt.

As a young businessman returning to Plains in 1953, he withstood not-so-subtle hints that it would be best for his business that he join the White Citizens Council. The people dropping the hints were the local chief of police and a Baptist minister. He was told that he was the only white man in town who hadn't joined, and friends even offered to pay the $5 membership fee. He refused, saying, "I'd rather flush the money down the toilet than pay it to you."

Driving through Plains one wintry evening in 1975 he pointed out the local school to a New York reporter. The school is totally desegregated. It was the hometown school of Carter's nine-year-old daughter Amy.

"Look how neat and clean they keep it. You won't see any vandalism at that school. Those kids don't know who's black and who's white. Sure, their parents have painful memories, but no one wants to go back to that old struggle. That would be debilitating and embarrassing and counterproductive. It's like an old wound that no one wants to reopen," he told the visiting reporter.

As governor of Georgia, he closed the wound on an old scar, hanging a portrait of the late Civil Rights leader Dr. Martin Luther King, Jr., in the halls of the state capitol in Atlanta. Dr. King had pastored the Ebenezer Baptist Church in the capital city and was buried there after being shot down on that Memphis motel balcony in 1968. Carter joined the singing of the black anthem "We Shall Overcome" in the same gold-domed building that was once a haven of segregation. Even then, however, many Georgians refused to sing along.

And in the 1930s, A.W. Davis felt it better to sneak away to the balcony.

Miss Julia Coleman and Coach Y. T. Sheffield influenced many.

The Unforgettable Miss Julia

There's nothing unusual about dreaming of a way out and of escaping the town you call home, especially if you're isolated in a small town whose world stretches only as far as the county line. In the Plains of Jimmy Carter's boyhood, many dreamed, but few escaped the rhythmic rotation of the crops, the red clay that every rain turned into quicksand, the hot Georgia sun that wrinkled even the young, the feeling that your life was all charted out and that your chart was no different from your father's or his father's.

Escape was something many of the young people talked about. Some of them found their escape in Miss Julia's reading list. Some found it watching Buck Rogers on the screen of the Rylander Theater over in Americus. The more private ones kept it their own secret. Most of them—if they'd admit it—knew that except for maybe time away at college, Plains would always be their home.

Jimmy Carter had his own dream. Lillian's brother Tom was in the navy. He had joined, and he was seeing the world. The arrival of a Tom Gordy postcard was an event sure to cause excitement. The postmarks were from exotic spots of the world. Tom Gordy didn't just dream. He had found a way of escaping, and his was more than a dream.

In Tom Gordy, Jimmy saw all that he wanted to be. Uncle Tom was traveling. He was free. He was doing things others only talked about. He was lightweight boxing champion of his unit, and a photograph of him and the challengers he defeated held a place of honor back in Plains. Even before he started to school Jimmy planned a navy life.

"Uncle Tom was my distant hero, a man thoughtful enough to send me small mementoes of his visits to foreign, exotic places. From the time I was five or six, the only goal in my life was to go to Annapolis.

"Even in grammar school I read books about the navy and the academy. I wrote off for the entrance requirements, not telling them my age. I almost memorized the little catalogue. I planned my studies and choice of library books accordingly," Carter says, thinking back to those boyhood dreams.

With all his hopes young Jimmy had doubts. First there were his teeth. The catalogue talked about a "malocclusion of teeth." Every bite from an apple made him fear his now-famous teeth would keep him home. Then what about his feet? No one with flat feet was acceptable. Thinking his were flat, Jimmy rolled them over Coke bottles to strengthen his arches. At 120 pounds he thought himself too light, so he adopted a banana diet and took to lying in bed to conserve energy and pounds.

In his family, college was a foreign word. Earl Carter had gone through the 10th grade and—going back through the family tree—no male had even finished high school. Jimmy Carter had chosen a rocky path.

Jimmy read Miss Julia's Six Great Books as a high school sophomore.

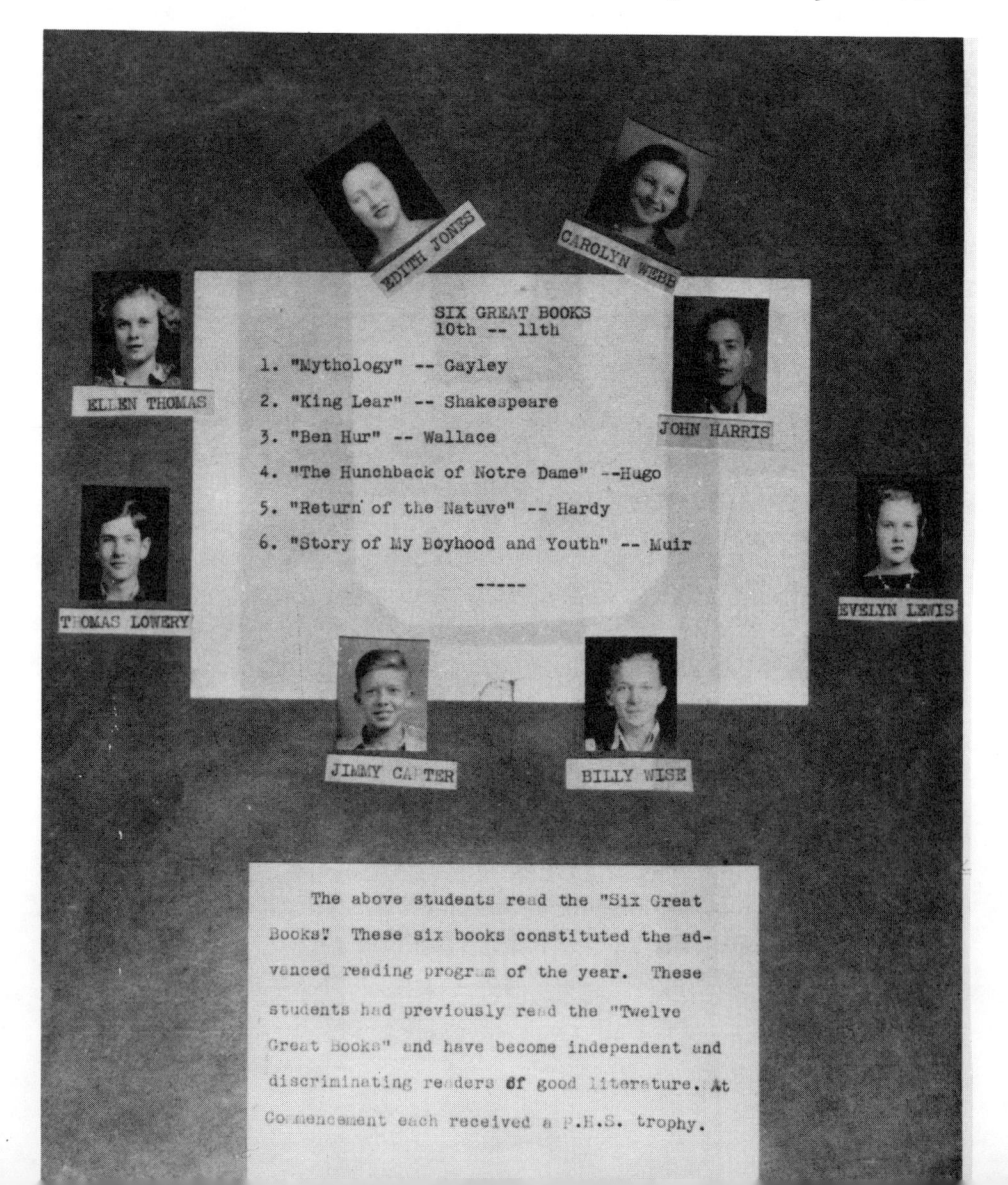

His first roadblock was Miss Julia. Through the years Julia Coleman was teacher, principal, and superintendent, although most remember her more as a teacher. She was short and slightly crippled. Poor eyesight forced her to read with the aid of a thick magnifying glass. Yet, she had that ability to make books she read aloud come alive. She had that special gift only a few have, a way of seeing through the mischief and indifference of a child and bringing out that talent which was stored inside. When she found it she was able to add a dose of desire, so that the talent would not go to waste.

In Jimmy Carter she saw ambition. He wanted to go to the Naval Academy. He wanted to be a navy officer. She saw, too, a mind that could absorb any book passed before him. To her, that was the greatest gift. Books and her students were her life. Any child who loved books was loved especially by her. Miss Lillian had instilled a love of reading into her boy, and Miss Julia taught him to respect it. As a high school sophomore, he read her Six Great Books, earning a gold star. Later he was to follow this up by reading the works on her list of Twelve Great Books, earning an award for this at graduation. But his love affair with books had begun much earlier.

"When I was 12 years old I liked to read, and Miss Julia was my principal. She forced me pretty much to read, read, read classical books. She would give me a gold star when I read 10 and a silver star when I read five. One day she called me in and said, 'Jimmy, I think it's time for you to read *War and Peace.*' I was completely relieved. I thought it was a book on cowboys and Indians. Well, I went to the library and checked it out, and it was 1,415 pages thick, I think, written by Tolstoy about Napoleon's entry into Russia. I've read it a number of times since," Jimmy Carter says.

School under Miss Julia was more than the "Three R's," however. She produced plays, pageants for every occasion, and special projects—most directed at showing the young people that literature wasn't just thick books about ancient subjects. It could also be fun. Like most of her students, Jimmy had his day on the stage. As a junior high student he was the "Barefoot Boy" in a May Day pageant. Students in this out-of-the-way school were exposed to a classical education, although Miss Julia also sprinkled in agriculture, religion, and especially good citizenship. During World War II she formed the Victory Corps, and her students proudly donned uniforms and participated in war bond sales.

This old-time patriotism was part of every school day. The day would begin with a student formation outside the red brick building. Youngsters would stand as erect as the white columns on the schoolhouse as the flag was raised and the pledge repeated in unison, hands over every heart. A devotional would be given before the students marched to their rooms, class by class.

Many of the students would arrive even before the sun to work on the

Jimmy portrayed barefoot boy in one of Miss Julia's plays.

Friendship Garden, a project that turned the school grounds into a nursery. Each child would plant a flower in honor of a newborn child in town. It was theirs to care for until the child was old enough to come to school and care for it himself. Of her garden, Miss Julia quoted this verse: "The child who planteth a seed and watches it blossom forth in beauty gains knowledge." She was dedicated to passing this knowledge on to the young minds, even organizing a traveling library that would deliver books to the steps of the farmhouses.

Jimmy's sisters Gloria and Ruth were part of the traveling library program, and Jimmy had his own way of spreading around Miss Julia's knowledge. "I always told Jimmy he was a mama's boy because he was so good. He was never in a fight. But nobody picked on him, because he had a way

Jimmy (rear left) held flag on Honors Day at Plains School.

Friendship Garden turned Plains School into a park.

with words. Did he ever love to read. Many times, when I asked him to come and play, he'd say, 'Come in here and I'll give you a reading lesson,'" remembers A. W. Davis, the black youth who grew up as a neighbor of the Carters.

But even his own ambitions didn't keep Jimmy from giving into the lure of spring of 1941. There's something about spring. Flowers begin to feel their growing pains. Birds start testing their vocal repertoire. Animals decide to store their winter coats. School children grow restless as the walls seem to close in, the clock goes into slow motion, and a magnet outside seems to lure them into the lukewarm sunshine. That's what happened to Jimmy and nine of his classmates that spring. The lure of spring and a day at the movies in Americus was too much. Playing hooky from school, they headed for Americus. When they returned, they discovered they had indeed been missed. "When we got back to town and school, we discovered that we had got caught. The principal paddled every one of us, including Jimmy," remembers William Wise, one of those 10 who took part in the Americus Adventure and still a resident of Plains. Carter was relegated to second in the Class of '41, behind Eloise (Teeny) Ratliff, and lost the honor of being the class valedictorian.

When the class gathered for its 35th reunion in the summer of 1976, they could look back and laugh at their escapades. As they came together at the Best Western Motel in Americus that June, they were remembering the good times...and Miss Julia. Not what she had injected into them, but what she had drawn out of them. The last time they had celebrated was in Georgia's governor's mansion. Miss Julia was too ill to attend, but she had sent a letter which was read. Now, with the network television lights heating up the crowded room, they were recalling their dear old golden school days.

"I remember those debates she made us have every Friday," Jimmy

As a freshman, Jimmy (rear center) was basketball all-star.

Except for a day at the movies, Jimmy (front right) might have been No. 1 in class.

Carter told his old classmates. "And I remember how we always dreaded preparing for them. And I remember, too, how we always liked them. Kids don't get that coming along these days. We had a code of our own. It prepared us to go out in the world and do the best we could. We're small and isolated down in Plains, but you can learn just as much coming to Plains as you can from any of the people in New York City. We lived together, played together, fought together, and learned together," Carter told the 21 surviving members of his 23-person graduating class.

He was one of them. The guy in the class most likely to succeed. When they had gone around the room putting up-to-date names on once-familiar faces, he had stood and introduced himself this way: "My name's Jimmy Carter, and I'm semi-retired. My family, though, is in the lemonade business. We have three sons and an eight-year-old daughter named Amy. I have one grandson, Jason, born in August. He can already walk and say 14 words. He's the finest grandson ever born in Georgia."

It was a long way from Miss Julia's school in 1976, but Jimmy Carter had survived. But surviving wasn't enough to him, and part of the reason was what he had learned in her classroom. And he's not the only one. Through the years her school has turned out a surprising number of graduates who

As a member of the Class of '41, Jimmy was solemn.

went on to college. For her efforts she was rewarded with numerous honors, but the ones she cherished most were those her students received.

Don Carter was one of those students. The eldest son of Alton Carter, he's a vice president of the Knight-Ridder newspaper chain. But when Miss Julia died in 1973, he was editor of the *Macon Telegraph* in Georgia. In a moving column, he described her this way:

> She signed the diploma Julia L. Coleman, but we pupils knew her simply as Miss Julia. She was superintendent, principal, teacher, friend—all that fine education involves with young people growing up.
>
> For most of her life, she taught and directed a little school at Plains, in Sumter County, Ga. For years, from her classrooms poured young men and women who pushed far beyond the usual horizons of a small Georgia town.
>
> Miss Julia's subjects were literature and English. She could remember more poetry, talk of great literature, and teach grammar better than any college professor I can remember.
>
> She also had that greater quality of inspiring her students to reach for something more, to see opportunity, to want to serve. She could spot the flaws in life, but she found the beauty to offset it.

When he learned of her death, Don Carter went through his files and found a letter she had written him 10 years before. She wrote:

> I am not joining in the current line. Stop the World, I Want to Get Off. I still enjoy life. Home for me is a haven. I realize that, before too long, there must be a change. I may reside in some home for aging people. My plans will mature gradually as the need appears.
>
> I marvel over the service of modern machinery. I see operating here now a fantastic cotton picker which I prefer to dub the "grand dragon." I miss the old days when pickers gathered the cotton crop, singing as they worked. I miss many fine things we had lost, as we have made our way up to the space age.
>
> But never mind—I like this NOW of ours. I am well aware of a host of evils, negations, confusions and conflict. But I still see much good shining through the mists. I deplore all the evil, but I firmly believe in the ultimate triumph of the Greater Good.

Her letter could have been a page out of Jimmy Carter's favorite campaign speech. Her belief that the "Greater Good" would finally triumph comes through in his philosophy today. It's easy to see her mark on him and on the entire town of Plains.

But to the funeral director, she was just another dead person, just another old person who had died in a nursing home. He didn't bother to phone the funeral announcement in to the newspaper. She had no family.

His dream of the Naval Academy finally did come true.

Who would care?

A few people did hear of her lonely death in 1973. They came. But hundreds of others who had been touched by this limping lady who had to read through a magnifying glass knew nothing of her death.

She hasn't been forgotten, however.

After her death, friends went through her belongings. They found stacks of scrapbooks, now yellow with age, chronicling every event at the Plains School and charting the lives of those who had sat in her class. Those who knew her best say she'd stay up late at night, carefully pasting items into the book.

"She'd do special books on students she had lots of hope for," a former student said. One of those books was on Jimmy Carter.

Miss Julia watched her protege go to Georgia Southwestern College in nearby Americus for a year of catch-up work in math and science. Then to Georgia Tech in Atlanta as a Naval ROTC student, where, he said, the strict requirements made the Naval Academy seem almost easy. Then, at last, to Annapolis.

Annapolis was another world for the shy but determined plebe. He was labeled a "Cracker" when he refused to sing "Marching Through Georgia," a song considered obscene back home. Upperclassmen hazed him repeatedly. At mess he was told to "shove in," that is, sit and eat without actually touching his chair. Never did he show his emotions to the hazers. He would just turn and march sternly back to his room, where he would take out his frustrations listening to classical music, mostly Wagner.

The discipline of navy life came easy. His father's regimented household was a perfect training ground. Miss Julia's and his mother's appreciation of books had long since rubbed off on him, and studying came easy. Free time was spent running cross country or racing boats. He was known among his classmates as a quick study, able to absorb data at a rapid rate. His grades bounced between A and B, and when he was graduated in 1946 he was 59th in a class of 820.

As a young navy officer, this ranking and his pride in it was to come back to haunt him. In his autobiography Carter describes this episode. Admiral Hyman Rickover was grilling him to see if he was worthy of the navy's new nuclear submarine program. Carter, in his book *Why Not the Best?* describes the meeting this way:

"...It was the first time I met Admiral Rickover, and we sat in a large room by ourselves for more than two hours, and he let me choose any subjects I wished to discuss. Very carefully I chose those about which I knew most at the time—current events, seamanship, music, literature, naval tactics, electronics, gunnery—and he began to ask me a series of questions of increasing difficulty.

"In each instance, he soon proved that I knew relatively little about the subject I had chosen. He always looked me right into my eyes, and he never smiled. I was saturated with cold sweat.

"Finally, he asked me a question, and I thought I could redeem myself. He said, 'How did you stand in your class at the Naval Academy?' Since I had completed my sophomore year at Georgia Tech before entering Annapolis as a plebe, I had done very well, and I swelled my chest with pride and answered, 'Sir, I stood 59th in a class of 820!'

"I sat back to wait for the congratulations—which never came. Instead, the question: 'Did you do your best?'

"I started to say, 'Yes sir,' but I remembered who this was and recalled several of the many times at the academy when I could have learned more about our allies, our enemies, weapons, strategy, and so forth. I was just human.

"I finally gulped and said, 'No sir, I didn't always do my best.'

"He looked at me for a long time and then turned his chair around to end the interview. He asked one final question, which I have never been able to forget—or to answer. He said, 'Why not?' I sat there for a while, shaken, and then slowly left the room."

The admiral's question became the title of Carter's autobiography and the slogan for his presidential campaign decades later.

And he was later accepted into the nuclear submarine program, too.

Jimmy sent this inscribed photo home to Rosalynn.

Before he entered active naval service, however, other changes in his life were to come. The summer before his senior year at Annapolis, he went out on a date with Rosalynn Smith, a friend of his sister Ruth. It was just another date, or so it seemed.

But once he dated Rosalynn he never dated anyone else, carrying on a romance by mail through his final year at Annapolis. After that first date, he told his mother he had met the girl he was going to marry. Marry they did, on July 7, 1946, at the Plains Methodist Church after his graduation.

Then they went off to Pensacola, Florida, where Carter had a most unglamorous assignment of flying blimps. Next it was to Norfolk, Virginia, where Ensign Carter spent two years as electronics officer on experimental gunnery ships, first the *Wyoming*, then the *Mississippi*. It hardly was the life he had charted for himself through Uncle Tom Gordy's letters.

Submarines became his new hope. He tried unsuccessfully for a Rhodes Scholarship, even thought of quitting the navy. Then in 1948 he applied for submarine school. He saw it as his final chance to grab the gold ring he had been chasing those many years. He was accepted, and he finished third in a class of 52 at New London, Connecticut. Four rewarding years lay ahead.

Leaving Rosalynn behind in Plains, he reported to Hawaii for service aboard the submarine U.S.S. *Pomfret*. Two days later they were bound for the Far East.

The young officer was seasick for five days beneath the stormy seas. But as much as one might want to die while suffering, seasickness isn't fatal. On top of the ocean, life could be deadly, Carter was to discover.

While the ship was recharging batteries, someone had to stand watch above while the engines whined. One particular night Carter was on duty on the bridge, 15 feet above the ocean. He held tightly to the hand rail as the ship bounced and swayed.

Suddenly, an enormous wave jerked him loose from the rail. He found

Rosalynn and Miss Lillian pin on bars upon graduation from the Naval Academy.

Sister Ruth congratulated Jimmy on graduation day.

himself swimming inside the wave, not knowing if the ship was below or not. He came to rest 30 feet aft of the bridge on top of a five-inch gun. Had the wave hit at another spot the navy might have been minus one officer.

During this same stormy period a message came across the *Pomfret's* damaged radio: "To all ships in the Pacific. Be on the lookout for floating debris left by the submarine *Pomfret*, believed to have sunk approximately 700 miles south of Midway Island." The *Pomfret* could not transmit on her

As a midshipman, Jimmy still had boyish features.

radio to correct the error.

From the *Pomfret* Carter moved to the K-1—a prototype strike sub—then into the nuclear submarine field under Admiral Rickover. Life was demanding but enjoyable. This was the life he had dreamed about while standing at the mailbox back home. He was qualified for his own command but never senior enough to gain one.

His superiors gave him top ranking. His fellow officers regarded him as a serious-minded, ambitious sort of guy who stayed in the background until he was needed. All of them agreed that he knew the definition of work and didn't fear it. His navy career hadn't found its summit.

"I always thought Jimmy would go as far as he could in the navy," his mother says. Colleagues thought he had set his sights on being Chief of Naval Operations.

Then a call came from home. Earl had cancer. Daddy was dying. Daddy. Had it been that long since those days when they pulled peanuts together? Had it been that many years since they hunted and fished together? Plains seemed so far away, not just in miles but in time. Since leaving for Annapolis in 1943–10 years earlier–Jimmy Carter had considered Plains only as the place he had been born.

Jimmy and Rosalynn took an emergency leave and returned to Plains. Back home. By now they had three sons: John William, James Earl, III, and Donnel Jeffrey, born in 1947, 1950, and 1952, respectively.

For the first time since he was a teenager Jimmy and Earl talked, really talked. A year before the cancer was discovered Earl had been elected to the Georgia House of Representatives. They talked about this...and they just talked. Making up for that lost decade. Soon it was over. On July 23, 1953, Earl Carter died. He was 59.

What Jimmy Carter saw then saddened him and scared him. Driving around the family land to tell the sharecroppers about "Mr. Earl's" death, he was welcomed by tears. Soon the house was crowded with mourners. They'd shake Jimmy's hand and tell him about their personal memories of his daddy.

Earl Carter had lived one of those quiet lives that are sometimes not noticed until they're gone. He had bought—anonymously, of course—graduation gowns for girls who couldn't afford them. He had quietly helped families who had sudden needs. He had kept a ready supply of candy in his desk drawer to give kids who'd come by every day after school for a sample. Before dying he told Jimmy to forget certain debts.

Looking at the mourners Jimmy began to ask himself what would happen should he himself die. "Would anybody care? Would anybody even notice?" he asked himself. He found himself asking another personal question. "With Earl gone, who's going to run the business?"

His brother Billy was still a teenager. Uncle Alton was in his sixties. Cousin Hugh had other interests. That left only Lt. Jimmy Carter. The alternatives were clear. Jimmy and Rosalynn went back to Schenectady to weigh them.

Their decision was agonizing. Jimmy suddenly felt that roots thought dead still lived. He felt an obligation to his mother and brother...and to his father. Rosalynn could not agree. She loved navy life, the travel it offered, the unlimited horizons. Plains she remembered as a narrow horizon, close to parents who might not let them live the free life they had become accustomed to. It was the first real confrontation of their marriage.

A navy friend told newsmen years later that Carter's decision was agony. "His father was the mainstay of the community—the banker and the landowner. He was a baron in a feudal situation. Jimmy had a strong sense that nobody in the family could hold it together but him. He felt that if he didn't go back and take the burden, the town would die," William Lalor told *Newsweek* magazine. Other friends remember Rosalynn bursting into tears when the decision was made.

Daddy's death brought Jimmy home from the navy.

"I didn't advise him to come home," his mother now says. "But he knew we might lose everything. About a week after they had gone back up there, he called me—about two o'clock in the morning—and said they'd be home as soon as they could."

Jimmy still remembers his reasoning.

"I had looked at my daddy's life. There was a significance to it. He was an important part of his community. He had roots. You have only one life, and I began to wonder if I should spend mine engaged in war, even if I could rationalize it as the prevention of war."

He was coming home.

A Homecoming In Plains

Jimmy Carter had left Plains a scared but ambitious boy, the same freckle-faced Tom Sawyer who peddled peanuts to hungry checker players gathered downtown and the same boy who played boyish pranks on his sisters.

Eleven years later he came home a man. Not just older in years but with a wife and three young sons to support and with the experiences of the Naval Academy and the navy reshaping the boy who had packed his bags over a decade before.

Plains, he was to find, was still Plains. Most of the folks he had left behind were still caught up in the same routines they had followed for a lifetime. The world may have changed around it, but Plains had put time in a bottle.

It has been written that you can't go home again. That's not true, you can. But Jimmy Carter began to wonder if you should. All that he had learned sitting in Miss Julia's school was still there with him. Only he had added to this his own ideas of what life should be.

It would have been easy to hang a "For Sale" sign on it all, pack up Rosalynn and the boys, and go back to where he would be around those who thought like he did. But being back here where Earl Carter had walked made Jimmy Carter remember all that his father had been. Quitting was a foreign word to Earl Carter, and his son had never learned its meaning either.

Jimmy and Rosalynn threw themselves into the peanut business, not relying on the experience they didn't have but learning by their mistakes. When the long days in the field and warehouse were over, they would return to the $30-a-month public housing unit they called home and continue to talk business.

Rosalynn handled the books, learning accounting as she went along. She wasn't just a wife. She was his partner. If they made it, they'd make it together. If they failed, they'd go down together.

Meanwhile, Jimmy had things to learn, too.

"I had so much to learn. I checked out books on agriculture from the library, talked with the county agent, wrote away to the University of Georgia for literature, talked with Uncle Alton, and watched what others were doing. It was a difficult time," Jimmy says, looking back on 1953.

Not only was it difficult for the young Carter family, but the family business itself was hardly on firm ground. A business such as theirs was built on variables—the weather, good harvests, the good will of the surrounding farmers, and what they thought of the man at the helm. Folks around Sumter County had grown to respect and trust Mr. Earl. Jimmy may have been his father's son, but he had yet to prove himself.

That first year the business netted only about $200—a hard-earned $200. But slowly Jimmy was proving himself to his judging peers. They were watching, and what they saw was work. Side by side, Jimmy and Rosalynn put in 18- and 20-hour days, being on the job at dawn or whenever a farmer might want to bring in his peanuts.

Jimmy Carter was a mixture of Earl's stubborn drive, his mother's compassion, and his own intuition and ability. It was a blend folks came to like and respect. He never had his hand out to anybody. Never sat back and waited for business to knock on his door. And it paid off. Mr. Earl's business grew into a multi-million-dollar operation that now encompasses over 3,000 acres of farm and timber land across three Georgia counties, grosses $2.5 million a year, and supplies peanuts worldwide.

A favorite Carter ploy during Jimmy's presidential campaign was to pick up a handful of peanuts and tell folks around him that, likely as not, one out of every two nuts in his hand came from his farms back home. And he may have been right. Peanuts leave Plains by the tractor trailer full, ending up in candy, peanut butter, peanut oil, and other items around the world.

As the business prospered, the Carters began to find more time to reenter the mainstream of life in Plains. Most of the life revolved around the church. Soon Jimmy was teaching a boys' Sunday School class, telling them the Bible stories he had learned from Miss Julia during school devotional periods or from Mrs. Erma Jennings and O.V. Hogsett, the teachers who had made the biblical characters come alive so many years before. He became a church deacon and was active in the Men's Brotherhood organization.

He joined the Lions Club, the town's only civic club, and soon became an active Lion throughout the state. It was the Lions who enticed him to become involved in his first civic project—construction of a public swimming pool.

Carter raised most of the money for the pool and called on John Pope,

Coming home, Carter proved that peanuts and politics do mix.

a close friend from Americus, to help with the labor. The pool is still a gathering place for the people of Plains. It was only blocks away from the modest duplex where the Carter clan lived then, midway between there and the spacious ranch-style house they later called home.

There was more growing inside Jimmy Carter than just thoughts of peanuts, though. Maybe it was the time he had spent in Washington as a navy liaison to Congress. Maybe it was an unspoken vow to finish all that his father had left undone. One by one he took on civic ventures.

There were the hospital board and the library board. "I was one of the library's biggest customers, so it seemed natural," he says. There was the school board, where he faced racial problems as a moderate, quiet voice against what county blacks were forced to endure. "Separate but equal" was the rallying cry, but somehow the equality was usually lost in the shuffle. Two of his six years on the school board were as chairman.

As a church deacon, he joined other members in visiting neighbors' homes to invite them to church, even going on a missionary excursion into Pennsylvania one year. Later it was that state which was to put him over his biggest presidential campaign barrier. Around home, folks began to figure "Miss Lillian's boy must be getting ants in his pants again."

There was also time for pleasure. The Carters, the John Popes, and the Billy Hornes of Americus became a familiar trio. Giving into Rosalynn's love of dancing they drove 40 miles to Albany whenever possible to dance, trying current fads like the twist. Although his taste ran more to the waltz, they also joined a local square-dancing group. Life again was fun.

When Jimmy and Rosalynn had time, they would walk together through the fields, hand in hand. Where once they might have talked about that navy life that never was to be, they began to realize that their life was here. Still, there was that restlessness inside Jimmy, the feeling that life had even more to offer. Finally in 1962 he told Rosalynn he wanted to run for the state senate, the job his daddy never had time to finish.

She realized it was something he needed and wanted. Yet she also knew that the burden of the business would fall on her slender shoulders while he was away in Atlanta. She accepted the challenge.

So did Jimmy. He may have been new to politics, but he wasn't naive. Homer Moore, who ran a business similar to Carter's in Miss Lillian's hometown of Richland, 18 miles away, was the incumbent. Moore had courthouse savvy, and he had friends. Not just hand-shaking friends but first-namers in the right political cliques. He knew his way around the district, and the only reason he was up for reelection in 1962 was that the courts had ordered Georgia to reapportion its political districts.

Though the decision ultimately would be his own, Jimmy sought help from others. From his mother. From his cousin Hugh. From friends. From a preacher who came to town for a summer revival at the Plains Baptist Church.

After evening services, Miss Lillian invited the minister home for coffee. Relaxing in her living room, Jimmy told him of his plans.

"You don't want to go into such a discredited profession," the preacher said. "If you want to be of service to other people, why don't you go into the ministry or some honorable special service work?"

This put Carter on the defensive. His answer was a question. "How would you like to be the pastor of a church with 80,000 members?" he asked, referring to the newly divided 14th district.

His mind made up, he went to work. Cousin Hugh became his campaign manager. The Popes, Hornes, and other friends volunteered for duty. He was known in some of the district's churches and to some of the neighboring farmers, but when he finally qualified, the 38-year-old businessman had plenty of work ahead.

Searching for something that could capture the flavor of his life, he adopted a standard speech on the roast beef-green peas circuit.

"I could think of only two things: that my Carter ancestors had settled in Georgia in 1750, and that I lived in a small town and could speak with the true voice of a southwest Georgia farmer.

"This line went over pretty well in little towns like Parrott, Preston, and Gooseberry, but after I'd made the speech before a civic club in Americus, the largest town in the district, one of my friends told me I'd better change it.

"He had overheard somebody say that 'If the Carters have been in Georgia 200 years and haven't gotten any further than Plains, it's time one of them did something,'" Carter says, laughing at himself.

So he did. The hard way.

Carter spent election day driving the district kissing last-minute babies, and shaking last-minute hands. When he arrived in Georgetown, he sensed that something was wrong. A county official warned him he was staying home, that he wanted nothing to do with election day. Carter called John Pope and asked him to hurry down to Quitman County.

"I couldn't believe what I found," says Pope. "There were no booths set up. A man named Joe Hurst was running the election. He had set things up in the ordinary's office, right out in the open.

"Joe would meet the voter at the door, put his arm around their shoulder, and take them on into the office. At the table the poll manager, Doc Hammond, would say, 'Strike out Jimmy Carter's name. Joe wants you to vote for Homer Moore,'" says Pope, still a close ally to Carter.

The candidate hurried back to Georgetown to see for himself. He called a Columbus newsman—long since departed—who came down to investigate. This was another victory for Hurst.

"The reporter went inside to look at things, and when he came back Joe had his arm around the guy, taunting us," Pope remembers. "Jimmy told Joe he wanted an honest election. 'That's all we run down here. They always do what I say,' Joe said.

"The clincher was the absentee ballots. Just before the polls closed I asked a lady how long it would be before they had any results," says Pope. "'It might be midnight because we have about 100 absentee ballots out,' she told me. At that point only 322 people had voted, and Hurst had told me privately that he had forgotten to mail out the absentees."

But when the votes were counted, 433 votes had been cast, and naturally Homer Moore had won by a landslide. It was to be weeks before Carter and Pope discovered how. (An Atlanta attorney, Charles Kirbo, had been added to the team. Kirbo became Carter's senior advisor during his presidential campaign.)

"We were down there going through the records. I was calling out the list," Pope recalls. "It got be a chant. Suddenly it dawned on us why. They

After a disputed election, Carter took oath as senator in 1962.

had voted, supposedly, in perfect alphabetical order. We got in touch with a reporter at the *Atlanta Journal*, John Pennington, and the next day the story was on the front page.

"People started calling Pennington saying their relatives' names were on that list and had been dead for years. Some of the folks were in prison, it turned out. The publicity made things easy from then on," the Americus businessman says.

After some political maneuvering and court orders, Carter and Moore had a return bout just like the judge instructed. This time the newcomer won overwhelmingly.

Fourteen years later Homer Moore doesn't like to talk about that election, although he professes no grudge against his opponent. He even went to Maryland in the spring of 1976 to speak out for his old foe. Still, there's something in his voice that more than hints that Homer Moore has looked at the rise of Jimmy Carter and asked himself what that guy he defeated 14 years ago was doing running for President.

When the South Georgia dust had cleared, Jimmy Carter had a reserved seat in the Georgia Senate. Soon he was putting into practice all he had learned from a Georgia Southwestern College speed-reading course and fulfilling a campaign promise by reading every bill that passed across his desk.

Word spread through the capitol that this new guy Carter was a worker,

At 41, Carter was a member of the Georgia Senate.

someone to be reckoned with. Within three years he was voted by his Old South peers as one of the five most effective legislators in the General Assembly.

He worked particularly hard on educational measures, helping to turn Georgia Southwestern from a junior college into a four-year institution. Here he clashed with an old foe, Howard "Bo" Callaway. Callaway was a member of the board of regents of the Georgia university system. He and Carter had met before when the LaGrange textile executive was leading the Georgia Young Republicans and Carter was in the Young Democrats.

Carter and Callaway were neighbors, the Goldwater Republican coming from LaGrange, but there the similarities ended. Callaway had gone to West Point, Carter to Annapolis. Each of them felt the need to outshine the other.

Callaway left the board of regents and became one of the first Republicans to represent Georgia in Congress since the days of Reconstruction. In

While a senator, Carter read every bill that was introduced.

1966 Carter began to plot a race against his old competitor. Carter wanted his job. Or at least he thought he did.

"When I first got into politics, it was as a school board member appointed by the grand jury. Folks back home always thought I'd end up in the state legislature, like my daddy. But when I was in the navy and with the Atomic Energy Commission, I worked closely with Congress. It intrigued me, and I guess Congress was in the back of my mind when I first entered politics," Carter says.

His eyes were trained on the Third District seat. But not for long.

The job likely would have been his. Callaway and his GOP friends wanted to move into Georgia's governor's mansion, so Callaway gave up his seat in Congress and joined what was to be a crowded 1966 race for governor, especially on the Democratic side of the ballot. And the crowd included State Sen. Jimmy Carter.

"I was getting ready to go to India with the Peace Corps when Jimmy offered to drive me over to Albany so I could take some tests," his mother says. "I knew something was up the way he was acting. On the way back from over there he told me he was going to run for governor instead of Congress."

It is difficult to understand his decision. Even with Callaway in the Third District race Carter would have made it a neck-and-neck struggle, for some of the Goldwater fervor had subsided by 1966. With Callaway out of the way it would be clear sailing.

Democrat Jack Brinkley—who had asked Carter to keep him informed about his own plans—entered the Congressional race and 10 years later still represents Carter's home district.

Meanwhile the governor's race was well stocked with proven Georgia thoroughbreds. Ernest Vandiver was the pre-race favorite until the former governor had a recurrence of heart trouble and his doctors forced him to drop out. There was another former governor, Ellis Arnall, a hero of the moderates in the 1940s. There was Lester Maddox, a frequent local candidate around Atlanta and still remembered for his pistol waving when blacks had tried to desegregate his cafeteria years before. There was also former Lt. Gov. Garland Byrd and segregationist newspaper publisher James Gray of Albany.

Then there was Carter. Unknown outside his own doorstep and entering as a late bloomer, few took him seriously. Gathered around him were the same friends who had rallied when he made his first senate race. An office was set up in his old warehouse office on Main Street in Plains. His sister Gloria managed it, keeping score on their lists of potential supporters. Hugh Carter was again his campaign manager.

Covering the state from the mountains to the shore, Jimmy and Rosalynn shook as many hands as they could find, and he went on the civic club circuit trying to answer the question, "Jimmy Who?" Still no one took the candidate too seriously. No one except his opponents. Carter figured Arnall and Maddox were the men to beat.

"I'll never forget that election night," attorney Milton Jones of Columbus says. "We were gathered at an Atlanta hotel watching the results. There was no doubt in our minds that Jimmy would be in a runoff. A lot of us went to bed that night thinking we were in.

"The next morning, early, I heard a commotion outside my room. It sounded like crying. I opened the door, and folks were looking at the front page of the *Atlanta Constitution* like they couldn't believe what they saw. Ellis Arnall and Lester Maddox were in a runoff. We didn't know what to do."

Carter did. His mother remembers his crying, just like he did when as a

Carter's hard work made him a surprising third in 1966 governor's race.

youngster others would catch the biggest fish. He had let the big one get away, by 21,000 votes. But when the tears were shed, he told Georgia that he was the first announced candidate for governor in 1970.

Maddox went on to defeat Arnall in a runoff on the Democractic side, then faced Callaway in one of the most memorable elections in Georgia history. It was a dead heat, a photo finish. It would be up to the Georgia legislature to look at the pictures and decide who would be the winner, as if there were any doubts. In 1966 the Georgia General Assembly was hard-core, old-line Democratic. It was the same tired faces that had been there for decades. They believed in the Democratic Party. Most of them believed in segregation. That equaled Lester Maddox.

To see this enigma of state politics become governor hurt Carter even more. It also riled him. Put it together and you have enough momentum to keep his hopes alive for four more years.

His day was still to come. And Lester Maddox—though ineligible to serve more than one term as governor—was to play a role in Carter's performance.

Progress For A Georgia Turtle

Revival ministers have this nasty habit of asking embarrassing questions. The preacher who steps behind the pulpit every Sunday has to deal with his congregation every day, so he's a bit shy. But in the tradition of Southern Baptist hell, fire, and damnation ministers, an evangelist can take off the gloves and swing with both fists.

The physical strain of the gubernatorial campaign—he lost 22 unaffordable pounds—and the mental stress—he had never learned to lose—were still taxing Jimmy Carter when a revival preacher slammed on the pulpit and asked the congregation this question: "If you were arrested for being a Christian, would there be enough evidence to convict you?"

Sitting there on the hard wooden pew, Carter began to squirm. There was evidence he was a Christian. Hadn't he been a member of the Plains Baptist Church since he was 11? Wasn't he a Bible-toting deacon? Hadn't he gone on missionary crusades seeking converts?

But while the minister spoke, the 42-year-old Carter finally came to grips with himself and the answer.

"It was a definite 'No.' I had never fully committed myself to God. My belief and my faith were superficial, based primarily on pride. I never had done much for other people. I was always thinking about myself," says Carter.

It was not a textbook theological decision. To someone who has never undergone the emotional trauma of coming face-to-face with his life in a religious experience, it may seem like emotional hogwash. To Carter it was very real. Too real.

By this time in their lives Jimmy's sister, Ruth Carter Stapleton, was the wife of a Fayetteville, North Carolina, veterinarian. Late in life she had begun to move toward a full-time commitment to Christian work. Hers was a deep, personal relationship with Christ. She was then building a reputation as an evangelist and faith healer. Back at home for a visit Ruth and Jimmy walked the sun-baked fields as they had when life was much simpler.

"Ruth asked me if I'd give up anything for Christ, if I'd give up my life and my possessions—everything I had accumulated. I told her I would.

"Then she asked if I'd give up politics. I thought about it, it seemed like for hours. I had to admit I would not. She warned me that until I was willing to make that decision, I'd have doubts," Jimmy relates.

In a 1976 interview with Bill Moyers, Carter described those doubts. "I was going through a stage in my life there that was a difficult one. I had run for governor and lost. Everything I did was not gratifying. When I succeeded in something, I got no satisfaction. When I failed at something, it was a horrible experience for me," he said.

Pouring out his heart to his sister, he finally realized he must be willing to give up this dream of being governor if he was ever to find peace. Only then would he be able to find again the old satisfaction.

"Since then I've had just about a new life. As far as hatreds, frustrations, I feel at ease with myself. Now that doesn't mean I'm a better person, but I feel better off myself," he says.

But old-time religion seldom guarantees success at the polls. Realizing this, a mended Carter began to mend political fences. Before the sound of Maddox's inaugural address had stopped echoing he was back at work.

Going back on the civic club tour, he spoke seven or eight times a week all over Georgia, becoming a familiar face among Rotarians, Lions, and Jaycees. He was keeping alive old friendships and beginning new ones. He was talking. He was listening. He was looking back. Mainly he was looking ahead. He had built a mental card file on what was happening across his home state.

On April 3, 1970—making official what he had promised four years before—he called a press conference in a hearing room at the state capitol.

"I announce today my candidacy for governor of Georgia. After traveling in every part of the state the past four years and meeting with the people, I am confident I will win," he said.

In the way of that confidence, however, were two major obstacles—former Gov. Carl Sanders and Atlanta TV newsman Hal Suit. When Sanders had left office four years before, he had been considered one of the state's all-time popular governors. Sanders was obstacle No. 1.

Suit was running his first political race, but he had certain things in his favor. With no Republican opposition he could save his energy and resources. Neither did he have name recognition problems, for WSB-TV was powerful enough to bring him into living rooms across the state.

Carter's campaign against Sanders is one of the most debatable sides of his political career. Perceived as a liberal in 1966, the 1970-model Carter sounded a little like Georgia campaigners of the past. He was trying to appeal

Republican Hal Suit, here with Carter, debated Carter and lost.

to the conservative followers who had helped elect Lester Maddox four years before in Georgia and who sympathized with their Alabama neighbor, Gov. George Wallace.

Sanders was pictured as the darling of the Atlanta newspapers—or as most Georgia politicians have always said: "Them lyin' Atlanter newspapers"—the rich, a pawn of the establishment. The Atlanta lawyer, whose firm was tied to Georgia's big business, was tied to Hubert Humphrey, especially when it was disclosed that Sanders' campaign buttons were recycled HHH pins.

Meanwhile Carter was going to where the people were. He'd show up at

Carter took his gubernatorial campaign where the people were.

pre-dawn shift changes, greet shoppers as the stores opened, eat lunch at the factory cafeterias, go into barbershops, supermarkets, high school football games, or wherever two or more would be gathered. Between him and Rosalynn they estimate they shook the hands of 600,000 Georgians.

Bill Shipp, then a reporter for the *Atlanta Constitution* and now the newspaper's associate editor, described the strategy this way: "...He later passed up the Civitan and Rotary speeches in favor of shaking hands at factory gates and rubbing shoulders with the good old boys around service stations and garages all over the state.

"The factory foremen ran him away from their gates. The workers looked at him as if he were trying to sell them something they didn't want to buy.

"But he and his wife Rosalynn and his mother, Mrs. Lillian Carter, 72, persisted. They were there at dawn and at midnight, handing out pamphlets (when the factory officials would let them) and looking as if they didn't have a friend in the world. All three often campaigned nonstop from 6 a.m. to midnight six days a week."

It wasn't a big money campaign. Carter and his staff would stay with friends along the way and eat in roadside diners. It was in sharp contrast to the Sanders' operation that gave the appearance of a well-oiled, well-financed machine.

As Carter figured, he was in a runoff with Sanders. Here the controversial tactics intensified, Sanders, a natty Brooks Brothers dresser, became "Cuff Links Carl." Carter was the working man's candidate, which around Georgia meant someone who stood for law and order with a slice of segregation.

Sanders, after going out of office, had become a part owner of the Atlanta Hawks basketball team when the National Basketball Association franchise was moved from St. Louis. Actually his dollar-and-cents interest was small. Primary owner Tom Cousins needed Sanders to insure that the team could play at the state-controlled Georgia Tech coliseum. That deal was to become a part of Sanders' downfall.

When the Hawks won the NBA Western Division title, Sanders joined the locker-room celebration. As is customary, more champagne was being used as shampoo than was being drunk. The lens of an *Atlanta Constitution* photographer caught Bill Bridges and Lou Hudson, two black stars of the Hawks team, dousing the former governor with bubbly. By the time the picture was circulated quietly in the Georgia backwoods, Carl Sanders was in deep political trouble.

Carter has always denied having any part in distributing the photo. However, insiders think some of his young, overzealous staffers did. Whoever sent it, the photo meant suicide for Sanders.

Upsetting former Gov. Carl Sanders gave Carter momentum.

Near the end of the hot campaign Sanders tried to recoup. Going before the TV cameras to take off his coat, roll up his sleeves, and symbolically go to work, he made the mistake of wearing a shirt with French cuffs. "Cuff Links Carl" was to be a haunting memory to Sanders, who never again was a major factor in Georgia politics.

Yet, despite this negative side, the Carter campaign was actually based on hard work, something that seems to follow the early-rising farmboy. While some may say he ran a "Redneck" campaign, he still had ample support from the black communities who remembered his senate fight to abolish voting restrictions. And despite an ill-advised feud with individuals at the Atlanta newspapers—particularly *Constitution* editor Reg Murphy—he received good support from the state's news media.

To get to the core of it all you return to the hard work of the candidate and his staff. They stayed on the road, not dwelling on the newspaper editors, the courthouse crowd, or the bankers, but spending their time with the common voter.

One particular aspect of this side of the campaigning was called the "Hi, Neighbor" program. Milton Jones, who had been a 1962 classmate of Carter

Flags and banners waved for Carter and Maddox ticket.

in the Georgia General Assembly, was among his staunchest supporters in 1966 and 1970. The Columbus attorney remembers how his own doubts about this program were changed.

Made up of a group of those who knew Carter best, the team would gather at an Americus shopping center before dawn. Most of them were from Sumter County. Many of them shared his church pew or had known him since he was a freckle-faced boy back home. From there they would go in various directions across the state to hand out brochures and shake hands.

"When they told me about the idea, I told them not to send that bunch to Columbus," Jones says. "We didn't need that kind of help, I thought. Frankly, I didn't think the idea was worth taking up time with.

"Then late one week somebody called me up and said a group would be coming to Columbus that Saturday morning. I argued, but nobody would pay any attention to me, so I thought I'd get them set up at a local shopping center, then take off.

"I figured they'd fall flat on their face, but I met them and took them out to the mall that Saturday morning. Well, I started listening to their conversations, and I couldn't believe it.

"People were impressed with the fact that these people, who knew Jimmy Carter so well, were spending their time that far away from home to help him get elected. I had to eat a steady diet of crow after that," said

Jones, who briefly served as the newly elected governor's executive secretary during the transitionary period of Carter's administration.

Sanders, meanwhile, became just another former Georgia governor who had failed in a comeback try. Four years before—when he was ineligible to attempt reelection by Georgia law—he had been at his peak. Now Sanders was only another Atlanta lawyer. The only hurdle still to be cleared by Carter was Republican Suit.

When Callaway and Maddox had dueled in the previous gubernatorial showdown, the GOP had had high hopes. They also were optimistic about Suit, especially after Sanders was out of the way. The Republicans soon learned they still had some growing up to do in Georgia as Carter mauled the ex-broadcaster by more than 200,000 votes.

But at the same time that Carter was piling up a landslide victory, Lester Garfield Maddox was readying a move from the governor's office into the lieutenant-governor's chair. He had his heart set on moving back into the mansion four years later, and he needed something to keep him busy and

Lester Maddox looks on as Carter receives oath of office in 1970.

feed his healthy ego during the wait.

While campaigning Carter had embraced Maddox, saying he was "proud to be on the ticket with him." At the windy, cold inauguration that January afternoon, they posed for photographers, each smiling his best victory smile.

Maddox, who had based his professional and political life on a hard-line segregationist platform, quit smiling when Carter—fully sworn in as Georgia's new governor—stepped to the microphone. He was talking to the crowd that was gathered on the historic capitol grounds, but Georgia was to learn that the nation was listening.

"I say to you quite frankly that the time for racial discrimination is over. Our people have already made this major and difficult decision.

"No poor, rural, weak, or black person should ever have to bear the additional burden of being deprived of the opportunity of an education, a job, or simple justice," Carter told Georgians gathered around the capitol steps.

The national press made Carter into an instant cover boy. When Georgians shopped at their news stands the next week, their governor was peering out at them from the cover of *Time* magazine. Used to hearing variations on the "Segregation, yesterday, today and tomorrow" theme, Carter's words struck a new vein. Across the South a new breed of governor had been elected...Askew in Florida, Dunn in Tennessee, West in South Carolina, Bumpers in Arkansas, and others. Carter managed to become the spokesman of this New South.

Criticism came, too. Remembering the "Redneck" strategies he had used to oust Sanders, people began wondering out loud if they truly knew this man they had just elected. Had he been speaking out of both sides of his smiling face?

He answered them this way: "I can't truthfully detect any profound changes in my political philosophy, except those subtle changes that have come through the constant human learning process. The actions I have taken as governor have been completely consistent with the goals I worked out over a long period of difficult campaigning.

"Possibly the reason some people think I've changed my political posture is that in my inaugural address I expressed for a national audience what I had frequently expressed to the Georgia people during my campaign. That is, that the Georgia people had already decided for themselves that the time for evasion of federal laws against racial discrimination was over. Our people had been struggling against this problem and had decided, often reluctantly, to come together and seek racial harmony.

"When I pointed this out in my inaugural address, it wasn't anything new to the Georgia people and didn't get any extraordinary publicity within the state. But when the people saw the emphasis placed on it in the national

Inaugural speech called for end of discrimination in Georgia.

Carters enjoyed first dance at Georgia's inaugural ball.

magazines, they reacted in a very human way. They assumed there was a major new emphasis being placed on civil rights. This was not the case," Carter said.

Also to react in a very human way was Lieutenant Governor Maddox. Maddox had just spent four years living in the governor's mansion, and he intended to move back there in four more years. Georgia's constitution stipulated that a governor could not succeed himself—an amendment since changed—so the former restaurateur decided to find work upstairs as the state's lieutenant governor.

In Georgia the primary job for the lieutenant governor is to preside over the state senate, and Maddox realized this would be a good way to keep his power base firmly entrenched. He also saw it as a way to control what was going on in his old office. When Carter said he would honor his campaign pledge to reorganize the state's overgrown government, he did not know what lay ahead, and his biggest obstacle was to be his own lieutenant governor.

Reorganization had been a popular theme across Georgia during the campaign. The public was well acquainted with a state government that had grown steadily through the years, mostly in the wrong places. It had been 40 years since then Gov. Richard Russell last realigned the state bureaucracy, and the list of agencies had swelled to over 300. Carter proposed to slice the list to 22.

Even before he had officially taken office Carter had a team of experts led by Harold Hill (now a member of the Georgia Supreme Court), Bill Harper, Milton Jones, and Bert Lance (later to become a member of the Carter Cabinet) formulating how the realignment would be carried out. The first bill of the 1971 legislative session—introduced while the Carter family was still moving into the governor's mansion—authorized the governor to draft a reorganization program and present it to the 1972 legislature. The House passed the measure, swinging solidly behind Carter.

Enter Lester Maddox. The volatile lieutenant governor readied his forces in the senate for their showdown with his successor. Maddox found sympathetic support among many state officials.

"I shouldn't have been surprised at all of this. Why should reorganization have been popular with people who were losing their jobs? But we proved an interesting point—you can go over their heads, to the people," Carter says in retrospect.

"We told them this is what we have, and this is what we could have. They liked what they saw and heard. This taught me that when you have a tough decision, you don't go to the special interest groups, you go to the people."

Carter won the first round, and for the next nine months, teams of

Jimmy Carter took over governor's office from Lester Maddox—who became a foe.

experts, some of them "borrowed executives" from private industry, worked out the reorganization program. If fully implemented, Carter said it could save taxpayers $50 million annually.

Meanwhile Maddox and his supporters were searching for a weak spot in Carter's reorganization armor. They thought they had found it in his proposed merger of public health, welfare and vocational rehabilitation services into a massive department to be known as the Department of Human Resources (DHR).

Even some supporters of reorganization had their doubts over this portion of the plan. When the house first went over the measure, it failed to fully implement the DHR. At this point the speaker of the house, the late George L. Smith, entered the picture. Through compromise Smith got the Department of Human Resources through. But it still had to face Maddox and the senate.

With the DHR as its rallying cry opponents of the plan seemed confident they would defeat the program and strike a knockout blow against the governor. All seemed lost when Sen. Floyd Hudgins of Columbus broke a tie vote. The DHR question was answered, and reorganization was to become a reality.

"Really I can't take that much credit for all of that," Carter says. "Georgia was just ready for a change. It was a time that only comes along every few decades. Reorganization was only part of it. The people expected us to express and reflect new attitudes—socially, racially, and in every way."

Maddox wasn't through yet, however. He was to be a four-year roadblock for Carter. Their relationship worsened, and before the term was over it had turned into a name-calling contest, a situation that did nothing to create harmony at the state house. Carter won those first two battles on reorganization, but before their terms were up Maddox was gaining the upper hand more often than not.

"It was a unique situation to have an ex-governor down the hall. He had been there, and he knew what he would do in each situation that came up. It was especially unique to have an ex-governor around who wanted to be governor again in four years," Carter said in a conversation at his state capitol office just before moving out.

It wasn't just Maddox, however. Though the makeup of the Georgia General Assembly had changed drastically and has continued to change, the legislature in 1970 was hardly up to date with that "New South" everyone was talking about. It had been reapportioned, but it was still controlled by the rural representatives. A poll had ranked it 45th among the 50 state bodies. Add Maddox to this mixture, and it was a deadly concoction.

"Overall, the legislature accepted my programs, but that's not what people will remember," says Carter. "What they'll always think of is their disgust with the atmosphere that pervaded in Atlanta between the lieutenant governor and me.

"You can't really second guess your individual decisions without having total recall of the situation and time, so my bickerings with him are the things I'd like to go back and change.

"I take my share of the responsibility. I first tried not responding to his statements, but I finally started talking back. Neither strategy really accomplished anything. I regret the whole situation."

While Carter was to move out of the governor's office and begin moving toward the White House, Maddox's moves have not been so fruitful. He confidently ran for governor in 1974. Though he finished on top in the Democractic primary his margin was narrow, and forecasters predicted his doom in the runoff against Rep. George Busbee of Albany. How right they were. Busbee swept into office, leaving Maddox a bitter, disillusioned cafeteria owner in Atlanta. And by the time Carter was settled in the White House, word was out in Atlanta that Maddox's cafeteria was for sale. The former governor was facing still another change.

Sitting in his Sandy Springs place of business, Maddox hardly looked his swaggering, acid-tongued self when a reporter visited him one afternoon in early 1976. There were reminders of the past on counters nearby—autographed axe handles (he calls them Drumsticks), Lester Maddox watches, recordings, books, and photos.

But the old edge was gone from the sharp tongue that once put down TV talk-show hosts like Joe Pyne and Dick Cavett—until the conversation turned to Jimmy Carter.

"He's a hypocrite," Maddox said bluntly. "He tried to seem like he was a friend of Lester Maddox during his campaign. But right after he was in office he called me down to talk. He hadn't asked for any help of any kind up until then, so I thought he might need some help. He didn't say hello or anything, just began telling me what he wanted done. He's a hard, mean man."

That particular Saturday, former *Atlanta Constitution* editor Reg Murphy—now editor of the *San Francisco Examiner*—had been guesting on an Atlanta radio show the night before. As Maddox walked through the cafeteria refilling his customers' iced tea glasses, he talked about what Murphy had said.

"Did you hear old Reg?" Maddox would ask. "Never thought I'd agree with him, but when he said Carter was the biggest phony he had ever seen, I clapped out loud."

Maddox later traveled into New Hampshire and Florida spreading the gospel according to Maddox, a gospel that left Carter far short of sainthood. Carter eventually carried both states, and as Carter's fortunes continued to rise Maddox emerged as the presidential candidate of the American Independent Party. It was to be an effort so futile that the outspoken former governor could not even get on the ballot in his home state.

But in 1970 Maddox was an obstacle of another kind, one who was to hamper every move taken by Carter's administration. Yet despite him Carter was able to hammer out a progressive, efficient four years as governor.

His improvements within the prison system, in mental health, budgeting, the merit selection of judges, education, and his Heritage Trust environmental program are programs which should benefit Georgians in years to come.

"You know, it was even better than I thought it would be," Carter said before leaving office. "I guess I've been surprised most at how easy it is to get things done. I'm not talking about in the legislature. I'm talking about how people outside of government rally behind you and help."

As an example, he pointed to a move to place the state of Georgia's bank deposits on a bid basis, an action that earned the state $28.2 million in interest in 1974 compared to $8 million in 1970.

"We thought this would cause the state's banks to howl. Instead, they seemed to appreciate us removing the politics from the practice. They cooperated fully. This was typical of support we had from the business and professional community," he said.

His breakup of the traditional depositing practices wasn't Carter's only financial innovation. He also formulated a "Zero Based Budgeting" plan which has since been initiated in Texas, Missouri, and other states. During the 1976 presidential campaign, people such as Sen. Edmund Muskie of Maine were making sounds like the federal government might move in the same direction. Under the plan departments justify all programs—old and new—annually.

"I just wanted government to be run like a business. You have to set priorities," Carter said. And the environment was another Carter priority.

His Heritage Trust Program protected over 18,000 acres of Georgia land from the bulldozers. It was Carter, too, who blew the whistle on a proposal to build a controversial dam at Spewrell Bluff in Upson County, Georgia. This move received national attention.

What kind of governor was Carter? The jury is still deliberating that one. His reorganization plan never was as effective as he envisioned it, but the legislature sliced it up drastically. His pet project, the Department of Human Resources, has proved a bureaucracy within a bureaucracy and was so cumbersome that Governor Busbee moved to split it up in the fall of 1976.

Yet that same reorganization plan cut administrative costs from 9.6 percent in 1971 to 5 percent in 1974. The number of employees annually added to the state payroll decreased from 14 percent to 2 percent.

Two revealing points which don't show up on the statistical sheets give a hint to his philosophy. They concern his cousin, State Sen. Hugh Carter, and the home area that Jimmy Carter loves so well.

Soon after Carter took office the beloved Sen. Richard Russell died suddenly, and Carter, as governor, was to name his successor. There were political pressures for him to name former Gov. Ernest Vandiver, but he withstood those. A move was to develop within the state capitol, however, which would be even more difficult for him to ignore.

Many members of the Georgia Senate told the governor that his cousin Hugh would be an ideal choice to succeed Senator Russell. They presented a petition to him saying just that. Others seconded the idea. Instead, the job went to Atlanta attorney David Gambrell, who was to be soundly defeated by State Rep. Sam Nunn of Perry in 1972.

"I would have loved to be a Senator. I think I could have been a good

Carter welcomes President and Mrs. Richard Nixon to the Georgia capitol.

one, too, good enough to get reelected. But I understood. I know what people would have said and thought. That's not the way Jimmy thinks or operates," a philosophical Hugh Carter says today.

A ride through his home county shows the lack of personal favors Carter tossed their way. Plains is still the same Plains it was when he moved to Atlanta. Those who know him best say the area will not prosper from personal plums while he's in Washington either.

Perhaps the most discussed criticism that followed Carter during his term as governor was his stubbornness, his inability to compromise his own standards or his own beliefs. Critics point to his running feud with the General Assembly and his dealings with other state agencies.

As one long-time member of the Georgia senate put it: "He just won't compromise...he's the worst governor in the entire history of the state. I've tried to deal with him, but it's impossible."

Carter answered this way: "Being the worst governor in history for that particular senator may not be inconsistent with being a pretty good governor for the majority of the people of Georgia."

He still wouldn't give in.

Ben Fortson has been secretary of state for as long as most Georgians can remember. He's the mediator, the man in the middle, for most governors. Sitting in his familiar wheelchair, he described Carter to the General Assembly in the midst of the reorganization wrangle.

"Jimmy Carter is a gentleman. He's polite and soft-spoken and doesn't lose his temper. But I've known him for a long time, and I want to tell you something you'd better remember. Don't be fooled by that soft voice and that smile. That man is steel inside. When he thinks he's right, he's the most determined fellow you'll ever see," Fortson drawled.

Using an analogy the Georgia assemblymen would understand, he continued. "He reminds me of an old South Georgia turtle. Did you ever see one come up against a brush pile or a limb in his path? He doesn't stop and back up. He doesn't even worry about trying to go around. He just starts pushing, and he keeps at it until before you know it that limb is laying off to one side, and he's heading down the same path he started out on," the colorful Georgian said.

That hard-shelled, determined turtle could be any number of folks down South. The Southerners of Carter's generation are leathery types not afraid to work to get what they believe in. That's something they're taught from the time they were big enough to swing a hoe. It's that religious work ethic in practice instead of words. These people aren't especially ruthless, they're just determined. They're not exactly vindictive, they just need to surround themselves with people who have that same inner drive they were born with.

But they are a little stubborn.

Ralph McGill was a spokesman for a lot of things this so-called New South stands for in the days when the Old South was still young. The late editor-publisher of the *Atlanta Constitution* wrote words which inspired generations of Georgians. Some were inspired to new ideals and plateaus. Others to hatred.

Decades ago McGill wrote about stubbornness, comparing the horse—

which he considered unreliable—and the mule—which he respected. A mule, he would say, practiced the art of the possible. It wouldn't lunge and strain against too heavy a load. It would give its utmost, but it would not let itself be driven beyond its strength. Nor would it ever commit the utterly idiotic act of rushing back into a blazing stable, seeking security, as would a horse.

There was a streak of mule in Jimmy Carter. He practiced the possible. He wouldn't give in to a heavy burden. He was part turtle, too, never veering from that path he had picked out for himself.

But when word leaked out in Georgia that Jimmy Carter was thinking of running for President, many folks began to think he was practicing the impossible and had chosen a dead-end path.

Jimmy's Running For What?

The sign on the road said this was the Americus-Sumter County Airport, so this must be the place. But there was no terminal. No stewardess. Not even any sign of the ever-present Secret Service agents. Yet, according to the schedule, Jimmy Carter was due to land there within the hour. The day before he had won the New Hampshire primary, the nation's first taste of presidential politics. But this desolate airstrip hardly looked like the type of place you would expect to find a potential President. The skies may have been friendly, but mainly they were lonely.

Ten miles away in Plains there were bands, banners, and buttons. Here a lone phone booth gave out the only light and was the only hint of civilization. There was a stray dog, wagging his tail, the only welcomer other than a sparse turnout of local news people.

First to arrive was Rosalynn Carter. She was winging in from Florida. Shortly afterwards the candidate's small craft landed. Climbing out over the wing someone handed Carter his suit bag and his luggage. He carried it on to the waiting car.

In Plains a flatbed truck had been turned into a speaker's stand. Main Street had been roped off, and the town's single policeman was directing latecomers into what few parking places were available.

The festivities had been organized by Mrs. Maxine Reese, a neighbor of the Carters. "We were just sitting around the breakfast table, listening to the news. We decided we should do something for Jimmy, so here we are. This is the best way to do things. It all happened so fast that there wasn't time for anything to go wrong," Mrs. Reese explained.

The crowd roared as Carter mounted the platform. Secret Service men, trying to blend into the crowd, stood out like sore thumbs in their unwashed blue jeans and neatly ironed flannel shirts.

The Americus High School band played while Jim Head, an elementary

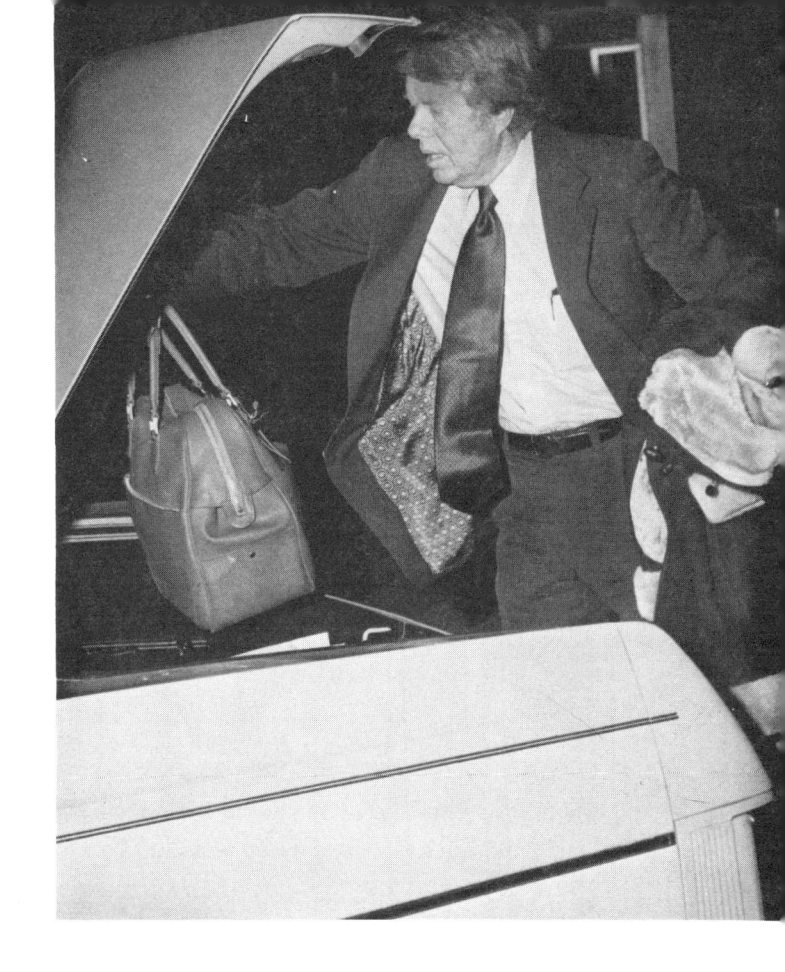

From beginning to end, Carter carried his own bags.

Jimmy helped Rosalynn down from a plane on a dark night in Americus.

Local gospel singer Leonard Wright helped welcome Carters home to Plains.

school principal from Americus, sang the National Anthem. The Reverend Bruce Edwards, pastor of the Plains Baptist Church, gave the prayer. It was nothing but home folks. And the final speaker was one of them, too.

"You'll never know what it means to me to come home, late at night, as tired as all of us are, and see all of you. You're the difference in my campaign and others'. People back home, praying and loving...that's the difference. I don't know how to treat you. I can't keep you up every Tuesday like this. We need to work out something. This could get boring," Carter told them.

Caucuses already had been held in Iowa, Oklahoma, and Maine, along with the startling win in New Hampshire. Even Puerto Rico had gone to Carter, giving him five wins in five starts. By this time Georgia was beginning to sit up and take some notice.

It had not been that way in the beginning.

Word that Carter planned to run for President had leaked out late in November of 1974. Bill Shipp, associate editor of the *Atlanta Constitution,* was the one who got the advance word, and when the state's largest morning newspaper spread the story across its top eight columns folks around the state started to snicker. Some didn't even bother to laugh.

By the time a Georgia governor is ready to leave office he has usually worn out his welcome. People are beginning to look ahead toward the new man. Outside of the late Gene Talmadge few former governors have ever been able to mount a comeback. The state constitution at that time limited a governor to one term, and people were saying it was just as well for Carter that he couldn't run again, that he couldn't be reelected anyway.

Long-time ally Milton Jones discounts this attitude.

"I remember some time in 1973 when people were saying Jimmy had lost his popularity and had lost touch with the people. He called me one day and said he was going to be in Columbus in the next few days, and he wanted to see some people.

"I thought he meant party leaders, the courthouse crowd. He said no, that he just wanted to go to some shopping centers, anywhere he could just meet and talk to people. When we got out there, people crowded around him just like they always had. I knew then that no matter what people said or what newspaper polls showed, that Jimmy and the people would always have a love affair going."

But that didn't keep Georgians from having their private laughs. Some began looking for other motives. They could picture him as Vice-President, that must be what he's after. Others thought he might be laying the groundwork for a Senate campaign against Sen. Sam Nunn, a former Carter team member who had run against and defeated Carter's appointee David Gambrell. Some thought he'd be a stalking horse for another Democrat. Some few thought the strain had been too much on him, that he should be retired quietly to his peanut fields.

Carter's popularity back home was hardly at its peak, and the defeat of Bert Lance, the outgoing governor's personal choice as his successor, was ample evidence that he did not have a lot of support among Georgia Democratic leaders. Lance, who had served as chairman of the Department of Transportation while Carter was governor, later became president of the National Bank of Georgia in Atlanta. There'd be more for him to do later, however.

It was difficult for Georgians to take Carter seriously. Through the years they had seen a parade of politicians make a mockery of Southern politics. They'd fight an outsider who criticized one of Georgia's political heroes, but deep inside they knew most of them were out of the same well-worn mold.

In 1824 William Harris Crawford was the nominee of the Jeffersonian Republican Party—predecessor to our current Democratic Party. The Lexington, Georgia, resident had been Secretary of War under President James Madison. But when he became the presidential nominee in 1824, he was an outsider. Foes called him an intriguer and manipulator. He was defeated by Andrew Jackson.

Crawford can hardly be called a product of the mold. Tom Watson can. In fact, it may be Watson whom later Georgia politicians emulated. Ironically, Carter's grandfather, Jim Tom Gordy, was a diehard supporter of Watson who nurtured the Populist movement in Georgia and served in both the House of Representatives and Senate. Watson was an exponent of rural mail delivery, fathering the Rural Free Delivery plan. Gordy, in fact, was to serve as postmaster in Richland for many years.

It's his views on race that cause Watson to be remembered, not the birth of RFD. Watson was an enigma. He was a tragic figure, one who began as a champion of brotherhood and died a venomous preacher of hatred. He went from a Populist candidate for President to a defeated candidate in his home state. Populists never saw this side of him. They only remembered him as one who died "fighting all of the sons of bitches in the world." He had been a man who cared not for the frills, the pomp, the fancy side of politics. He fought against the wealthy, privileged sector that overran the less privileged. He was more interested in the people.

In the beginning, Watson believed in political equality for blacks. He called for full citizenship. He spoke out harshly against lynchings, at a time when Georgia was hanging more blacks than any other state except for Mississippi.

Somewhere along the line, however, Watson lost his earlier perspective. Opponents had defeated him for Congress by openly buying black votes. He was to turn his back on all that he once stood for. He was to become the symbol of all who feared and hated. He proved he could holler "nigger" louder than his opponents.

In Georgia, this was to become part of a politician's strategy. Issues, campaign promises, who donated to your campaign, these questions were not asked. How you stood on segregation was the key.

The events of the past had left Georgia a bit ashamed of her political heritage. She had little confidence in what her candidates had to offer, and the rest of the country agreed, or so most thought.

Southerners had seen what happened to their own who thought they would be President. Estes Kefauver of Tennessee won a string of primaries in 1952, but he had to settle for applause at the convention. Richard Russell, the late Senator from Georgia, was qualified to be President, but the closest he came was a favorite son nomination in 1952.

Then there was George Wallace.

The Fighting Judge had become a symbol of things past. Though he had mellowed and moderated, he still was thought to be out of that old mold of segregation—Now and Forever. He had found support outside the South for his brand of politics, but even before that assassination attempt in Maryland in 1972, it had become obvious he would never take his message all the way to Washington.

How could a grits-eating peanut farmer from Georgia hope to be President? Folks back home asked themselves this question, and Carter offered an answer.

"There's still some of that old stigma attached to the South, but it's outweighed by that old fascination with Southern politics. But the fascination is not a handicap anymore. I've gotten this feeling from talking to just plain people on the street, all over the country.

"Mainly it was a removal of our racial barriers. That helped our stature tremendously. People accept Southerners as representative of the nation's thinking," Carter said, even before he had packed up and left the state capitol.

Carter had served as a National Democratic Committeeman for a time, and one of his chores was to travel across the country campaigning for any Democrat who needed help. He said that no longer did people single him out for ridicule just because he happened to be from the South.

"Someone took a poll recently," he said at the time. "They asked if the person would prefer a Southerner to be President. Only four percent gave a negative reaction. The era of Southern prejudice is over. It's time a Southerner can be elected President."

Even those who bought his reasoning pointed to George Wallace as that Southerner. From his wheelchair, Wallace still stood tall in the minds of some.

"He's no threat," Carter replied. "He's had the same level of support for 11 years—about 17 to 25 percent. He's only a threat in certain areas. He can't be on a national ticket."

However, few really believed Carter's contentions on December 12, 1974, when he gathered together his followers at Atlanta's Civic Center to make official what people had been speculating.

"I am," he said, "as of this moment a candidate for the presidency of the United States. When my duties as governor are completed on January 14, I will totally devote my time and energy to an aggressive campaign for that office."

At noontime that day he had spoken to the National Press Club in Washington. It was part of the Carter strategy to make the announcement in Atlanta rather than the nation's capital. Already he was seeking to disassociate himself with the political establishment. He sought in that speech to establish himself not as just another candidate. He wanted to be something different.

"Being President is not the most important thing in the world to me. There are a lot of things I would not do for any office or honor in the world. If I ever mislead you, if I ever place political favor ahead of what is right and best for our country, if I ever fail to apply the highest standards of personal integrity, openness and honesty to this campaign, then I do not deserve your support or the office I seek," he said.

Watergate was a recent memory. He promised integrity and talked of the kind of America he would like to see.

"Our people expect great things from our country—and they should. Our people have become disillusioned because they believe government and politicians have too often failed to live up to these expectations—and they are right....

"Americans are concerned about the basic integrity of government, the exclusion of the people from governmental decisions, a lack of administrative and executive competence, and the almost total absence of well-defined and clearly understood national purpose and goals," he continued.

A host of familiar faces were on hand, even astronaut Buzz Aldrin. Many were the enthusiastic followers who would be the backbone of his two-year effort. Even more persons were there out of courtesy to their fellow Georgian.

The media in his home state front-paged Carter's announcement, giving him polite applause. But skeptics outnumbered the optimistic. The *Columbus Ledger-Enquirer's* veteran capital correspondent, Beryl Sellers, had scheduled his vacation for that week and was not inspired enough to forego it. *Atlanta Constitution* editor Reg Murphy was there, however. His column the following morning was bannered with a now-famous headline: "Jimmy Carter's Running for What?" In this column Murphy said, "Gov. Jimmy Carter's timing was just right. The state needed a good bellylaugh, and Carter obliged by announcing he would run for president." Months later Murphy was fed a steady diet of his own words.

An old adversary of Carter, Murphy mentioned the timing as if it were accidental. But nothing the Carter forces did in those early days of the movement was by chance. Most of the events had been carefully charted months, even years, before.

Just who first came up with the notion that Jimmy Carter might be presidential timber depends on who is telling the story. Some say it was young Hamilton Jordan, one of his top aides. Some say it was psychiatrist Peter Bourne, a close friend of the former governor. Whoever actually broached the subject, it was a 70-page memo written by the 32-year-old Jordan that plotted the course.

In this 1972 memo he outlined what Carter would have to do to be ready to make his move when he left the governor's office. He talked about his establishing a national reputation as a thinker, of cultivating national newsmen, of even writing a book. Quietly Carter and his staff began putting the recommendations into practice.

At the same time Carter was giving himself a cram course in important subjects. He was reading daily the *New York Times, Washington Post, Wall Street Journal,* and other publications which gave in-depth coverage to national and world affairs. He was working on his personal weaknesses.

"Jimmy Carter's Running For What?" a headline asked.

Columnist William Buckley even reports that Carter was coached in his diction so that his Southern accent would not be so noticeable.

Atlanta advertising executive Jerry Rafshoon was so successful in marketing the Hollywood epic, *Cleopatra*, that he opened his own agency. He had also been so successful at selling Carter's 1970 gubernatorial campaign that he was now in the inner circle of advisors. It was Rafshoon who had noticed the similarities between the Carter smile and the Kennedy smile. He mobilized a campaign that would capitalize on the similarities. He even arranged a 1973 appearance for Carter on "What's My Line?" Carter stumped the panel, Arlene Francis saying, "We can assume, can't we, that you're not a government official?"

All of this was history when Carter, flanked by his entire family, made his 1974 announcement. Already on paper was the battle plan. It was simple, really. Election reforms indicated that more states than ever before would be having primaries in 1976, and Carter intended to run in each. He had mapped out a 250-day schedule for 1975. He was training for the rigorous

Stepping into wrestling ring in Columbus, Georgia, Carter sought support.

year like a fighter, even swearing off his occasional drink of scotch for the duration.

In the beginning he knew he would have to depend on friendships around his home state. To foster these relationships Carter met with some of his friends in late 1974 to share his plans. The Democratic Mini-Convention was coming up soon in Kansas City, and Carter needed their help.

Milton Jones remembers that meeting well.

"I laughed to myself when he told some of us what he was planning to do. Not that I didn't think he could be a good President. It was just that this was the presidency, and it seemed so impossible and so far away. Then I listened to him lay out the plan for us. The more I listened the more I started to get enthused. This was right after the worst of Watergate, and so he was dwelling on it. He also was convinced the race would boil down to between him and Teddy Kennedy. He was sure he could beat him, too.

"To hear him describe his plan, you thought of a football coach standing at the blackboard diagramming a play. On the board everything goes all the way for a touchdown. Everyone blocks his man. Everyone carries out his assignment. Jimmy convinced me that if we all did what we were assigned to do, that he could go all the way, too," the former Georgia legislator says.

Their first assignment was to get themselves elected as delegates to the Mini-Convention. Jones and Mrs. Janet Barker of Warner Robins, wife of a state senator, were elected from Carter's Third District. What they saw in Kansas City was eye-opening.

"Each one of us was assigned a state to work on," Jones says. "We were supposed to locate the state chairman or anyone we might know and somehow wrangle an invitation for Jimmy to talk to their caucus, to sit with them on the floor or visit them some time while we were out there. I had Pennsylvania, and I always take a lot of lighthearted credit that it was Pennsylvania that finally put him over. Anyway, he spoke to them the first night out there, and I had a chance to just follow him around the rest of the time.

"It was eye-opening to me. He had something I couldn't understand. He had also done more with that Democratic committeeman job than anyone of us realized. It seemed like someone in every state knew him. I remember him going before the Colorado caucus. Gary Hart told them that this was the man who did more to get him elected than anybody else. Jimmy got a standing ovation when he was through," Jones said.

There were problems to be overcome, too.

"When he went to speak to the New Jersey group, they almost booed him when he got up to speak. All of them thought, 'Oh, no, here's another George Wallace or another Lester Maddox. What are we in for now?'

"He gave the standard eight- or nine-minute speech he was using then. When he finished talking, they gave him a loud, standing ovation. I was convinced. When we got home, I couldn't wait for the first primary," Jones said, relaxing in his Columbus law office. He and Mrs. Barker sent out a letter expressing that optimism once they were back in Georgia. It said in part:

"...We can't close without mentioning the Carter presidential situation. As many of you know, both of us are rather close to Jimmy Carter, so perhaps our prejudices are coloring our judgment. We really don't think so, however.

"From what we saw with our own eyes and heard with our own ears in Kansas City, Jimmy has a much better chance of being elected President than we had previously thought. He was very well received by delegates from all over the country. We watched how he, and the vast majority of the Georgia delegation, worked and compared it to the other leading contenders.

"Whether you are for him or not, the main report we bring you from Kansas City is that, at least in our opinion, Jimmy Carter has the best chance of any Southerner in the last 114 years of being elected President...," the letter told Georgia Democrats.

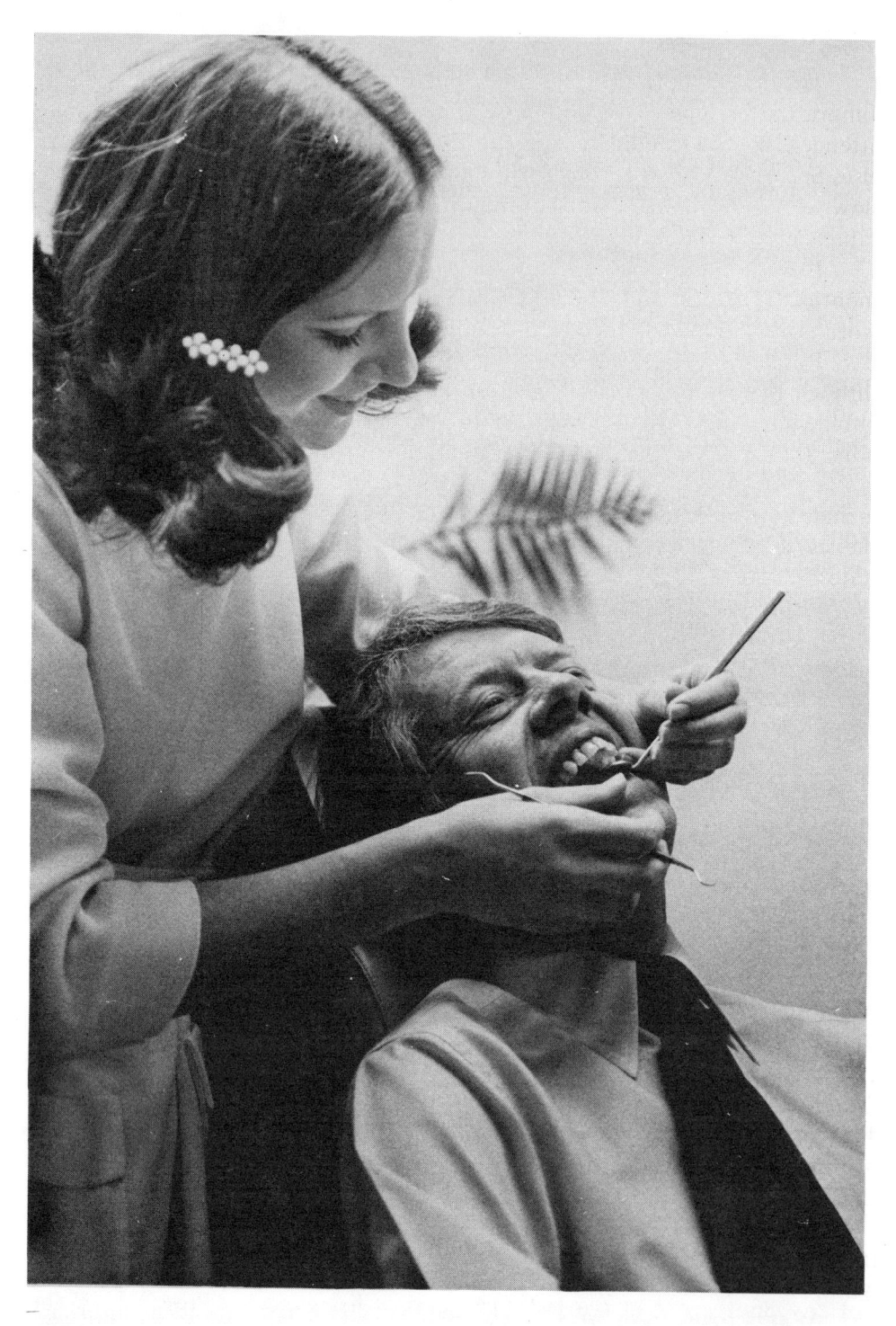

Columbus, Georgia, dental aide Jan Ceranski checks out million dollar teeth.

They were optimistic, excited, but there were to be moments when Jimmy Carter must have doubted. A press conference in Philadelphia was attended by the candidate and press secretary Jody Powell...and nobody else. Speeches echoed through half-empty halls. He was building, but it was slow, very slow. It was a word-of-mouth foundation, not unlike his statewide campaigns in Georgia.

It was a typical Georgia July when Carter came home to regroup after 6 months, 37 states, and 300,000 weary miles. He was dressed in a pair of worn jeans and mud-stained clod-stompers when he greeted his guests.

Rosalynn Carter was puttering in the kitchen as a break from going through the mounting mail. Nine-year-old Amy was busy chewing a fistful of bubble gum and begging her father to help her build a spook house. It was a home that could be the dream of a situation comedy producer.

Carter moved away a stack of records he had been going through. They included Gregg Allman and Frank Sinatra albums. The records put away on the stereo, Carter excitedly talked about those first six months on the road, state by state.

"Rosalynn, how many counties have you visited in Florida so far?"

"All of them north of Orlando," she answered from the kitchen. "I've made four or five trips there."

"She's turned into quite a campaigner, probably better than I am," Carter said. He also pointed out that his three sons had joined them on the road, although their paths were all different.

"I'm still the same, though. I just know more about campaigning now. I understand how the media works and can cooperate with them better now. I've been preparing for this campaign for two and a half years. I know the issues and have a steady stream of information coming in to keep me up to date," he said.

His comfortable, book-shelved den offered evidence. Stacked up along a couch were newspaper clippings, divided up by issue or by state. Carter's Atlanta staff—at that time hidden away in the rear of attorney Robert Lipshutz's Peachtree Street law office—kept close tabs on the nation's press.

"Just look at the national press coverage we've received. The *New York Times* has done three major features on the campaign. The *Christian Science Monitor, National Observer, Washington Post, Los Angeles Times*, and a lot of others have followed us. Wallace gets headlines, but we get serious articles all over on our campaigning and on the issues," he said.

Of course, he learned some more light-hearted lessons, too. "I have to travel light. I don't have time to wash so I bring the laundry home for Rosalynn," he smiled.

At this point there were no plugged-in Secret Service agents monitoring his every wave, and he was traveling light, worrying about a clean shirt. But he was building, although it wasn't the traditional foundation.

"While the others have been building a money base, we've been building a people base," was the way Carter put it. It was to prove a firm foundation.

Peanuts Can Grow
In New Hampshire

Every four years politicians knock on her door, and New Hampshire says welcome. The campaigners fill up her hotels, eat in her restaurants, and drink her booze. The visitors pour upward of $60,000 into the state's treasure chest.

Usually the visitors are students, recruited off the college campus, ready to give out pamphlets, knock on doors, do whatever it takes to win for their candidate, whoever he may be that trip. Some, you see, are fickle. On one trip they may be leading the cheers for a Eugene McCarthy, and a few weeks later they may have pledged their allegiance to a Hubert Humphrey.

Living through this invasion has turned the New Hampshire resident into a sophisticated, almost blase, voter. There are faded posters on telephone poles all over his state, crumpled-up brochures in every waste can. The voter there sees himself as more than a Gallup statistic. Because state law dictates that he'll go to the polls before the rest of the country, he wants to be sure of his choice.

"I had breakfast with Fred Harris, lunch with Jimmy Carter, dinner with Moe Udall and turned down seven others," explained Bob Raiche. "It's no wonder we're blase. We know that every four years someone's going to be knocking on our door."

A waitress offered Raiche more coffee, but he refused. He had to gather his thoughts. The noisy visitors were almost through with their lunch, and soon the former New Hampshire legislator would be asked to give them a briefing on his home state.

Around the crowded dining room at the Wayfarer Inn in Manchester, New Hampshire, was a 100-person invasion force from Georgia. Right now they were marveling at the mounds of snow on the ground, but for the next five days they would be walking the streets of Manchester and Nashua offering personal testimony about Jimmy Carter.

Atlantan Steve Selig checks in for Carter charter to New Hampshire.

"That's why this project is so unique. It's unusual for someone from the candidate's home area to say anything good about him, much less come this far to say it," said Raiche.

The Georgians were from all walks of life, housewives, teachers, doctors, stewardesses. They were in New Hampshire at their own expense. The project was the brain child of Carter's national campaign director, Hamilton Jordan, a spinoff of the successful "Hi, Neighbor!" program which had proved so successful during Carter's 1970 gubernatorial campaign.

"It's an interesting undertaking. People had been saying they wanted to do something to help. This trip, which is something no other candidate has ever attempted, is the result. Canvassing is nothing new up here. New Hampshire gets hundreds of people during every presidential year, mostly busloads of college kids or paid supporters. We think the wide variety of people coming all the way from Georgia is going to be inspirational," predicted Mrs. Connie Plunkett, Carter's Georgia coordinator, herself an unpaid volunteer.

The invasion force had been duly warned about the weather, but most of them still couldn't believe all that snow. When they deplaned in Manchester, groups of them got into snowball battles, to the delight of the TV cameras which were grinding.

The snowball duel was to cause one Georgian trouble back home. His kids saw him on TV and, remembering his reasons for not taking them, wondered how such a busy man could be out there in the snow having that much fun.

Inside the Wayfarer, however, it was all business. Teams were formed and assignments made in the two cities they would be covering. Raiche and other local Carter supporters gave the teams insight into what to expect. There was even a cram course in French for those who might be canvassing French neighborhoods.

Their goal was to contact 25,000 households, or 30 percent of the Democratic households in New Hampshire. If each canvasser averaged 55 households per day—about four hours' work—that goal might be reached. Should they choose to rise early, they might greet the 5 a.m. shift change at local factories.

A few enthusiastic souls ventured out that evening. Mrs. Dot Padgett of Douglasville, accompanied by CBS cameramen, went door to door in a Manchester neighborhood, and all she attracted was the police. I.D. Engram of

Columbus, Georgia, lawyer Ben Phillips waits outside New Hampshire door.

Fairburn hurried to a nearby W.T. Grant's and stocked up with a flashlight. But he found he needed more than light in the dimly lit streets and the icy winds, especially after his first fall on a slick snowbank.

Not even Mrs. Padgett's scrape with New Hampshire justice or Engram's introduction to New Hampshire snow sent any of them packing for home, and the next morning they reported for duty. And they looked like something out of an L.L. Bean Catalogue. All that was missing was Sergeant Preston and that dog of his. This group was dressed for the Yukon.

When Milton Jones' team arrived in the Boston bedroom community of Nashua, 25 miles from Manchester, they found it something out of Currier and Ives. Jack London must have done the landscaping. It was beautiful... and it was cold. On Jones' team were Mrs. Ann Singer of Lumpkin, Mrs. Margaret Broun of Athens, Miss Julianna Winters of Decatur, and Miss Mary Bell Wilkins of Atlanta. They were armed with a bundle of prospects and a willingness to spread the Carter gospel.

Georgians found scenes from Currier and Ives in the snowy North.

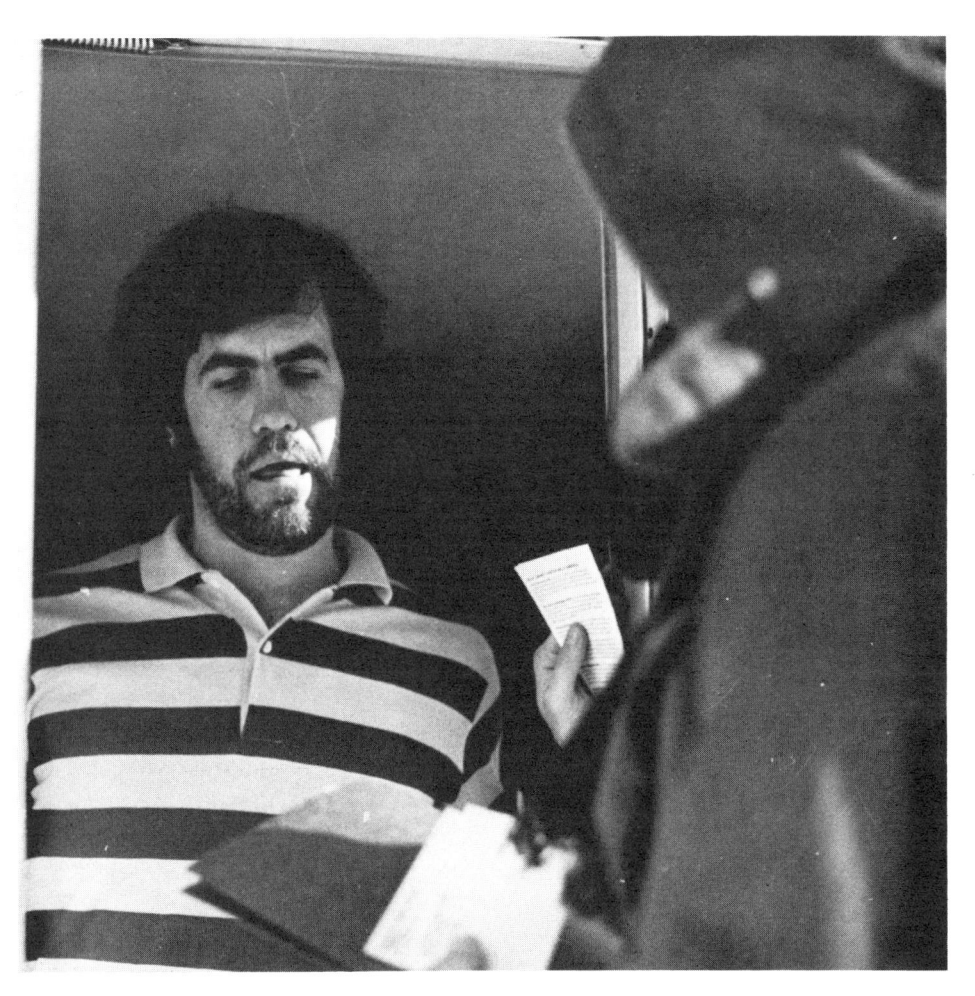

New Hampshire voters were shocked Georgians had come so far.

    Responses to their efforts ranged from addressee unknown to slammed doors, to invitations for coffee to unanswered bells. Inching their way along the icy sidewalks, which were almost invisible beneath the fluffy snow, they began to make their way through the stack of name cards. Word that they were in the neighborhood spread, and many residents not even on the workers' lists came to the door to find out if those strange people slipping and sliding down their streets were from Georgia.
    "Is it cold enough for you?" one woman asked Julianna Winters.
    "Yes, and do you have a brochure?" the Emory University student replied.
    Mrs. Singer even found that if she mentioned her home was near Ft. Benning, Georgia, a popular stop on the army's infantry tour, they knew

where Lumpkin was.

Shielding her small child from the chilling wind, Mrs. Kathryn Ruisinger gave Jones her impressions of Carter.

"He's been on a couple of talk shows out of Boston, and I watched him both times. I liked the way he sounded. If he could get rid of the bureaucracy in Washington like he did in Georgia, he's the man we need," said Mrs. Ruisinger, who had lived in Nashua only three months, coming from Nebraska.

Not all of the people answering the door were so talkative, but most were cordial. Southerners always brag about their hospitality, but that week they received a lesson in what hospitality is truly like.

The five Carter workers continued to knock on doors even after the sun had made its daily exit at 4:30 p.m. With the sun at rest, the cold took over. The temperature dropped below zero. Sidewalks became even more treacherous, and the cold was also to have an effect on other things.

Jones was making one of his final calls on a darkened Richmond Drive. If he thought it was cold, he should have checked with his glasses. As the temperature dropped, his lenses began to contract, and as he left the home of a man appropriately named J.R. Snow, one of the lenses popped out.

"There I was, on my hands and knees groping around in the snow. Finally, I knocked on Mr. Snow's door again, and he was kind enough to come out and help. We finally found it," the Georgian said.

For the 100 invaders it went on this way from Monday through Thursday. By day they braved frostbite. By night they braved writer's cramp, composing follow-up letters to those they had met that day. Mail was being carted out of the Wayfarer headquarters by the boxful.

When they were through, 18,295 homes had been contacted. Of that number 606 had said to count them among Carter supporters. Another 1,439 were termed favorable, and 4,686 were uncommitted.

That was the report card Carter himself received when he arrived in Manchester for a visit with the folks from back home. Jimmy Carter was 1,200 miles from Plains, but it was plain to see he was among friends.

Bulbs were flashing. People were inconspicuously trying to get in line for a picture with their candidate. Women were standing on tiptoes for a kiss on the cheek. To the folks in that room those moments were worth the aching muscles, scratchy throats, and writer's cramp.

Carter circled the room, stopping to chat with everyone. He questioned what the charts on the wall meant, and when he was told those were the scoreboards his smile broadened.

After greeting his old friends, Carter moved toward the hotel ballroom for a meeting with some new friends. When he arrived, Bill Shaheen, a New Hampshire native but an Ole Miss law school graduate, called for attention.

Carter found Sumter County neighbors waiting in Manchester.

"Y'awl be quiet," the local Democrat joked. "I want to introduce to you the next President of the United States...." But there was no need to finish.

"I'm proud to call each of you a friend," Carter began. "This means so much to me. I wish Rosalynn and my whole family could be here to share this evening with me. At the beginning of last year there was nothing to distinguish me from the rest of the candidates in New Hampshire. Now I'm known as the one with the love, friendship, and support of his folks back home. People might forget me, but they won't forget that all of you cared enough to come through the ice and snow."

The New Hampshire primary was only six weeks away, and he predicted that the group which came to be known as the "Peanut Brigade" would have their impact. How right he was. When the New Hampshire votes were counted February 24, 1976, Carter was on top, Morris Udall a soon-familiar second.

Carter's Campaign Express was rolling, thanks to his friends who had invested in "Long Johns" and come North to spread his word. Earlier he had been among the honorable mentions when the candidates were rated. Now he was on top. His opponents were learning things about Jimmy Carter.

His friends from Georgia learned, too. In the coming months they would be taking similar trips. But none would be like that first one. In the New Hampshire snow those who might have previously doubted became convinced, those who were lukewarm became enthusiastic, those who thought it would be a lark found politics hard work.

Yet, the most important lesson was summed up best by Dean Fowler, a nursing home tycoon from Montezuma, Georgia.

"You know, if these people didn't talk so funny, I'd think they were from Georgia," he said, turning on his best Southern accent.

As Carter put it, "You paid the people of New Hampshire the ultimate compliment when you said, 'They're just like us.'"

And so they were.

Clearing One More Hurdle

School was out, and youngsters, books in hand, began their afternoon invasion of Milford. It didn't take long for the peaceful atmosphere of the snow-covered New Hampshire village to be echoing with the sounds of the children celebrating the end of another dear old golden school day.

The youngsters were loosely marching in groups of two and threes, moving toward the historic town square, when a visitor stopped them and promised them a chance to meet the next President of the United States.

"Just wait right here, he's inside the beauty shop," the man said.

"The beauty shop?" one of the kids giggled.

"Oh, he's in there giving out brochures," the fellow hastily explained.

As promised, Jimmy Carter emerged from the beauty shop. Preceded by an entourage of Secret Service agents and photographers, he moved past the waiting youngsters. But an aide told Carter the youngsters had been waiting for him, and he walked over to the service station lot.

"Hi, I'm Jimmy Carter," he said.

"Are you really the President?" one of the excited youngsters interrupted.

"Not yet. But I will be if you'll help me," he answered.

Figuring that a button and a brochure would send them happily home, Carter continued his walk around the icy Milford square. How wrong he was.

"You guys come here. The new President of the United States is over here. We just met him," the youngsters told their friends. A mob of Milford school children was waiting outside the drug store when the candidate came out.

In a matter of minutes he had gone from the next President of the United States to the new President of the United States. If only it were that easy.

That was a January Thursday, but it might well have been any day in

Milford students thought Carter was already the President.

any town during Carter's two-year quest for the White House. His days weren't his own. They belonged to the mimeographed schedule that carved up his days into neatly packaged sections, down to the minute.

This day had begun at 7 a.m. when Carter guested on a local radio program. Remembering the discipline of the farm, his days began early. To some, time is money. To a candidate, time is votes.

As Carter candidly told his sister Ruth: "Honey, I can will myself to sleep until 10:30 and get my ass beat, or I can will myself to get up at 6 a.m. and become President."

The night before had been spent at the Dennis Boyer home in Nashua. Following the habits of his gubernatorial campaigns Carter usually stayed with supporters in whatever town he might be visiting. Even that was regimented. "He usually gets to a home about 10:30 or so, spends a few minutes chatting, then is in bed by 11 o'clock. He's very regimented. He holds to a pretty rigid schedule, being up by at least six the next morning," explained Ellis Woodard, a New Hampshire volunteer who was to become a full-time staffer by the end of the campaign.

The radio interviewer asked the predictable questions, and Carter fired back the predictable answers. Only when callers began to phone in questions did Carter begin to warm up. He was at his best one on one with the people.

Then he moved from radio to shoes, leading his motorcade to the J. F. Elwain Company in Nashua. He marched up and down the rows of workers at the shoe factory, stopping at every sewing machine to chat with the smiling females.

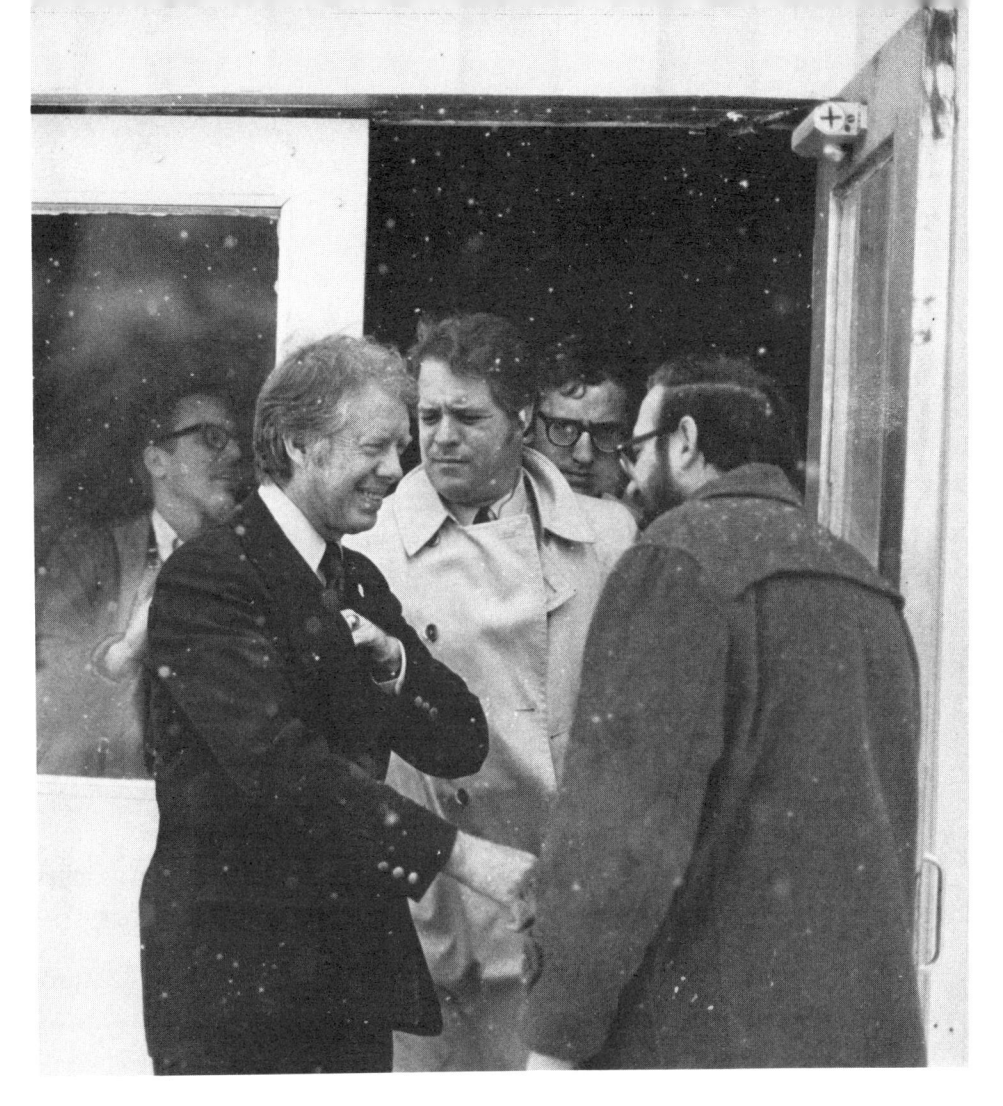

The New Hampshire snow didn't seem to bother this Georgia farm boy.

"Look at that profile. Doesn't he look like a Kennedy?" one told her neighbor at the next machine.

"He's better looking in person," another said.

This was to be his day-long pace. Before the day was over he would shake hundreds of hands and give out a like number of brochures. And the smile never left his face. Not even when he left the shoe factory, only to be greeted by a band of sign-waving questioners.

They called themselves the People's Bicentennial Committee. They had been following candidates all over New Hampshire, asking a series of questions on nuclear energy, the environment, and other issues that interested them. Photographers began taking pictures, and the TV lights warmed up as the committee members talked to Carter. Calmly he tried to answer each of their questions. No one seemed to notice that as he talked he was moving toward the waiting car. He would, however, see more of them that day.

"At least he talked to us," one of the picketers said later. "Reagan just

People's Bicentennial group found Carter willing to talk.

pushed us aside and Udall tried to pretend we weren't there. Carter seems like kind of a nice guy, really."

At Edgecomb Steel the talk was not about the candidate's resemblance to the Kennedy Clan. Here they asked more pointed questions.

"Didn't you do something about the bureaucracy in Georgia?" a computer programmer asked. His aides were shuffling their feet impatiently as Carter ran down his ideas on government reorganization.

The pitch was usually the same..."Hi, I'm Jimmy Carter, I want to be your President." Most of them listened. Most said they'd read his brochures. Some tucked them away for future reference. Some tossed them into the trash before Carter was hardly out of sight.

Every stop began to blend together for those tagging along, but Carter never slowed down. He seemed relaxed talking with the women about stitching shoes and equally at home talking with a hard-hat about the heavy lathe he was operating. He seemed to speak the language of each. The old clock on the wall was nearing noon, and reporters asked what Carter did about lunch.

"He doesn't usually stop, but since we're running ahead of schedule, he may stop and eat in one of the factory cafeterias," Ellis Woodard predicted. And so he did, picking out a can of beef stew and munching on potato chips while talking with a reporter.

"This is the only kind of lunch I ever eat. We don't usually stop," he said, taking a drink of milk from a carton. "This is the way I like to campaign. I've always enjoyed meeting factory shifts or going into the plants to meet people where they work. I think people appreciate that. I really believe these visits are among the most important things I can do. The polls everywhere show there's a great deal of undecided voters left, and most of them are right here in the factories and shops."

Before reporters could make their selection from the vending machines and get their dollar bills through the changer, Carter was on his feet, asking about the next stop. There were to be eight more that afternoon.

Leaving behind the whirling machines and hard-hatted workers the Carter Caravan moved to Milford, where he visited the local newspaper editor. This was to be a private interview, and the rest of the group waited outside the editor's office.

It was the first break the Secret Service agents had had all day. Lighting

Carter spoke language of hard hats and of the shoemakers.

up a cigarette, one of them talked about the differences in following Carter and the other presidential hopefuls.

"This man keeps you moving, all the time. You never know what to expect. Take Udall. You know he's right there in his hotel room waiting for you, and you know he's going to follow his schedule to the letter. In the afternoon he's going to go back to his room for rest and conferences. He's probably not going to go back out except for dinner meetings. But Carter's moving all the time," the agent said.

Leaving the editor behind, Carter followed aide Greg Schneiders up the hill toward the Milford town square. Walking into a dry goods store, he began his usual spiel. But the woman behind the counter interrupted.

"You don't have to tell me who you are. I met your wife and son a few weeks ago. They were right here in my store," she said, reaching under the counter and producing a green Carter pamphlet.

He was to find that in this town he was among friends, not necessarily voters, but friends. The thousands of miles his family had been traveling were beginning to pay off.

Back in Nashua he spoke to local supporters and members of the Peanut Brigade from Georgia who were opening his local campaign office. While the Secret Service shift changed and a new group punched the federal time clock, Carter made a few quick phone calls before packing up for a trip to Boston, 50 miles away. His day was to end there.

The three stops there were distinctly different. The first two were in

If you tried to keep up with Carter, you ate a quick lunch as he did.

troubled Roxbury, a Boston suburb where busing was a fighting word. The other was in stylish Cambridge, where busing is intellectually discussed behind Harvard's vine-covered walls.

Deep in the ghetto it was strange for a Georgia newsman to see a neighbor talking about Civil Rights to an all-black audience from Boston. After being introduced by Rep. Andrew Young, a black Congressman from Atlanta, that was to be Carter's subject.

"The greatest thing to happen to the South was the passage of the Civil Rights Amendment. It gave people the right to vote, to work and to advance, rights they should have had all along. In the end it freed the white Southerner as well as the black man," Carter said, words that made a neighbor from down home stop taking notes and listen.

Later Young explained how he came to support Carter.

"I think the stand Jimmy Carter made on Civil Rights in the 1950s and 60s was a more courageous stand than my votes in Congress. When he was standing up to the Klan and to the White Citizens Council, it was anything but comfortable or popular. I admire him for it, although I must admit that it was difficult for me in the beginning to be speaking out for a man from deep in Georgia. I had to overcome some prejudice of my own," said Young, later to become a member of the Carter team as U.S. Ambassador to the United Nations.

After his two visits in Roxbury, Carter was again on the move. It was only across Boston, but it might have been across the world. From the crowded ghetto they moved to Cambridge, home of Harvard and of the affluent. He was guest of honor at a reception hosted by Henry Morgenthau, a wealthy television producer and son of a former FDR cabinet member.

Carter seemed as at ease talking to the mink-and-diamonds set as he did to the ham-and-potato-salad crowd. It was enlightening to note that people in the sprawling mansion were interested in many of the same issues as the folks in the inner city.

The ride on the press bus back to New Hampshire turned into a nap. Still, coming across the radio was a familiar voice. Jimmy Carter was on the air, taking questions from listeners. He was ending the day just as he had begun it 17 hours before. Reporters had long since put away their pads, but he was still talking. Amazingly he was still in good voice, and, more surprising, his answers sounded fresh even if the questions were by now stale.

Jimmy Carter had a dream, but he was being forced to live a nightmare to see it fulfilled. That day in January 1976 was one of about 700 or so days he endured to get to the White House.

It began to pay off that January 19 when, despite sub-zero temperatures, he got 28 percent of the delegates in the Iowa caucus, putting early pressure on Henry Jackson, Morris Udall, Birch Bayh, Fred Harris, Sargent

Georgians raised money for neighbor with Manchester cattle auction.

Shriver, Terry Sanford, Lloyd Bentsen, George Wallace, Milton Shapp, Frank Church, Jerry Brown, and the other Democrats who had presidential dreams.

Terry Sanford was the first to yield, dropping out on January 23.

On January 25 Wallace showed he would not go down without a struggle, when he took the majority of delegates in Mississippi. Polls still showed Hubert Humphrey and Ted Kennedy leading the Democratic pack, and they were not even announced candidates.

On February 2 Carter showed his power in New England by leading the pack in Maine. He did the same on February 9 in Oklahoma, Harris's home state.

On February 10 Bentsen departed.

On February 24 the friends Carter had made in New Hampshire showed up at the polls. In the nation's first statewide primary, Jimmy Carter was a winner.

There was talk that he couldn't be beaten. Foregoing his recommended strategy Carter began to use words like win, lead, and other unretractable phrases. He was to learn his lesson in Massachusetts. He had not intended to campaign heavily there, concentrating instead on Florida. Feeling confident, he bragged about Massachusetts.

He finished fourth...behind Jackson, Wallace, and Udall, although on that same day he did win in Vermont.

On March 4 Bayh gave up the ghost, leaving Carter, Jackson, Wallace, and Udall to fight it out. Jackson was revitalized after Massachusetts, and Wallace had always run strong in Florida, so the Sunshine State was an important one. But Florida was the knockout blow for Wallace as his Georgia neighbor swept the state, even the Panhandle, which in the past had been diehard Wallace country.

A week later Shapp dropped out just before a Carter win in Illinois. Then Shriver threw in the towel on the eve of Carter's victory in North Carolina. One by one Carter's opponents were falling aside. All that was left was Jackson, and their shootout was to be in Pennsylvania.

Carter prevailed, and his old friend from Washington joined Sanford, Bayh, and the others on the sideline. It was that week in April that the old warhorse Humphrey tearfully confirmed he would not enter the race. Carter thought the nomination would be his "unless I do something to muddy the waters."

Carter didn't muddy the waters, but Church and Brown almost did. They entered the race and began knocking the tiring Carter off here and there. The Idaho Senator took Carter twice, and the youthful California governor won three. But Ohio was to be Carter's knockout blow. It was his 17th primary victory, coming on the final grueling night of the primary season. Then a travel-weary, battle-scarred Carter returned home to Plains to

Miss Lillian listens while her son confers with George Wallace.

the welcome of thousands of friends and supporters.

It was after three o'clock in the morning when he stepped from the car on Main Street. By that spring night in June he had been shaking hands and smiling at potential voters for 18 months. It showed on his lined face. But coming home always seemed to give him a second wind. Mounting the steps at the depot he talked to the cheering crowd, then moved through the street greeting old friends.

P.J. Wise was one of those old friends. His son Phil was one of Carter's shrewdest advisors. When P.J. stuck out his hand, Carter must have thought it was just another handshake. Wise, however didn't want to shake his hand. He had a message. Handing it to Carter, Wise waited for a reply.

"Did he want me to call tonight?" Carter asked.

"He sure did, no matter how late it was. Said the phone was right beside his bed," Wise answered.

The message was from George Wallace. Carter quickly made his way to the depot, and finding phones in the outer office taken, he moved up the steps to a more private cubicle. With his mother sitting on the desk beside him he called Wallace in Montgomery. That evening no one was to know the nature of the conversation.

Carter embraces old friend John Pope after clinching nomination.

At a press conference the next morning everyone found out. The press was crowded onto the depot loading dock waiting for Carter. The rostrum was to be an old pulpit rescued from a nearby church by John Pope, a friend of Carter. The background was to be a picture of the candidate, a permanent fixture on the outside of the depot. His family flanked him. When the candidate arrived he was wearing a denim jacket, blue jeans, and plaid shirt. It was a not-so-subtle way to show that this man was not a candidate of the usual establishment.

But his message was establishment. Governor Wallace had called to say he was recommending that his supporters turn to Carter. Chicago Mayor Richard Daley had called to say he was supporting Carter. Senator Henry Jackson had said he soon would release his delegates to the former Georgia governor.

The day was June 9, 1976. The Democratic Convention was still a month away. But overnight on June 8 Jimmy Carter had captured the nomination. That night, plus 17 victories and 18 months of non-stop travel.

Coming down from the depot steps Carter paused to talk to a school teacher from Indiana who had a busload of students he wanted Carter to meet. There was not time then, he explained, but Miss Lillian said she'd be a stand-in. Secret Service men ushered him toward his car.

Turning back one more time, he saw John Pope. Pope had been with him since that nearly aborted state senate campaign 14 years before. Hardly a word was spoken, and then they gave one another a bear-hug embrace.

Together they had cleared one more hurdle.

The Coronation Of Jimmy Carter

Beforehand, everyone thought the Democratic Convention would be like going to a movie after your best friend had told you everything about it, from the quality of the popcorn to whether chewing gum was stuck to the bottoms of the seats. All that was left was the coronation. After that Wednesday in June when Jimmy Carter was so busy on the phone, the smiling man from Georgia was the signed-and-sealed nominee.

Those of little faith didn't know Jimmy Carter, however. While everyone knew the ending, they didn't know the script. That would be written by Carter. Since he also was directing the show, he carefully arranged the week so that no one would know who his co-star was going to be, and he carefully cast the people who would wave from the Madison Square Garden podium so that every faction of the party would have its moment to cheer.

Carter began his play on July 5 when Sen. Edmund Muskie of Maine winged into the Plains airstrip, a pasture formerly reserved for crop dusters. Muskie was the first to be interviewed in Carter's tedious search for a Vice President. Two days later Sen. John Glenn of Ohio—the former astronaut—and Sen. Walter Mondale of Minnesota arrived. All three spent time closeted with Carter at his home, then got a tour of downtown Plains and the surrounding peanut fields. By the weekend Carter was in New York. The countdown had begun. Still to be interviewed were Sen. Adlai Stevenson of Illinois, Sen. Henry Jackson of Washington, Sen. Frank Church of Idaho, and Rep. Peter Rodino of New Jersey.

Hundreds of news personnel were in New York trying to tell the Democratic story. The reporter with the best and closest contacts to the Carter camp was a special correspondent for the *Columbus Enquirer,* back in Georgia. She had been a reader of that newspaper for nearly five decades. Instead of reading about the convention, she was writing about it. Her name was Mrs. Lillian Carter. Throughout the week, she would scribble down

John Glenn got lesson on peanuts from an experienced teacher.

notes, file away events in her mind, then sit down with Carrol Dadisman, the *Enquirer's* executive editor, to put her day into words. Who could tell the events of that week in July better than she?

Well, I want to tell you the funniest thing. I asked Jimmy if I could tell you this. He said it'd be all right. Well, Rosalynn had said, "Grandmommy, we'll be by for you at quarter till 12." I was dressed and ready. I was sitting in the dining room looking out the window. I saw the State Patrol and then I saw all these cars going by. And I said, "By golly, they have left me." So I had sense enough to call the Secret Service. I have their private number. And I said, "They've left me."

This boy said, "I know they haven't." I said, "Yes they have. They're gone." So he said, "I'll call you right back." He called me and said, "They have gone but wait now, hang on the phone. I'm going to get them word." All the time he was talking to the car Jimmy was in, so I heard Jimmy say, "Oh, my goodness." And in a few minutes, I heard somebody say, "Tell her to stay right there, we're sending somebody for her."

"Well, I just might not go," I said, just being facetious. And in a few minutes I could hear Jimmy say, "Well, tell Mother I am just so sorry." So in a few minutes Jimmy called and said, "Mama, I didn't know you were waiting. I thought you were going with somebody else. Rosalynn forgot to tell me. We'll wait right down here at Howard's place." That's a house about five miles down. So this man came for me and we went about 100 miles an hour to get down there quick as we could.

Jimmy said he never had been so happy to see a smile on anybody's face, 'cause you know I'm really funny and sensitive. I said, "A year or two ago I would have just said no, I'm not going."

But we had a good trip up there. It's the best ride I ever had in my life. I was invited to sit up in the cockpit, which I did. On the way up, every once in a while Jimmy said, "Mother, I declare. I'm so glad you're not mad." He was so embarrassed.

I'll tell you something else. The stewardess is one of my friends. I met her in Americus. We go up there and eat at Faye's place. Did you ever eat there? Anyway, she filled my pocketbook full of wine. When I got to New York, I had eight bottles full of wine. I couldn't lift the pocketbook.

Well, we got to New York, and, of course, everybody met us. We came on to the hotel, and oh, have you ever seen so many people? Jimmy spoke to the crowd and it was real warm. He was introducing all of us and when he introduced me, I think every black person out there screamed. They're my friends. It just gave me such a warm feeling. I noticed out there in the crowd different banners. One of them said, "We want a President who can chew gum and make decisions at the

Miss Lillian caught up and made it to the plane for New York.

same time." And I saw one out there that said, "Gay People for Jimmy Carter." I said, "Oh, my!"

* * * *

The Carters were encamped at the Americana Hotel. Security was airtight on the 21st floor where the family was housed. Color-coded badges were required. A small army of receptionists answered the house phones and only a few select persons had the numbers for the private lines in the candidate's suite. If anyone wanted an audience with any of the family, there was a stack of forms to be filled out. Interviews with the vice-presidential hopefuls were scheduled. The invasion had begun.

* * * *

Yes, I've met all the vice presidential candidates Jimmy has talked to so far. I like them all very much. It's hard to say which one I like the most.

I met Mr. Muskie when he came to Plains. I didn't get to stay with him long, because I had to go on back to the office—the headquarters, you know.

Then Mr. Mondale came down, and when Jimmy introduced us, he put his arm around me. I said, "Mr. Mondale, you're a heap better looking than your picture." And I carried on a few words with him.

Then the next one who came down was Mr. Glenn. When I talked with him, he was very low key. And I told him how much I had always admired him for what he did. I felt like I was talking to somebody like Billy Graham. He is so quiet, and he's very nice-looking. I like his wife, too....

Then yesterday, I walked in Jimmy's room and Scoop Jackson came out. I had met him before at the convention down in Florida (1972). I said, "Well, Scoop, it's nice to see you." That's all I said to him, but I talked with Mrs. Jackson.

So this afternoon, I went in and Mr. Rodino was there. And I told him how much I respected him for what he did during the Watergate hearings.

I think they're all real nice....

Oh, let me tell you about Saturday night. I had dinner with Jimmy and Rosalynn in their suite. You haven't seen their suite, but oooh, it's gorgeous. It has two bedrooms, two baths, a huge living room and then a room for his interviews, and a dining room. Well, I hadn't eaten frog legs since my husband died. They cost too much. So, we had frog legs. Amy didn't. She said, "I wouldn't eat a frog leg for anything on earth—those dirty frogs."

Then afterward, we had finger bowls. Amy had seen them before, and she said, "Well, I know what to do with them, but I don't know how—whether to dip a napkin in it or what." So the waiter came by and showed her.

This morning, we went over to the delicatessen across the street, because the food here is so high. While we were over there, this man behind me said, "Do you know who that is over there? It's Norm Crosby"—you know, the one who does double talk on television—and Norm heard him. So he said, "You're Mrs. Carter." You know, people know me everywhere I go.

So we began to talk to Norm. Amy's very friendly, and she went over and sat in his lap and he asked her for her autograph and she asked him for one for "Go-Go." That's what we call my daughter Gloria. After awhile I got a piece of apple pie and Amy got a tuna fish sand-

wich. She just ate a little, so we wrapped it to take back to the hotel.

* * * *

The interviews continued, following the prescribed script. There were receptions, parties, gatherings, all designed to make down-home tourists feel at home. A Sunday night party for the 5,000 delegates was an old-fashioned picnic, right out on the Hudson River Pier. Dress ranged from after-six finery to cut-off jeans. "We wanted folks to feel at home. We had fried chicken and greenery and plenty of peanuts," one of the organizers said, 250 pounds of peanuts to be exact. Fresh and raw. The kind Jimmy grows. Also on the table were 10,000 pieces of chicken, 2,000 pounds of cole slaw, 500 pounds of cold cuts, 900 gallons of cold beer, and 45 gallons of soda pop. There might be a hunger for suspense, but not for food.

* * * *

Well, I started out Sunday and Hamilton Jordan said, "Come and go with me to a labor party." I said, "What do you do at a labor party? I'm not in the mood for that." And he said, "It's a labor party downstairs." It was just cocktails. Two women and about 25 men. I like that. I thought they were going to talk about...you know...labor. But they didn't.

Then later we went to that big party for all the delegates. I stayed in the receiving line for a few minutes. I have had a broken wrist, you know, when I went to India. And I have broken my shoulder. So they kept shaking hands, and this man caught my hand—he was just being friendly—and turned it. I thought my wrist was broken again. It like to have killed me, so I got out of line. Then I saw they had somebody come over to take care of me every few minutes, to keep people from speaking to me. They'd say, "She's awfully tired." And one fellow just said, "Go back." So I said, "No, let me talk to somebody. I'll go crazy."

Then today, we went back to the delicatessen across the street. You know, I was telling you about Amy and the friend over there where we ate. He had invited us back over for breakfast, and he told Amy he'd have her some funny books. So I went to Jimmy's room this morning, and they were eating. "Where's Amy?" I said. Jimmy said, "She's getting a bath to go with you. Now, Mama, make her behave. Make her be nice."

So we went over, and it was just spotless. They had this table ready for us, all fixed up with flowers on it and everything. And he said, "Amy, come over," and he gave her 15 funny books. 'Course she just jumped up and kissed him right in the mouth. The breakfast I ate would have cost me five dollars and a half. But it didn't cost me a penny. I told Joe, the little bodyguard, to tell the owner we can't come back unless he took the money. Well the man got insulted. He came over and said, "When I invite guests, I intend to give them the meal free. If you come back tomorrow, I'll let you pay." That was his way of getting us back tomorrow.

At lunch we went to Newsweek. *They said it was casual, so Rosalynn put on slacks. This is interesting to women. How Rosalynn dresses, that seems to be the cue. I already had on my slacks. So we went on over to* Newsweek, *and let me tell you who all I met. That was the grandest thing.*

I met Ben Bradlee of the Washington Post, *and I met the owner or publisher of the* New York Times. *And Sally Quinn was there, too. Yeah, I met Sally. I like her. Mrs. (Katherine) Graham was the hostess, and she was just wonderful. She took me around to meet everyone.... Barbara Walters was at the luncheon. She said, "Oh, Miss Lillian, I'm glad to meet you. I'd like to talk to you while you're here." I said, "Barbara, I'm sorry. I can't possibly see you this time."*

Anyway, the crowning point of my day was Walter Cronkite. He came up to me and said, "I have been dying to see you." And he took me and kissed me, and he said, "You're going to be sitting in my box Wednesday night." He had asked me and there was a little controversy. Jimmy thought I ought to be with the family when they're taking pictures over there in his suite of rooms Wednesday night. But I'm going to be with Walter until the balloting. Then they're going to rush me back over to the hotel to take pictures with the family. I said, "I'm gonna do that or bust, because I just love Walter Cronkite." He's just so nice.

* * * *

While Jimmy Carter was locked away in his suite, Barbara Jordan stole the show. For a day, she owned New York and the Democratic Party. It was her high-pitched opening speech on Monday evening that set the stage for the entire week. The Congresswoman from Texas could have named her pay. Some were even willing to offer her the vice presidency. Senator John Glenn followed her and that was a job no one should have had. As the week drew on, South Dakota Senator George McGovern, Maine Senator Edmund Muskie, the late Chicago Mayor Richard Daley, Idaho Senator Frank Church, and Alabama Governor George Wallace all had their turn at the podium.

But none matched the smiling woman from Texas.

* * * *

Before the Convention Monday, Jimmy had the family over to Mamma Leone's. It was just the immediate family—Jimmy and his wife and the boys and their wives, my sister Sissy and I. It was a private dining room, and it was beautifully decorated—just a gorgeous thing. I've got what we had for supper written down here—antipasto, fettucine al fredo, veal piccata, Mamma's special ice cream and veridicchio.

The owner presented me with a dozen roses. He came over and said, "From one Mamma to another." At the dinner, Chip gave the toast, which is a secret. We were all surprised and very happy. (Later, it was told to one and all that Chip and Caron were going to present Jimmy and Rosalynn with their second grandchild.) So then, we went to the Convention.

Well, at the Convention, I couldn't hear a thing. You know that. I sat right by Mrs. Bob Strauss and her son, and right across the rope from me was Mayor Daley's wife. So I had a nice conversation with both of them. Which was great. After we had been there for—well, just before Barbara (Jordan) spoke—I said, "Amy, why don't you cry, so your mother will let us go home?" So she said, in a whiney voice, "Mama, I'm so tired." So Rosalynn said, "Is Grandmomma ready to go?" I said, "I am ready." So we left the others over there.

I had the funniest feeling sitting there in the Convention. The newsmen said to me: "We've talked to you at every plateau, and we want to know exactly what you feel about Jimmy now." And I told them, "Tonight as I looked out, I had not realized exactly the enormity of what he is doing. I saw that huge crowd and heard all those speeches and realized they were talking about Jimmy, and I had the queerest feeling." I don't know. It was a kind of awe. It was such a deep feeling. You know, I felt it was a sacred thing I was looking at.

I felt that way all the way home. I came home, and thank goodness, we went to Jimmy's room, Amy and I. And he was in there in his shorts—his walking shorts—barefooted, eating and looking at the television. And I said, "Oh, Jimmy, I'm glad it's you." I had felt like he was out of the universe...

Jimmy said, "Mama, I heard you were giving something to the Columbus (Ga.) Enquirer *every day. Will you tell me what you're doing?" I said, "No." He said, "Well, I've got to see that, because I know it's a mess." And I said, "No, it's real good, Jimmy." He said,*

Delegate Milton Jones was interested in his crackerjack prize.

"Well, what do you do? What do you tell them?" "Nothing," I said, "just things." And he said, "Mama, please let me know." And I said, "I'll let you know when it's all over."

* * * *

The love-in was still in bloom. People of all persuasions were mending old fences and forgetting old grudges. The past, they all claimed, was forgotten. This was a new year and new times. Jimmy Carter was love. And if you wanted to be a Democrat, you had to have some of that love in your heart. Until he got elected, anyway.

* * * *

Shirley MacLaine called me Tuesday and invited me to her show. It was a marvelous show. Afterwards she asked me to her dressing room, where we met, oh, so many people. The only thing about it—I had this pretty pocketbook somebody had made for me. It had Jimmy's name on it in his writing, and it had two big peanuts, and I loved the thing. I hope whoever gave it to me is reading this so she can give me another one, 'cause Shirley said, "I just love that pocketbook," and I said, "You can have it."

To myself I said, "Lord, don't let me give her anything else." She made such a hit with me. But she looked inside and said, "Here's something else in the pocketbook, Lillian." I saw it was a little spare peanut

Democratic gathering brought out some strange sights.

pin that I always wear. "Would you like to have that?" I asked. She said, "Yes, I'll have earrings made of it." She was the most gracious person I have ever met. I just fell in love with her. Great.

Later on, we went to be on the "Tomorrow Show." The Convention made it late, and while we were waiting out there, I met Jane Fonda and her husband, Tom Hayden. Well, I'm gonna tell you right now, I never met anybody that I liked more. I told Jane, "Maybe the reason we're getting along so beautifully is that we're both controversial." Before we left there, I had made friends with both.

When Tom Snyder talked to me, he was the easiest person I ever talked to. He is a wonderful person. He asked me many questions including, "Who's going to be vice president?" And, of course, I didn't know. We got home about 3 o'clock Wednesday morning. Just as I came in, I turned on my television, and there was Tom Hayden saying, "How can Jimmy Carter lose when he has Miss Lillian? Miss Lillian with all her lovely ideas about Civil Rights and her liberal ideas which we have been fighting for all these years." It scared me to death. I was 'fraid Jimmy was listening...

This morning early, I went up to see Jimmy, and I stole his paper *with the thing in it about me seeing Tom Hayden and Jane... I came down to my room and just as I got there, the phone rang, and the Secret Service said, "Miss Lillian, I hate to tell you, but the governor says when you get through with that paper, he wants to read it." So it scared me. But he didn't fuss at me about it...*

I had planned to go and sit with Walter Cronkite tonight. But NBC and ABC said they would like for me to do it, too. So we solved it. Jimmy called me this afternoon, and he said, "Mother, I have two women in my life—you and Rosalynn." Which touched me, you know. I could just cry about that. He said, "Rosalynn needs to go over to the Convention with the rest of the family. I want you and Amy and Jason—Jackie's little boy—to be here with me. 'Cause simultaneously, the lights will come on here and over there." So that just solved every problem. Mr. Cronkite's gonna cry his eyes out when he hears it. But I'm sorry, Mr. Cronkite, Jimmy says for me to stay here. I think that's the best thing to do. After all, this is a special Jimmy night.

* * * *

A special Jimmy night it was. The countdown of the states began, ever so slowly. Alabama...Alaska...on and on. There was excitement and noise, but the only real suspense was wondering which state would put Jimmy Carter over the top. That honor belonged to Ohio. For months, there had been various people issuing tallies on who might reach that magical number of 1,505 delegates. It was the people at the red, white, and blue Madison Square Garden who counted.

They selected Jimmy Carter.

Another hurdle had been cleared.

* * * *

That night, about 8 o'clock, I went around to Jimmy's room where Jason, Amy and I were going to be with Jimmy. They had 22 television cameras in the room. Twenty-two. They had about 10 newsmen in there all the time. They were asking questions all the time, and we were saying the different things.

And Plains. Let me tell you something. They showed Plains and Gloria told me there were about 3,000 people there. And today Billy called down there to one of his friends and he said there were 1,500 cars there. Which meant about 5,000 people waiting for tonight. Isn't that something? Jimmy just enjoyed that more than anything. The TV would switch from one thing to another, and when they'd switch to

All of Plains turned out to watch their favorite son get the nomination.

Plains, he'd say, "Oh, Mama, look at Plains." I think he was most thrilled when they showed Plains. Several times, tears came in his eyes.

Jimmy was so proud of Rosalynn. She was there at the convention hall and people kept coming up and congratulating her. Rosalynn said she was so thrilled, "but the only thing is, Jimmy's not with me. I just wish he were with me." And Jimmy said, "Oh, I'd just give anything in the world to be over there." It was a funny thing, you know, to see them just reaching to each other. And he had to be here, and she had to be over there.

Then Rosalynn, at the very last said, "Oh, I wish he was here." And the newsmen said, "Is there anything you'd like to say to him?" And she said, "Tell him we won." Tears rolled down his cheeks.

Jimmy was very thrilled, and he watched the whole thing. When the votes began coming in where he didn't do so well, he'd say, "That's all right. I knew that was going to happen." You know, he was explaining to me what was going to happen... When they showed the Georgia delegation, he just had a fit. He was grinning from ear to ear. He said, "Mama, those people made me what I am. They have just been great." Most of them were volunteers who had paid their own way and spent all their time on campaigning for him.

Georgia delegation had reasons to cheer at Democratic Convention.

After the thing was over, Amy was sleepy, so we came back home and I had just gone to sleep when they sent word for me to come back. They were having a party up in Jimmy's suite. When we went into the room, it was just the family and a few others. And Jimmy was seeing Rosalynn for the first time.

We were gathered in a circle. Jimmy said, "I have something I want to say to everybody." So we all got quiet. "There have been a lot of people all over the United States who have helped to bring about tonight. But the one person that I attribute to having the most influence and having helped me the most and done the most for the whole campaign is Billy." That was great. "Billy stayed at home, he took care of everything, and he was always there when I needed him." Jimmy started crying, and Billy cried, and they were there together. To me, it was the most beautiful thing of the whole thing. These two in some ways are opposite. Yet their love is so deep.

* * * *

The story was over, save the final chapter. Now the question would be answered. The suspense would end. The Democrats had themselves a nominee. They had all of that love building up. So much so that it was almost sickening. All they lacked was a vice-presidential nominee. Muskie? Mondale? Glenn? Church? Jackson? Rodino? Stevenson? Everyone had his personal favorite.

In retrospect you must remember which three men were given an audience back in Plains. There was Muskie, the tall veteran from Maine. There was Mondale, the almost-presidential candidate who had said he feared he couldn't spend every night in a Holiday Inn so he dropped out. There was Glenn, the silver-haired astronaut, still a magical figure.

Carter had said he wanted someone who was qualified to step in as President if needed, who was compatible with him, who would help the ticket... all of these things and more. That matter of compatibility was important to him. As governor he had seen what can happen when two men at odds are thrown together. He wanted none of that in the White House. But how do you gauge compatibility? Usually you need to know a person over a long haul, not just casually or in a controlled setting. That's where Plains came in.

Intuitively, Carter knew there was a lot of Plains in him. How could there not be? He figured that by bringing the candidates there, seeing how they reacted in that setting, among those people, he would learn a lot about the candidate, but more importantly, the man. Plains would be the judge.

Muskie was first. He arrived in the wee hours, talked with Carter for an hour, then went to bed. The next morning they talked some more. The Senator tried to be a part of life in Plains. He took off his coat and tie, put on his comfortable shoes, and tried to be just another visitor. Later they took a walking tour of the town, and some of the local judges said Muskie looked stiff and ill at ease.

Edmund Muskie took walking tour of Plains on vice-presidential interview.

Walter Mondale and Carter field questions in Plains news conference.

Then there was Mondale. He, too, was coatless and though his tie was still on, it was loosened when the Carters greeted their visitors from Minnesota in the driveway. They conferred, met the press briefly on the Carter lawn, then drove toward town. Mondale smiled and waved at anything that moved. "You're Billy's daughter, aren't you?" the Minnesota visitor asked 17-year-old Jana Carter. "How did you know?" she asked. "I saw your picture when you were out in that pond that day."

Moving toward the depot, he was introduced to Mrs. Maxine Reese. "How's your campaign coming along?" he asked her, referring to an unsuccessful attempt she made at getting elected to the Georgia House. Walter (Fritz) Mondale had done his homework.

John Glenn arrived later that day. He electrified the crowd wherever he went. When he got out of the car at Carter's house, the crowd of tourists out front roared. Carter waved a thank you, but the applause was for the popular Glenn. When they met the press, one of the first questions concerned both men's military backgrounds. It seemed to irritate both of them, and insiders say it was to be too much of an irritant for Glenn to overcome.

Back in New York, Carter built up an Alfred Hitchcock ending.

* * * *

Last night, I told Jimmy, "You've always told me you would tell me who the vice presidential candidate would be before you went in to announce it. He said, "Come in tomorrow morning just before I go and I'll tell you after I tell Rosalynn." I had to go to this place (ABC-TV) for this interview this morning. So I told them, "I have to get back before the press conference." And they hurried, and I got back over here at 10 minutes to 10. And the crowd down there in the ballroom.

We had to push our way in. It was just for the press. I came over there and somebody gave me a seat on the front row. The newsmen kept saying, "Who is it? Who is it?" And I said, "He hasn't told me." I didn't know. So when Jimmy walked in, he looked around. I heard him say, "Where's Mama?" And then he saw me. He motioned for me to come up there and he stepped down from the podium and he whispered, "Mondale."

So everybody said, "What did he say?" I said, "He told me to keep my mouth shut." They believed it. And I was so happy. I have to say now that Mondale was my choice from the first. I never told anybody. When Jimmy asked me who, I said, "You don't want to hurt me, and I don't want to hurt you, and if I were to tell you the man I want, I might get angry with you if you didn't choose him." That's the way it is all the time.

* * * *

Grits and Fritz. The Democratic duo. Banners seemed to roll off the presses instantaneously. The Democrats had themselves a ticket. That night, as Carter is quick to point out, Mondale got more votes than he did. The suspense was over. All that was left was the cheering. Hours after Carter tabbed Mondale, that would come. First, however, there were people to thank. People who had stood by him long before anyone outside of Georgia knew who this man Carter was.

Going to the City Squire Hotel where most of the Georgians were gathered, he met with the home folks. They presented him with a glass statue of a Democratic donkey so that he would remember them and that day. As if he could forget either. Hours later the world would be listening when he accepted the Democratic nomination. That afternoon he was speaking only to people who had been his friends long before his dream of the White

Gov. George Busbee presents Carter gift from Georgia delegation.

House was born.

"When I announced and began to campaign for the highest elective office, perhaps in the world, 19 months ago, not many people thought I had a chance, but a lot of you thought I had a chance. There were a lot of times when I was lonely. There were a lot of times when there was a great deal of doubt. We had some serious setbacks, and I made some mistakes, but I never had a feeling of loneliness or withdrawal or isolation or abandonment from the people of Georgia.

"For about eight months I was by myself. But later, when the going really got tough, you just can't imagine how it made me feel to get off a small airplane in an isolated airport and see some of you, standing there with signs waving back and forth in the snow and to see expressions of friendship and support for me. I could not have carried New Hampshire, which was a close election, without you. I could not have carried Wisconsin, which was a close election, without you.

"The strength of our political effort has been the closeness between me personally and voters around the country. Women in the shoe factories and textile mills. And men driving trucks and making electronics equipment and working on farms and cutting hair and waitresses in restaurants. To a substantial degree, they felt they could have confidence in me and that I was close to them. And there wasn't any political figure that stood between them, and possibly, the next President. And I'll never shake that intensely personal relationship, because I want to be sure that when I am in the White House, the American people will feel—that's my President."

There was hardly a dry eye in the room when Carter finished his remarks. They would hear him speak again, later that night—a much longer, more flowery, more political speech. Right then, that didn't matter. What he had just told them was what they wanted to hear. That made it all worthwhile, whatever happened in the future.

Clocks moved slowly that afternoon. To most of the people close to Jimmy Carter, it seemed like Thursday night would never come. To others, still frantically at work, they hoped it wouldn't. But it did. Madison Square was wall-to-wall Democrat.

First, Walter Mondale was introduced. He received one of the night's loudest ovations when he said that Americans have just lived through the worst political scandal in their history "and are now led by a President who pardoned the person who did it." The cheering section warmed up for the finale by giving the Minnesota Senator and his family a long, loud ovation. Now it was Jimmy Carter's turn.

A film chronicling his rise to that moment was shown, then Carter appeared before the convention for the first time. The smile was familiar and so was the greeting. The words might have been spoken to an auto worker reporting to work on the assembly line in Detroit or to an old person at a mobile home park in Florida. The words were the same.... "Hello, I'm Jimmy Carter. And I'm running for President of the United States...."

Smiles bounced back at him from the overtaxed crowd in the Garden. The tone was set. Happily. With a smile. Starting slowly, he began to overcome the nervousness that must have hit him when he realized he was speaking to the largest audience he might ever face, in the auditorium and around the world.

"It has been a long time since I said those words the first time," he continued. "I now come here, after seeing our great country, to accept your nomination. I accept it in the words of John F. Kennedy: 'With a full and grateful heart—and with only one obligation—to devote every effort of body, mind, and spirit to lead our party back to victory and our nation back to greatness.'"

Returning to the theme of his campaign, he continued.

"There is a fear that our best years are behind us, but I say to you that

Jackie Kennedy Onassis and Ethel Kennedy were among convention watchers.

our nation's best is still ahead. Our country has lived through a time of torment. It is now a time for healing.

"We want to have faith again!"

"We want to be proud again!"

"We just want the truth again!"

"It is time for the people to run the government and not the other way around...."

There was a feeling of old-time religion as he moved toward the conclusion.

"I have never had more faith in America than I do today. We have an America that, in Bob Dylan's phrase, is busy being born, not busy dying....

"I see an America on the move again, united, a diverse and vital and tolerant nation, entering our third century with pride and confidence—an America that lives up to the majesty of our Constitution and the simple decency of our people.

"This is the America we want.

"This is the America we will have...," he told the cheering Democratic family.

The Reverend Martin Luther King, Sr., gave the closing words. Behind him was a once-unlikely cast of characters...now bound together. Reverend King gave a simple Baptist benediction, in a style and reverence that only a black minister can offer.

Wallace, McGovern, Humphrey, Daley, Brown, Church...they all came together on that podium. It was there, for all to see. The Democrats were busy being born.

Politics In Their Own Back Yard

The smiling black face was unmistakable—a little older, more wrinkled, but unmistakable. The half-moon of hair was heavily sprinkled with white. But there was no doubt that it was Graham Jackson.

One April morning almost 32 years before, Graham Jackson, burdened by his accordion strapped over his army-green shoulder, had serenaded the flag-draped body of Franklin Delano Roosevelt on its last trip out of Warm Springs, Georgia, the quiet village that had brought peace to a troubled President. Jackson's tear-stained face became a symbol of a nation's grief.

Three decades later Jackson was back in Warm Springs, still carrying his familiar accordion, still playing, serenading a crowd numbering in the thousands circled in front of FDR's Little White House. There was little doubt that the man known as FDR's favorite musician would be playing "Happy Days Are Here Again." It was on the Roosevelt Hit Parade, and Democrats were hopeful it would be back on the charts again in 1976.

Labor Day 1976 belonged to Jimmy Carter, but he shared it with the memory of Roosevelt, a man whose strength still dominates the sleepy Georgia town.

Carter was there to launch his presidential campaign from the steps of Roosevelt's old retreat. On the front of the podium where he spoke was a copy of the famous unfinished portrait of the former President. Now a state park, the old grounds shook again with the fervor of presidential politics as Carter marched down a passageway through the crowd formed by the Peanut Brigade. He went to the historic porch, where he was greeted by two of FDR's sons, James and Franklin, Jr.

The Little White House through the years has become almost a Democratic shrine. It was here in the soothing waters that Roosevelt's polio-ravaged body found relief, and it was here that he found the strength to lead the Democratic Party to four terms of presidential power.

FDR's favorite musician, Graham Jackson, says hello to James Roosevelt.

It was here, too, that John F. Kennedy, a Catholic from Massachusetts, came in 1960 to open his Georgia campaign, entering a predominantly Protestant state which that fall was to give him an even greater margin of victory than his home state.

Carter was flanked by his entire family and a busload of friends from Plains, some 75 miles away. Seated to his right was Georgia's political chain of command: Sen. Herman Talmadge, Gov. George Busbee, Lt. Gov. Zell Miller, Rep. Andrew Young, Rep. Jack Brinkley, and a host of other home-state political leaders. James Roosevelt introduced Carter, as if anyone there really needed an introduction to him on that particular Labor Day morning.

"I'm sure you know what it means for me and my brother to be here for the opening of this great campaign. Our father would come here, before and after he was President, for inspiration. It's a pleasure for us to be back here on this moving occasion," Roosevelt said.

There was a revival fervor in the air as Carter began his 20-minute speech. Sensing the crowd was with him, the Democratic candidate used it to good advantage, playing off their applause and amens to good advantage.

As he began, Carter referred to "the most famous patient who came here looking for a new life.

"...Franklin Roosevelt first came to Warm Springs because he was physically handicapped, and the warm waters gave him strength and hope, just as later he gave strength and hope to an afflicted nation when he was President.

"His opponent in 1932 was an incumbent President, a decent and well-intentioned man who sincerely believed there was nothing our government could or should do to attack the terrible economic and social ills of our nation.

"But Roosevelt knew our country could be better, and with bold and forceful action he restored confidence in our economic system, he put our nation back to work, and he unified our people," Carter said.

Roosevelt wasn't the only Democrat Carter praised.

"Where does the buck stop? What did that sign in Harry Truman's office say?" he asked.

The crowd roared back the answer.

"Under Johnson and Kennedy, the inflation rate was two percent—and when Truman went out of office the inflation rate was one percent. Unfortunately, under this Republican administration, the inflation rate has averaged more than six percent. Is this what we want?"

And the crowd roared a unanimous "No."

It was an enthusiastic, partisan beginning. It touched a tone on both sides of the political fence. Andrew Young, seated in that row of Georgia political leaders, noticed this. He was just five seats away from Talmadge, once the voice of conservative Georgia politics.

"I looked down several times at Senator Talmadge. When I was clapping like crazy, he was just putting his hands together two or three times. When I was just lightly clapping he was clapping hard. But that's what this Democratic Party is all about," Young said.

FDR, Jr., was impressed, too, but for different reasons.

"Governor Carter seems to have the same concern for people my father had. Times change, and programs have to change also. He's simply brought some of my father's ideas up to date," said Roosevelt, a key Carter campaigner during the primary season.

Robert Strauss, then the chairman of the Democratic Party, was enthusiastic, also.

Carter—Ford duel began at the late Franklin Roosevelt's Georgia home.

"It was everything we could ask for. This is what we needed to get this campaign going. It was a tremendous kickoff, and now it's up to every Democrat to keep this momentum going," Strauss noted—which was not going to be easy.

Carter began that Labor Day with a comfortable cushion to rest on in the political polls. Some of his followers had been coasting since June, apparently treating the campaign as if their man had already moved into the White House. This attitude was to change dramatically as the figures began to change. Carter's cushion was wearing down to its springs. Gerald Ford was picking up that momentum Strauss had talked about at Warm Springs. The rabbit had stopped hopping, and the tortoise had pulled even. Overnight it had turned into a race.

Both men were to have their problems. From the beginning Ford's campaign staff had operated with a revolving door. The GOP was split down the middle, and a minority party can hardly afford not to be unified.

Carter, meanwhile, was running whistle-stop trains through the East—a

145

la Harry Truman—with unenthusiastic results. His TV ads showing him strolling across open fields were becoming shopworn. He, too, had to make changes.

It was hardly a classical campaign confrontation. People began to say that it would be won not by the guy who swung a knockout blow, but rather by the fellow who avoided punches and made fewer mistakes.

However, critics will long talk about the three presidential debates, those three evenings where for two hours the duelers in business suits poked and prodded at one another on TV. President Ford thought this would be his bailiwick. A veteran of three decades of congressional debate, he thought he would far outshine Carter, whose only experience in debating had been long ago with Miss Julia as his coach.

The first debate started off just the way Ford envisioned. Carter was nervous. He had won the flip of the coin and had the opening question. Later he was to regain his composure, but by that time Ford had scored enough points to be perceived as the opening game victor. Not even 27 minutes of silence while the embarrassed TV technicians repaired their equipment could change that.

The next confrontation belonged to Carter, however. It was here that Ford made his damaging slip of the tongue concerning Communist control in Europe. The final round was considered a draw, as each man seemed content to dance and jab instead of getting in close where a knockout punch might

Yes, in this day of Madison Avenue campaigning, they still kiss babies.

affect what happened November 2.

Back in Plains all of these battles were fought on 27-inch screens. Between rounds Carter would return home, and at other times he would be seen on the six o'clock news. However, two strange interludes were to bring the presidential wars closer to home grounds.

To trace the beginning of the first interlude, one must go back to a hot, summer, South Georgia afternoon. The press was headquartered at what was once the Carter Warehouse Office. Daily a schedule of the candidate's appointments would be posted on the bulletin board amidst messages for newsmen to call their offices around the world.

On that particular day Carter was to be busy. He had three major interviews. He was talking to *Reader's Digest, Rolling Stone,* and *Playboy* —which proves without a doubt that Jimmy Carter wanted to reach all sectors of American life. And the events that transpired would indeed make that a day to be remembered.

The interviewer from *Playboy* was Robert Scheer, an editor of *New Times* who was free-lancing a story for *Playboy*'s Hugh Hefner. Scheer and Carter were to meet three separate times for the *Playboy* interview, which followed the magazine's familiar question-and-answer format.

Along for that final visit at Carter's home in Plains was *Playboy*'s assistant managing editor, Barry Golson. As Scheer describes the events, the interview was over, and he and Golson were moving toward the door, exchanging good-byes with Carter. One last question was asked, a reworded query that they had asked the candidate over and over during their questioning: "Do you feel you've reassured people with this interview, people who are uneasy about your religious beliefs, who wonder if you're going to make a rigid, unbending President?"

What followed was a lengthy reply, covering Carter's Baptist background. He talked about autonomy, how he did not accept complete domination of his life by the Church, with a capital "C." He talked about pride, how no one should feel better than another. He talked about being saved by grace. Then he moved into the most quoted sectors of the interview.

His words speak for themselves:

"I try not to commit a deliberate sin. I recognize that I'm going to do it anyhow, because I'm human and I'm tempted. And Christ set some almost impossible standards for us. Christ said, 'I tell you that anyone who looks on a woman with lust has in his heart already committed adultery.'

"I've looked on a lot of women with lust. I've committed adultery in my heart many times. This is something that God recognizes I will do—and I have done it—and God forgives me for it. But that doesn't mean that I condemn someone who not only looks on a woman with lust but who leaves his wife and shacks up with somebody out of wedlock.

Columbus, Georgia, Boy Scouts greet an old scoutmaster from Plains.

"Christ says, don't consider yourself better than someone else because one guy screws a whole bunch of women while the other guy is loyal to his wife. The guy who's loyal to his wife ought not to be condescending or proud because of the relative degree of sinfulness."

The interview was to be published in the November 1976 issue, but *Playboy* wisely decided to release the contents early. Their decision was wise from a political standpoint—it might prejudice the vote on the eve of the election—and wise economically—people who read excerpts would want to see the interview in its entirety.

Comedians had a field day with the interview. Bob Hope quipped, "Carter said he had lust in his heart. Now we know why he's smiling." Political cartoonists hurried to their drawing boards. But what concerned Carter was the public reaction.

There was reaction to his salty terms and to his using worldly paraphrases in quoting Christ. There were people who thought it unpresidential, remembering that it was his language that condemned Richard Nixon in the ears of some as much as the other revelations on the Watergate tapes.

Mrs. Marge Thurmond, chairman of the Georgia Democratic Party, called the statements "disastrous." "I don't know why in hell he did it. That's the only way I can give it to you, baby," she said.

Senator Robert Byrd, a Democrat, said Carter should never have even granted the interview, much less said the things he did, while Senate Republican Leader Hugh Scott commented, "The trouble with Jimmy Carter is that when he says what he really thinks, it comes out pretty scary."

But wading through the partisan statements, the gospel according to Carter wasn't really against his Baptist background. Even if his language, as his local pastor, the Reverend Bruce Edwards, said, "wasn't quite the way I would have put it."

Carter was admitting temptation, which isn't revolutionary. And he was admitting he had "committed adultery in his mind," which is a common sin. As one newsman confessed, "If that's adultery, I plead guilty to committing it three times at lunch today."

What bothered a lot of folks back home was that Carter, a professing Baptist, granted an interview to a magazine that publishes graphic photos of nude women. The cover of that November issue had Jimmy Carter's name next to a busty, half-clad girl. Too, they were concerned that he talked about sex in public using the language of the streets.

In Plains, the November issue was still selling well into January. At the time, a local woman laughed when someone asked her if anyone in town

His faith in God became a campaign issue after Playboy *interview.*

would have seen the magazine had not portions been publicized. Definitely, she said, "It's always been in the barbershops here. Why do you think men get their hair cut so often?"

Just three months earlier, California Governor Jerry Brown—one of those Carter eliminated in the Democratic Sweepstakes—was the subject of a *Playboy* interview. There wasn't a ripple in California or elsewhere.

But Jerry Brown wasn't a Georgian or a Baptist. And although Hugh Hefner might not understand, therein was the difference.

The second episode was to hit home even harder. It did more than bring *Playboy* out of the barbershop and on to the coffee table. It hit at the heart of Plains—the church.

This final chapter began on October 24 when the Reverend Bruce Edwards talked about brotherhood in his regular Sunday morning sermon. Listening that morning was the Reverend Clennon King, a minister from Albany, 40 miles away.

That afternoon, unable to find Edwards, he tacked a message on the minister's door at home, promising to be back the following Sunday to offer himself for membership.

When the local Baptist church was founded in Plains, it was a desegregated congregation known as the Lebanon Baptist Church. Blacks and whites worshipped together, although sitting apart. But after the War Between the States the churches separated as did all churches in the South. Blacks worshipped together. Whites worshipped together. They might come together for funerals or weddings, but on Sunday mornings never the two did join.

So it had been in Plains. Carter and his family had led a fight to change that policy in 1965, but their struggle was unsuccessful. Carter's sister, Mrs. Gloria Spann, quit the church over the outcome of the vote, but Jimmy stayed on. When he was elected governor, a black State Patrol officer who was a Carter aide was welcomed into the church. During the presidential campaign black Secret Service agents had been seated along with black newsmen. But all of this was forgotten when King made his intentions known.

When the Reverend King showed up in Plains that cold Sunday morning, a line of newsmen was circling the churchyard. It was October 31, 1976, the Sunday before Tuesday's election. Services had been canceled, although members had attended Sunday School at 9:45 as usual.

During the preceding week, the Republicans had attempted to make political gain from the situation. Letters had gone out to black ministers across the nation. The GOP saw this as a chance to take the black vote away from the Democrats.

Again Carter's black supporters rallied to his side, just as they had the summer before after his ethnic purity statement. The Reverend Martin Luther King, Sr., father of the slain Civil Rights leader, condemned the

Carter couldn't even escape his followers at church on Sunday.

Reverend Clennon King as a political tool. Others accused him of being a paid performer. Clennon King's controversial background as a Civil Rights agitator caused him to be questioned by both blacks and whites. His history included being fired by an all-black college for criticism of the National Association for the Advancement of Colored People, time in jail for non-support, leadership of a Back to Africa Movement, a race against Carter for governor, and two presidential attempts. When he showed up in Plains, he called Albany home. By January 1977 King was calling Atlanta home, making an unsuccessful run for a congressional seat there.

Carter had said that no matter what happened he did not plan to resign his membership in protest. "This is not my church. It's God's church. I can't quit my lifetime habit of worship because of a remnant of discrimination."

To the rest of the members it was far more than just a political football to be tossed around in the headlines. Afterwards one member summed up the local feeling. "Most people knew that things would never be the same here if Jimmy won. But the church thing is the most painful thing a lot of folks here will have to endure," he said.

If you are going to measure how deep this pain cut into the soul of Plains, you have to understand the role a person's church plays in a small Southern town. Practically everyone has his name on the church roll and calls himself a Baptist, Methodist, or some other Protestant denomination. The man who leads the congregation in singing "Amazing Grace" on Sunday morning may be the guy who sells them fertilizer on Monday. The lady who bakes cakes for the covered-dish supper could be your mother's next-door neighbor. You can't divorce a church from the day-to-day life of the community. Hurt the church and you hurt yourself. The church is at the center of almost everyone's life in a small Southern town.

Through the years Civil Rights had taken on a religious connotation, too. Hard-line segregationists could quote scripture after scripture to support their beliefs. Blacks raising their voices in the old Negro spiritual, "We Shall Overcome," also could offer verse and number to back up their side of the problem. Right or wrong, it had evolved into almost a religious issue.

Ironically, though the name of God had been used often, most churches in the South had remained all black or all white. While the ministers were marching in the streets, the doors of the churches remained closed. This irritated many people in Plains. Editorial writers in faraway cities were pointing their fingers at the Plains Baptist Church, chastising it for a problem that existed throughout the rest of the South and the rest of the country.

Somehow Plains Baptist Church was to survive. The Reverend Edwards remained in the pulpit for the time being, hoping old wounds would be allowed to heal. Jimmy Carter remained an active member, saying he was proud of his church. During an emotional, tearful service, the antiquated bylaw excluding blacks was erased. The Reverend Clennon King was referred to a church "watch-care" committee that was formed to screen prospective members. After Carter's inauguration and after he had moved his church affiliation to Washington, the situation was to again become explosive.

But on that tension-filled Sunday on election eve, when the church doors were slammed shut, no one could be sure what lay ahead. The question of what effect that episode might have on the election remained.

The answer was in the hands of the American people.

The End And The Beginning

This was the morning-after, the morning after the once-peaceful village of Plains had seen its favorite son earn a four-year lease on the White House. It was approaching 7 a.m., and most of the crowd that lined Main Street in Plains had been there for nearly 15 hours, ignoring the November cold and the debris that covered the crowded street.

The party had really begun 24 hours before. A smiling Jimmy Carter had gotten out of bed on schedule and joined other members of his family at the old Boy Scout Hut where he once served as a Scout leader. On election day the block building is turned into the town's polling place. It is here that voters in Plains make their choices known.

Waiting in line behind his son Chip and wife Caron, Jimmy joked at how long they were taking. Finally his turn came, and he went behind the curtains to mark his own ballot. Coming out, someone wanted to know how he had voted.

"I voted for Mondale and his running mate," Carter jokingly answered.

Traffic in Plains was bumper-to-bumper throughout the sunny day. Television crews were preparing to beam the town worldwide. Tourists were looking for last-minute bargains. Workmen were readying a platform in front of C.L. Walters Grocery on Main Street. Cars were being waved into the schoolyard to park, and their drivers were being brought into town by shuttle buses. Meanwhile, the Carters were resting for the night and day that lay ahead.

By the time four o'clock came the town was teeming with sightseers. High school bands from throughout the area were tuning up. A rock band was entertaining people who had found a place close to the rostrum. Secret Service agents soon found their stations. In front of the speaker's stand an agent shed his stern face long enough to advise an elderly tourist how to set his camera. "I've got one just like it," the agent admitted. Newsmen were in

"Win or lose, we made history," Carter told an election day crowd in Plains.

place. This particular Tuesday the press was to outnumber the home folks.

At last Jimmy Carter made his way to 1901 Main Street. The message he brought with him was to be heard by the world, but most of it was aimed at his neighbors.

"This is the last day of a long effort on my part and on your part. I think win or lose we've made political history, coming this far from a town the size of Plains. I hope this sense of closeness that has spread among the American people from me to you will become the basis of my administration.

"You've made me rested when I was tired. You've encouraged me when we had temporary setbacks. You've corrected me when I made mistakes. But you've never lost faith. All I want to do is make you proud of me," he told the cheering crowd.

And so they were.

Atlanta was throwing him a party that night, and Carter soon was off to the Big City. Folks back home would be watching him on a giant TV screen that had been installed on the wall outside Thomas Grocery, counting down the states one by one.

While rock bands hammered out a strong beat and young people danced in the street. While peanuts were roasting along the sidewalks. While the aroma of reddened charcoal and sizzling chicken filled the cool night air.

Nobody's mind strayed far from the counting of votes.

There in Plains 580 people turned out to vote. The winner? A candidate named Carter. He polled 481 votes while Gerald Ford received 99. Across Sumter County Carter won 5,008 to 1,920. It was the same across the rest of Georgia and throughout most of the states east of the Mississippi.

By then the town had taken on the atmosphere of the infield on race day. It was wall-to-wall human flesh as insiders and outsiders took turns gawking at one another. An Americus civic club was selling barbecued chicken, but as the countdown began their business dropped off. All eyes were on the TV screen as states were added to the Carter column.

The clock was pushing 3 a.m. when United Press International proclaimed Jimmy Carter of Georgia the winner over Gerald Ford of Michigan. Plains celebrated. Plains gave thanks. Plains was now waiting to welcome him home.

On the platform at the depot there were hugs and tears. Then, on cue, they lined up across the dock, clutching their coats. This was the moment Mrs. Maxine Reese had been planning for. Weeks before, she had designed and ordered a jersey—not just any jersey, mind you, but one specially designed for the people of Plains.

On her signal coats were removed. The dock became a single file of green. White letters proclaimed "Jimmy Won!" In the middle was "76." The loudest cheer came when Miss Lillian slowly rose from her rocking chair. She

Friends gathered to tell Carters farewell on election day.

did a subdued mischievous bump and grind, then clowning some more, removed her coat. She, too, was wearing one of those new shirts.

It had hardly entered Maxine Reese's mind that Jimmy Carter might lose. But just in case, the folks had made a vow not to take off their coats and show anybody the jerseys should he lose. Either way, the shirts are now a collector's item in Plains, although copies are now on the racks.

When the TVs made it official, a few folks went home. Newsmen who were staying in nearby Americus went there for a quick nap. Others who had piled into campers returned to their home-on-the-road for the rest, too. But by the time 7 a.m. rolled around, the streets were again packed.

The sun was still asleep, but Plains was awake—not wide awake, but awake. Beds had been banned the night before, and when the sun stretched and yawned, a crowd was already milling along Main Street. The sleepy eyes of the Americus High School band tried to focus on the music, and fingers numb from the November chill made their way to the appointed notes. "Happy Days Are Here Again" echoed around town, even before the sun made its debut.

Given a new face when the campaign began, the historic railroad depot—oldest building in town—had become the symbol of Jimmy Carter's hometown efforts. Visitors had posed in front of it, tangible proof that they

When it was official, Miss Lillian and friends revealed special shirts.

The headline and the wide smiles tell the election story.

had visited this overnight headquarters for picture-taking tourists. Now the old green-and-white depot was being forced to bear the burden of a loading dock full of friends, neighbors, and relatives, most of them wearing their newly unveiled green jerseys.

Hours before Jimmy Carter had left a neighbor. He was coming home as President-elect.

The arrival of a cadre of stern-faced Secret Service agents foretold the homecoming. Joining them was seemingly every State Patrolman in Georgia. Three buses arrived carrying an entourage of newsmen. The Americus High band was in position. The Andrew College chorus was in tune. Cameramen were hanging from the scaffolding. Old friends hugged and beamed victory smiles to one another.

All were waiting. Jimmy Carter couldn't be far behind.

When he arrived electricity bounced through the crowd. Chants began. Necks strained for a glimpse of the tired but happy peanut farmer. Winding through the well-wishers, the smiling Carter made his way to the steps of the crowded dock, stopping there to give his mother a prolonged hug. Around him were the family and friends who had stood by him so long.

As he reached John and Betty Pope of Americus, she handed him a special street-sale edition of the *Columbus Enquirer*. The four-inch-high headline said simply: "Carter Wins." He held it high for the photographers, his broad smile echoing the hometown paper's headline.

The smile was still there as he stepped to the microphone.

"I told you I didn't intend to lose," he said, his trademark still filling his face. Suddenly the smile departed. Another emotion had taken over, one he had managed to keep in tow for so long.

"In 22 months I haven't been choked up...caught without something to say...but when we drove into town, and saw this many people foolish enough to be out in Plains...."

Words wouldn't come, only tears. Tears flowed freely across the platform. Rosalynn Carter hugged her husband tightly. The crowd in the street, which by now had begun to fight back tears, too, broke into prolonged applause. A Georgia newsman who had followed the Carter tracks found himself fighting off the threat of tears, too.

It must have been at that moment, that split second when he looked into the eyes of his friends, that Jimmy Carter—like those who were huddled in the shoulder-to-shoulder crowd—realized this was more than the celebration of a victory in some faraway state primary. That goal no one believed attainable—a pipe dream, they said—had become a reality.

Jimmy Carter soon would be President of the United States.

The smile returning, Carter went back to the microphone.

"All the others who ran for President didn't have people helping them who would stay up all night in Plains, Georgia," he began.

"All the others lost, too," a battle-weary Billy Carter chimed in.

Then Jimmy Carter became reflective.

"It's been a great two years. I've learned a great deal about our country, as you know. I know a lot about you, and you know a lot about me...I just hope I can be the kind of President who'll make the nation proud of me, just as I am proud of you," he continued.

Later there would be time to look toward the future. That morning Carter wanted to look to the past. Looking into the faces of those who had donated time, money, but more importantly a concerned love, he began to talk about the two years that had led them to that moment near dawn in Plains.

"I had the best organization any candidate ever had...the best family any candidate ever had...the best home community any candidate ever had...the best support of a home state any candidate ever had. And the only reason the vote's close is that the candidate wasn't quite a good enough campaigner," he said with a smile.

The sun was coming up over the rooftops as he talked. "I see the sun rising on a beautiful new day, a beautiful new spirit in the country...a commitment to the future." When that future is here, historians will analyze how Jimmy Carter did it. How overnight he moved from a one-term Georgia

By the time victory came in wee hours, Amy was too sleepy to care.

governor to the presidency. How he overcame an incumbent President. How he managed to sidestep the conventional, established routes to the White House. How this was a victory of the people. And around him that November morning were those people.

Oh, by then a few political glad-handers, some back-slapping hacks, had joined the crowd. But basically it was Plains and people who believed in Plains. There were farmers, laborers, merchants, housewives, blacks, and whites. Mainly it was home folks, the same group that had been by Jimmy Carter's side since he began selling peanuts on that same street.

It was fitting that the end and the beginning came where it had all begun.

"Don't It Make You Proud?"

As I jerked back the curtains in the camper, it hardly seemed possible that the sun was directly overhead. The morning had slipped by unnoticed. Outside, the warm November sun was sucking water out of the soft Georgia clay. A few hours before, it had seemed as if the sun would never arrive. The night had seemed as if it would never end. Except for a few minutes, leaning back on one of the camper seats, I had had little rest between Jimmy Carter's afternoon departure and his next-morning return.

The night before seemed like only a dream. The crowds that had celebrated and shivered together in the streets of Plains were by then back at home. The question was, had it been a dream, or was Jimmy Carter really the uncrowned President of the United States?

Slipping through the mud, I was at the back of Billy Carter's service station. Off-duty Secret Service agents were milling around the lot, sipping on beers. Billy, who by then looked like a soldier who had fought a war and lost, was there, too. Someone passing by might have thought that can of PBR had become a permanent part of his hand. Occasionally, you'd hear a faraway cheer, but except for a constant murmur that still seemed to fill the air, Plains was trying to recover.

Television trucks were still there. Newsmen were walking the streets, looking for that angle that somehow might have eluded their competitors. State patrolmen were stopping and starting traffic. Lines of tourists were in the shops, giving the town the look of a department store during an after-Christmas closeout.

Make no mistake. The night before had not been a dream. It was very real, yet very hard to believe. There were tell-tale signs all around that Jimmy Carter had been elected President of the United States less than 24 hours before.

Thinking back to that moment when Jimmy Carter was first sighted

Election night in Plains was a time of waiting and shivering.

that morning, it is difficult to describe the feeling. I had visited this town two years before, driven straight to his door, knocked, and been welcomed inside. Today, guards lurked behind the skinny pines, and electronic watchguards were hidden in the clay. Once I could call directory assistance, ask for the number of Jimmy Carter, and soon hear his voice answering on the other end. Today, I go through a monotone voice which explains that I'll have to leave a message. Once I had stood outside his church, casually talking and joining him for dinner on the church grounds. Today there were ropes around the churchyard. Once I had relaxed and talked with him, the only interruption coming from an eight-year-old who wanted to show her daddy what a big wad of bubble gum she had in her mouth. Today, multitudes of staff personnel, reporters, and Secret Service agents competed for his time. Once I could slip a newspaper clipping into an envelope, take it to the post office, and have faith that Carter would pull it out of the mailbox at the end of his unpaved driveway. Today, mountains of mail go untouched and unanswered. Once he was "Jimmy" or "Governor." Soon he would be "Mr. President."

If you had been around Plains and Georgia during those years of change, you could not have helped but feel the emotions fighting to come out. Journalists take the oath to walk the tightrope, not to become involved. We hear it from the time we first walk into Journalism 101. But all of the oaths and all of the textbooks can't keep me from losing my balance on that tightrope—I've seen this one from too close. For only an instant, I am a Georgia-born, Southern-bred human being.

When I admit this weakness, I admit my pride. Like his neighbors, I didn't really believe it would ever happen. But now it has. And I'm proud of Jimmy Carter, proud of Georgia, proud of the South, proud of America. All of that bitterness can be filed away. The South won't be needing it anymore. I'm proud. Dammit, I'm proud.

As Jimmy Carter spoke that morning, the tears came more easily than the words, and it was easy to understand why. Standing there, he was only a block away from where his parents first lived, where his father tended store, where he was baptized a Christian, where he sat in Miss Julia's classes, where he and Hugh sold peanuts. It was sobering to him and sobering to those who stood in front of him. Now it was time to say thank you.

All of that was history as people walked the littered streets. The Carters were at home. Reporters were exchanging typewriters for beds. The TV lights had long since cooled off. The clanging of the fire bell interrupted my thinking. Rolling up his apron as he ran across the railroad tracks, C. L. Walters, grocer, was turning into C. L. Walters, fire chief. The volunteer crew was already on board as he joined them. Some things were getting back to normal, whatever that was. It was time for the rest of the world to do the same.

In Chicago, Lewis Grizzard was trying to do just that. His address was Chicago, but his mind was on Georgia that November. Watching the snow fall and the wind blow, his thoughts turned toward his home state. He had grown up in Newnan, Georgia; attended the University of Georgia; and served as executive sports editor of the *Atlanta Journal*. All before becoming sports editor of the *Chicago Sun-Times*. He wasn't thinking sports, however, when he sat down and wrote the following words:

> I was born in Georgia. I was reared there, went to school there and worked there until a year ago when I moved Up North. No truer son of the red clay hills ever hiked to the top of Stone Mountain and picknicked on cold fried chicken and cathead biscuits smothered in sawmill gravy, by-God, than me.
>
> Frankly, the transition from Atlanta to Chicago hasn't been that difficult. They sell grits here. The Atlanta teams were losers. And Atlanta had a fat mayor.
>
> The big difference, of course, is the weather. My Atlanta friend Dorsey Hill warned me about that: "Snow navel-high to a tall Yankee." The other thing that has taken some getting used-to is most of the people I've met in Chicago talk funny....

Grizzard remembered Carter as governor and how he loved stock-car racing. ("That's a case of beer, six good ol' boys fighting in the cheap seats and Tom Wolfe quoting stocker hero Junior Johnson as saying he'd just as

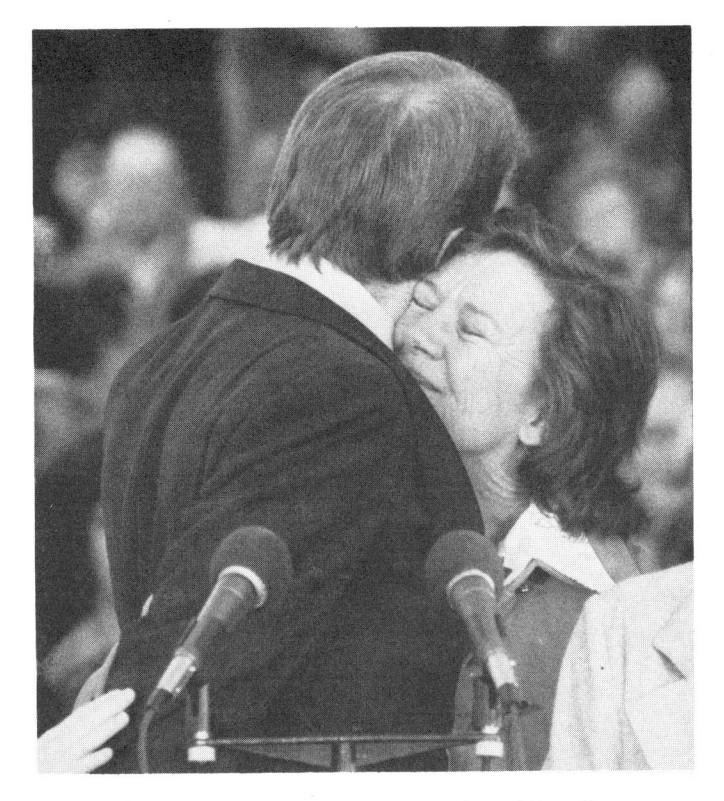

Gloria Spann receives brotherly hug before Main Street speech.

soon eat a bucket of the most distasteful substance imaginable as see a Ford beat a Chevrolet.") Grizzard, who has since moved back South as a sports columnist for the *Atlanta Constitution*, remembers that love of racing carrying over into the governor's mansion while Carter lived there.

> He used to give parties for drivers, their mechanics and sportswriters at the mansion in Atlanta. That's why I never trusted him. First one he had, he served an exotic Mediterranean fare with an accompanying rosé. An operatic trio performed afterward. A. J. Foyt was nervous and Fireball Roberts turned over in his grave. Next time, it was cold beer, barbecue and country music. Jimmy's no dummy.
>
> Of course, I thought he was crazy too when he announced he was running for President. Lester Maddox laughed at him on the 6 o'clock news. The editor of the *Atlanta Constitution* did the same thing in print the next morning.
>
> But Georgia—as did most of the rest of the South—eventually rallied behind Carter. And there can be no question many of us voted for him simply because he talks like we do and knows all the words to "Amazing Grace."
>
> We've been the nation's stepchildren for a long time, folks. We've been mocked, laughed at and looked upon as shuffling simpletons in straw hats, drawling and dawdling in a "Hee-Haw" society. It wasn't a true picture. Jimmy Carter is our living, elected proof.
>
> My stepfather lives in Moreland, Georgia—population 300, about

40 miles south of Atlanta. He has previously been an ardent supporter of both George Wallace and Lester Maddox. Were he to study the issues closely, he would find himself directly opposed to Carter on practically all of Carter's stances.

I was with my stepfather last weekend. "It's about time," he told me, "WE ran this country for a while."

But Dorsey Hill put it best.

"Sumbitch," he said, "don't it make you proud!"

Like Grizzard's stepfather, many Southerners neglected to compare much of Carter's platform with their own leanings; they only knew he was one of them. After a century of waiting at the altar, they just wanted to go on with the ceremony. Now the pronouncement had been made. North and South were family.

Oh, there were still to be reams of newspaper copy devoted to diagnosing and dissecting the South, poking fun at it often as not, not belly-laughing humor but the pointed brand. As B. Drummond Ayers of the *New York Times* did less than a month after Carter's election.

Wrote Ayers:

What is the rest of the nation, the non-South, to make of these Georgians soon to march north?

Must everyone plant a magnolia? Or learn to eat Moon Pies and drink Are-Ac-Cee Cola?

Relax would-be crackers.

The truth about the invaders lies somewhere between Margaret Mitchell's antebellum aristocrats with their white columns and black mammies and Erskine Caldwell's trashy folk in the share-cropper's shack down at the end of Tobacco Road, where the hard surface turns to rutted red clay.

In fact, a good case can be made that James Earl Carter Jr., is your prototypical, mean-average 1976 Georgian.

May the South grow up in kudzu if all of those words are true. But this was only one of many articles designed to explain what life was like in this faraway land called Dixie. Many of the articles were designed allegedly to translate Southern dialect into Northern English. There was even a book written on that subject. When Southerners read these articles, they sometimes felt they were being used as a pincushion. But they would soon get over the prickly feeling and realize that this was one of the rules of the game. For now, everyone on both sides of the Mason-Dixon was feeling one another out.

When your feet hurt, you can't wait, Allie Smith and Rosalynn Carter found.

You could see these attitudes being born months before in New Hampshire. The Southern visitors were a novelty to be put on display and allowed to drawl. Folks in New Hampshire quietly chuckled as they watched the Carter supporters slip and slide in the snow. The visitors, meanwhile, were marveling at how the local folk navigated in the weather, weather that would cripple a Southern town for weeks. They were talking among themselves about the friendly welcome they were receiving, from those supposedly frigid, uncaring Yankees. They were all learning.

You could see it in the way people around the country cross-examined Jimmy Carter wherever he traveled. Was he another Wallace? Another Maddox? There was a lack of trust that had to be overcome, and was overcome. You could see it in the way Southerners flip-flopped in their attitudes toward their Georgia neighbor. At first they thought he was another candidate saying he wanted to be President only to further another cause. Then he became an enigma. Was this a Southerner exposing these almost heretical philosophies? "He may have been born here, but he doesn't think Southern," some of them said. Later, when it was narrowed down to him and Gerald Ford, Jimmy Carter again became a home boy. Many felt they had to support him or betray their Southern heritage. They, too, were learning.

You could see this same type of attitude take over this small, once-peaceful town of Plains. When all of this began, visitors were welcome, but only if they stayed in their place. As the Carter candidacy grew, some of these visitors—namely the press—were necessary evils to be endured. In the

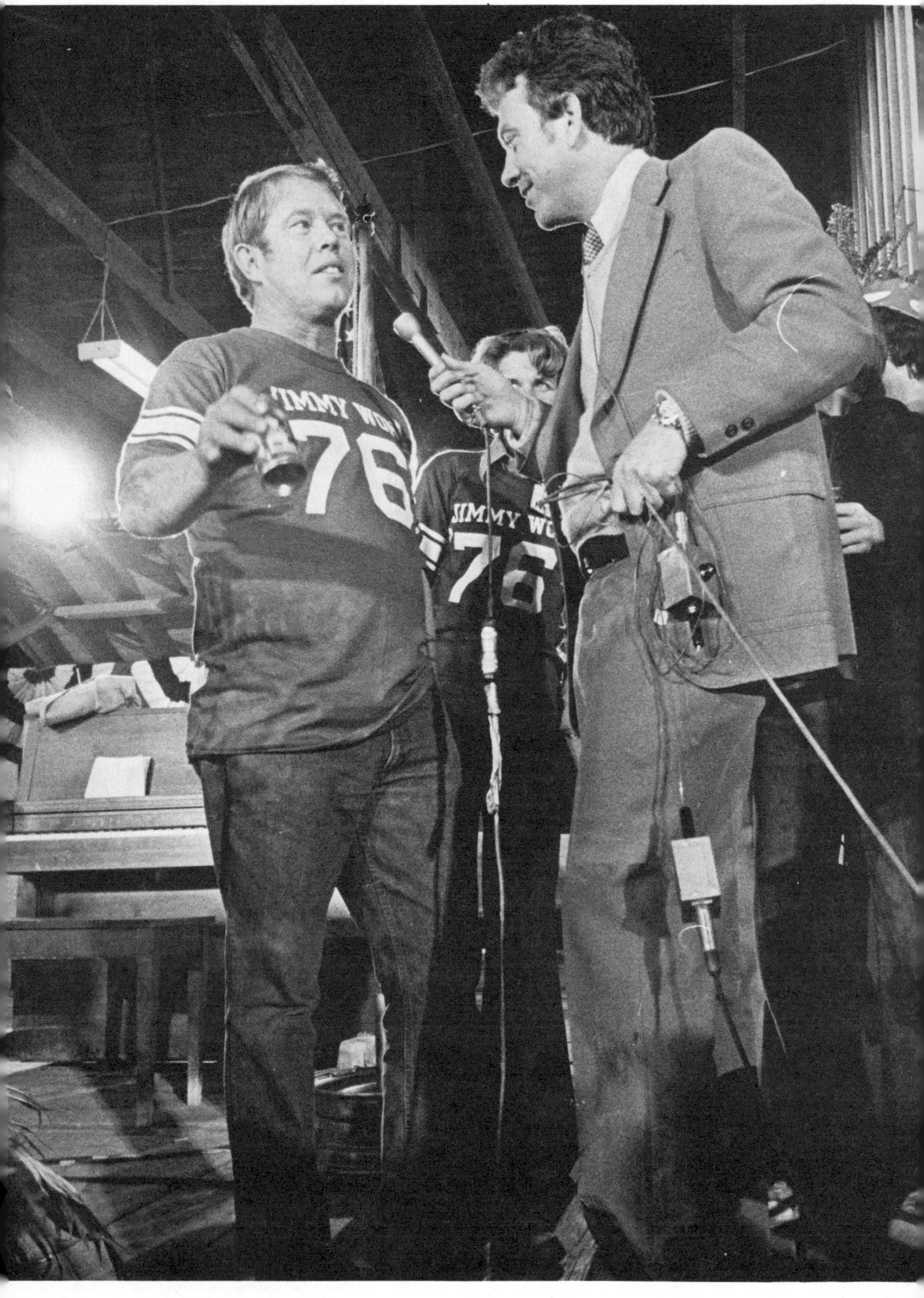

IMMY WO
76
IMMY WO
76

closing weeks these press-carded visitors were looked upon with scorn. They had intruded once too often into the life of these people's favorite candidate and into the life of this town. By now the hometowners could hardly be called naive. No longer could a reporter buy their time with the promise that they'd see their name in the paper. Many of the people in Plains had been introduced by Walter Cronkite on the six o'clock news, seen their picture in *Newsweek*, and met Barbara Walters. What was left? They had learned. Too much.

Coming back to earth, I was still in Plains, still in this town where it all began. Most of the stores would close that afternoon just as they do every Wednesday. Turner's Store still sells bib overalls. Walters' Grocery still cuts meat the way you order it. Billy Carter still loves his beer cold. Hugh Carter still auctions his antiques one Saturday night a month. Beneath the carnival surface, this is the same Plains Jimmy Carter has always known.

Still, it'll never be the same again. Plains has become an oversized Monopoly board—"I'll give you two houses on Bond Street for a hotel on Church Street." All because Jimmy Carter lives on Woodland Avenue. Many of its people are fighting to pass "Go" so they can collect again. They're being moved, but somebody else is rolling the dice. It's sad to see it all being disturbed this way. Sad to see those who started off as down-to-earth, small-town folks turned into money-grabbing media freaks, some because they wanted to, some because they were forced to, some because they couldn't help it.

The stark reality that so many have changed is the most saddening part. I can't help but remember that July afternoon when I stood on Highway 280 without wheels, with only the hope that a thumb and a friendly driver might get me to Americus. Don Oliver of NBC had the same problem. The second persons to notice us were Bo and Billie Cosby—but they were about to turn in the other direction, toward Preston.

"Where are you trying to get to?" Bo said, leaning out of the pickup truck window. "Americus...the Best Western," I told him. He turned back to Billie, and they talked for a moment. "Get in. We'll take you," Billie Cosby said.

Oliver, covered with mud from Carter's backwoods pond, wouldn't sit up front. He chose the windy rear. Sitting in the cab, the Cosbys talked about all that happened around here. We learned that man with the unlit cigar and comfortable overalls was a county judge in Webster County. We learned that his wife had been on "Peanut Brigade" excursions into New Hampshire, Ohio, Wisconsin, and a flock of other states. They were just folks. And around Plains, you find others who are that way. Good folks.

Beer in hand, Billy tells election night interviewer, "Plains is going to Hell."

Friendly folks. The kind of people who will go 30 minutes out of their way to help somebody in need.

Buford Reese was that way the day I ran out of gas on the way into town. I hadn't taken 10 steps when he screeched to a stop and carried me into Billy Carter's station for some gas, then five miles back to my car. That's just the way these people are. It saddens you to think they might become as callous as those of us who call the city home.

The haunting question as I continued that morning-after walk was how this peanut-growing, Bible-reading community bore a President. That is one for future historians to ponder. What makes Jimmy run? One can only look at the pieces that fit into the puzzle. Was it Earl Carter's obsession with the Christian work ethic and his penny-pinching attitude toward money? Was it Lillian Carter's compassionate attitude toward life and people? Was it Miss Julia Coleman's preaching that he had to fully develop and use every talent that God has given him? Was it seeing his daily bread come to him directly from the red clay he tracked into the living room? Was it Uncle Tom Gordy's letters from faraway places hinting of a promised land that lay beyond the Sumter County line? Was it his church, that taught him there was always Someone he could go to for help when others failed? Was it his friends, who were always there to offer encouragement? Was it a desire to escape Plains, or to look at it from a completely opposite way? Was it a desire to give the rest of the country the simple beatitudes of life that Plains always has had?

Consider Reg Murphy's description. Carter's old Georgia foe had changed to a San Francisco address by election day. Murphy, the publisher of the *San Francisco Examiner*, explained the newly elected president this way:

> Jimmy Carter is going to the White House January 20 because he is tougher than his critics, more ambitious than his rivals, and smarter than most politicians in American history.
>
> Tough: He once admitted that his most difficult job was to shrug off the snickers when he first declared his candidacy in 1973. But he went into the streets and stores asking personally for votes when it looked hopeless.
>
> Ambition: When the grey horde of senators joined him on the campaign trail, he simply worked them into the ground. He shook more hands and handed out more leaflets because he wanted to be President more than they did.
>
> Smart: Carter's mental capacity once was described by Adm. Hyman Rickover as one of the greatest in all his years of dealing with the Navy men who were the elitists in his nuclear submarine program. He out-thought both the Democrats for the nomination and President

This sign tells the complete story of Jimmy Carter's rise.

Ford for the election victory.

Still, does this explain why Jimmy Carter is tough, ambitious, and smart? Maybe we'll never know the real answer.

By mid-December all was becoming official. Carter had won the popular vote, beating Gerald Ford by 40,827,394 to 39,145,977, although Ford carried 26 of the 50 states. All that was left was the casting of the 538 electoral votes. Constitutionally, this would be the final, official step. Around the country, on December 13, 1976, the elected delegates met to cast their votes. Less than a month later, a joint session of Congress opened, inspected, and counted the ballots. All of this would finalize what 81,681,918 voters had started on November 2. Georgia's electoral delegates gathered in the state capitol to make their choices known. Governor George Busbee set the tone with a statement that sums up the attitude Down South.

"I view our votes," the governor said, "as a signal to the nation of the dawning of a new era. Our actions should express beyond a shadow of a doubt that the War Between the States is finally over and the South has finally joined the Union." He added that Carter is the "personification of the fact that the South is in the mainstream of American thought" and he "represents the hopes and dreams and aspirations of Southerners and the nation."

Busbee, the successor to Carter in Georgia's highest office, continued. "With his election, we are again a nation unified in our desire to fulfill the American dream. For too long we have been subjected to leadership based on division rather than unity....For too long, we have had leadership that looked backward rather than forward. Jimmy Carter will set national goals and priorities. He will attack our problems. And he will succeed because he knows that the strength of our nation, and the ability to solve our problems and meet our goals, lies not in partisan politics, nor in political deals, nor in pitting one faction against another, but in the people, regardless of where they live."

Busbee's words expressed the same kind of hope that the late Ralph McGill used to preach in the *Atlanta Constitution*. Maybe at last, the South would be pushing aside its proneness to wait for some kind of outside help, even heavenly help. "The earth is the Lord's, and the fullness thereof," McGill once wrote. "But it is man who must save the earth's substance." He would tell of a preacher who bragged on a congregation member's land. "You've got mighty rich land there, Brother Johnson. The Lord surely has been good to you." To which the farmer replied: "Yes, He has. But you ought to see what shape the place was in when the Lord had it all to Himself."

Jimmy Carter's success was proof enough that the South was developing its abilities and talents to the utmost, not waiting on the Lord or anyone else to develop its fullness. The days of hate, bigotry, white-sheeted Klansmen, brow-beaten blacks, and backward-thinking whites could be pushed aside—hopefully forever.

Walking around Plains that morning after, you could see it on the faces of those who had been working for so long for this day. It wasn't just Jimmy Carter who had received a vote of confidence. All of them could share in his success and stick out their chests when he placed his hand on the Bible and repeated the presidential vows.

The Greening Of Plains

Has Plains got a deal for you?

Say you're interested in a Jimmy Carter watch, eh? Well, here's one for you...made by the same people who brought you the Spiro Agnew watch. You do remember him, don't you?

How about a T-shirt? Don't like this white one, you say? Want something with some color? Well, there are a dozen other styles in all the colors of the rainbow. What about this one? It's just like Miss Lillian wore on election night. It's only $10.

Peanuts interest you? If you like them boiled, roasted, raw, in the shell, skinless...even bronzed. We've got anything you might want. Even one over six feet tall you can have your picture taken with.

Say you're a picky shopper. You want something for the person who has everything. Step this way. This is the item for you. You can be the first person in your Jimmy Carter fan club to have a bottle opener made in his likeness.

How does it work? Just put the bottle in that famous smile, and those million-dollar teeth will do the rest. You'll enjoy popping your tops with this little item.

* * * *

That's the commercial side of Plains, the carnival midway that once was a peaceful, God-fearing, small town. It's still the same inside. The people are still friendly. They go to church twice on Sunday, and Billy Carter's Service Station still can't sell beer on the Lord's Day. But since that Tuesday in November 1976, Plains has been harvesting greenbacks along with peanuts.

It really began sooner, about the time investors were offered a unique chance to become a Plains peanut farmer. Just $5 would buy you a one-inch

"Jimmy items"—like this made by Betty Groover—are popular in Plains.

square of land near downtown Plains. You too might grow up to be a peanut-growing President.

The idea was conceived by a group of investors in Plains, Americus, and Columbus, and the name that most people associate with it is that of Mrs. Gloria Carter Spann, the President's sister. She and her husband Walter were among the promoters, and it was she who felt the sting when Jimmy Carter publicly denied any part in the deal and condemned it as a distasteful money-making scheme.

His feelings, however, didn't stop folks from sending in their $5 bills. If you're among the gentlemen farmers who own land there, your neighbor might be Johnny Carson, Ed McMahon, Doc Severinsen, or Chevy Chase. Or it could be a druggist in Bismarck. Orders came in from throughout the country, although after Carter's condemnation most of the advertising was curtailed.

Once upon a time land in Plains wasn't in demand anywhere, and it was on the road to nowhere unless you had wandered off the interstate on the way to or from Florida and had gotten lost. Its people could see its beauty, but no one else bothered to come there and see it.

Fifteen years ago folks around Plains helped elect Jimmy Carter their state senator. He was a hometown boy. They were proud of him. Four years later they tried to help him get elected governor. He didn't make it then, but in 1970 he did. His brother Billy had hung a sign over a Main Street store in 1966. It originally said "Home of Our Next Governor." He changed the wording in 1970, erasing "Next."

Sometime in 1975 Billy had to hire more sign painters. Folks who happened down U.S. Highway 280 now read that Plains was "Home of Our Next President." But when November 2, 1976, became history, the sign painters were at work again. Overnight Plains had become the hometown of the new President of the United States.

By this time the folks back home thought they knew what to expect. When Carter first became a serious candidate, a few tourists would leave Interstate 75 around Cordele, Georgia, and make their way westward to see what Plains was all about. They wanted to see where this man Carter lived, where he went to school, where he went to church, where his folks were buried. As the tempo of the campaign picked up, they wanted more.

Tourists are a peculiar breed. Whenever one of us gets in the car and travels over a hundred miles from home, we're obsessed with having something to take back to our neighbors to show them where we've been. We invest in cameras and film and all that goes with it. We test the light, rearrange the shadows, get down on our knees, or anything else we have to do to get an unusual angle.

And that's one reason people driving into the town today don't see a rusty old water tower standing guard over downtown Plains. A daredevil group from Albany suddenly appeared in town in June 1976 and piece by piece dismantled the old beacon that was painted with remembrances from the Class of '68 and the Class of '71.

"We had to do it," Billy Carter said. "There were people climbing up it all the time to take pictures. One fellow got up to the top okay, but once he was up there and saw how high he was, he wouldn't come down. We had to send somebody up there and get him. It's just as well, anyway. We hadn't used it for years."

Some people want more than pictures, though. They want a postcard to send back to Peoria. They want an ashtray to go on the shelf next to a thermometer that looks like the Washington Monument. They want a sticker to add to the cavalcade of colors already lining their bug-speckled bumpers.

"When people started asking for things," local druggist Boze Godwin said with a grin, "I began stocking souvenir items. But when I started off, I never dreamed what kind of volume I would be moving. After the people started pouring in, it was hard not to stock these things. It's the peanut items that really sell. Can you imagine a drug store ordering 24 cases of peanut brittle? We can't keep it in stock."

Just two years ago all Plains had to offer a shopper were a drug store,

Photographers seeking better angle forced destruction of old water tower.

two groceries, an antique store, a dry goods store, a modern branch bank from Americus, a post office, and two service stations. Tourism has inspired two gift shops, a restaurant, a peanut museum, public rest rooms, and of course the depot that was Carter's campaign headquarters and is now a combination museum-gift shop-welcome center.

From the depot hourly leaves David Ewing's "Carter Country Tour." It hits all the local high spots: the birthplace, boyhood home, and other places where Jimmy lived; where his relatives live and work; Miss Lillian's Pond

As world spotlight turned on it, Plains took on a new face.

House; Jimmy's school; TV City; the world's largest worm farm; the haunted house; the location of Jimmy's treehouse; and the location of the family tennis courts.

Ewing, a gregarious Georgia Southwestern College professor, spices the tour with musical selections in his booming bass voice and a constant stream of chatter about Jimmy and the area. It began as a summertime lark but has turned into a thriving business. Lawsuits are considered against imitators.

You can't go into any of the Plains stores without finding an array of souvenir items, something to take home and gather dust. T-shirts have Jimmy's smiling face and an appropriate message. There are frisbees; yo-yos; buttons and badges of all shapes and sizes; jewelry; postcards picturing all the local sights; maps; books; and records.

One of the songs on the Carter Hit Parade is "Peanut Butter Man," by Frank Jones and Charles Cottles, a pair of country artists out of Jamestown, Tennessee. Jones does the nasal singing. It goes something like this:

> Now I don't mean to be talking bad,
> Remember the last few years we've had;

Pinto beans cooked to the bone;
Man can't live on bread alone.

Now join in on the chorus:

He's the PEANUT BUTTER MAN,
He's the PEANUT BUTTER MAN;
If anyone can do it, he can,
the Georgia PEANUT BUTTER MAN.

Everyone stocks the souvenirs. Even C.L. Walters' Grocery Store has postcards and pictures right across from the meat counter where the friendly, 38-year-old Walters cuts fresh meat to order.

"You have to stock the stuff. It's what people want to buy. Tourists don't want to buy groceries, not real groceries, 7-11-type items maybe, but not food. They come in here looking around, and if we want them to buy anything we have to have what they're shopping for," Walters says.

Main Street in Plains became a street with a parking problem.

There are other reasons, too. Town people once walked or drove downtown to pick up their groceries or do their other shopping. Now they're going to Americus or Albany. Mrs. Sandra Walters, who operates a craft shop upstairs over her husband's grocery, explains why.

"Women used to be able to come here even if they didn't have time to fix their hair or put on makeup. Now they feel like they have to dress up because they might end up being on the network news that night," she said, adding that their customers no longer can find a parking place along Main Street. Besides, the street has been turned into a 30-minute parking zone, complete with the once-unknown fear of parking tickets.

Attention was initially focused directly on Plains the day a Secret Service agent, assigned to Carter when he first was afforded protection, shopped in Ernest Turner's Dry Goods Store for some overalls. He said he wanted to blend in with the local folks. This riled the people of Plains, who were quick to point out that few people there really wore bib-style overalls these days. They kept their laughter under control when Johnny Carson began to poke fun at them about the incident. Neither did they laugh when a correspondent for the Cox Newspapers chain showed up at a Carter press conference wearing overalls, a red bandanna stuck in his pocket, a straw hat on his head, and a straw in his mouth. And to add to the problems a newspaper columnist wrote about the biblical display in Turner's front window, getting the press on the wrong side of the Baptists.

This made the town a little thin-skinned. Looking back, Walters feels otherwise.

"All in all I really can't complain about the way we've been treated. A few people used to be concerned that too much emphasis was being placed on the Carter businesses. People would come into town and expect to find the peanut warehouse, the antique store, and Billy's service station, and nothing else. But I can understand this. Anything to do with the Carter name was what people wanted to hear and read about," he said.

Rubbing his hands on his apron, Walters was not so kind when the subject turned to the attitude the national news media had shown toward Plains in particular and the South in general.

"It's natural, I guess. People up North think we all go barefoot down here and can hardly read or write. It's always been that way. Not long ago, the student editor of the *Harvard Crimson* was in town. He came in the store to talk. He glanced up over the meat counter and saw a Georgia Tech crest I've got hanging there.

"'You must be a Tech fan,' he said. I told him that I had to support my old school. He was really surprised to find out that I was a college graduate. He had this funny look on his face and said something about that he knew I was pretty articulate. Later on he went in the shop upstairs and was really shocked to find out that the clerk he was talking to had graduated from Georgia Southwestern College. He didn't know she was my wife," Walters said, laughing loudly. The *Crimson* editor might have fainted had he happened onto one of the town's Ph.D's.

It must have been surprising for other members of the media to discover that all the folks down South did not live on Tobacco Road and did not still worship Robert E. Lee. Some, however, never bothered to discover what life was really like. They were too content to write off the top of their head from inside the Best Western Motel in Americus, relying on past misconceptions and past prejudices.

One who broke this spell was Robert Sam Anson, political editor of *New Times* magazine. Anson was willing to venture out of his motel room and see for himself what the South was like. His 20,000-word article—he wrote twice that much but it had to be cut—took up almost the entire August 6, 1976, issue of *New Times*. Its title was "Looking for Jimmy." He went looking for Carter but found more.

"Down home. The South. More than anything, I guess it was what had secretly bothered me about Carter—that he was one of them, from there...that place. There was something about those people. They were not Americans in the same way we were Americans. That place was, in fact, a different country," he wrote in the preface, pleading guilty to harboring preconceptions of that faraway land he was to visit.

Anson traveled the interstates and the winding back roads searching for Carter. He found others who had a pleasant, boyish smile like Jimmy's. He found others who wanted to have roots. He found others who had been born again, who talked about Jesus and loving other people. He found others who had seen Civil Rights from the inside, through the eyes of marching blacks and unrelenting whites.

Robert Sam Anson went looking for Jimmy. Maybe he ended up finding himself.

"Starting out I had come to the South looking for its differences, and in the process, of course, I had ignored that which we had in common. By understanding that which set us apart, though, I had hoped to uncover what it was about Jimmy Carter that made him, well, so different," the New Yorker wrote.

What Anson may have discovered was that Jimmy Carter was not that different from a lot of the other folks back home. He had the same human frailties, the same stubbornness, the same respect for the work ethic, the same God, the same addiction with planting his roots.

Around Plains you can see this. There's a little bit of Jimmy in those Good Ole Boys who hang out around Billy Carter's station taking verbal jabs at one another. There's a little bit of Jimmy in the blacks who congregate

Primary night became party night in a happy Plains.

outside "The Night Club." There's a little bit of Jimmy in the peanut farmers who truck their crops to the warehouse. There's a little bit of Jimmy in the friendly shop owners.

Jimmy Carter is, simply, a product of this town, this region, and these people. And it's a love of that life style that brought many people back to Plains.

"I want my grandchildren to look at their grandparents and know them. When Christmas comes I want to be a part of them, not some person coming to visit from Charlotte, Atlanta, or Montgomery. I want them to know something about us and for us to know something about them. That's the way I grew up. That's what having roots is all about," explains Walters.

He has seen how the other half lives, too.

"When I graduated from Tech, I went the corporate route. It was promote and move, promote and move. We lived all over. It was a good job, really, but it wasn't the kind of life I wanted, I discovered.

"My dad had bought this store in 1942, when I was four years old. He wanted to retire, but he wanted to sell it to somebody in the family. I bought it from him, and we came back to Plains. I had been raised in this store. I thought I knew what people wanted. But mainly it helped us get back home.

"We're small-town people. Anyone who lives in a big city doesn't really

New uniforms, new faces: Kenneth Franks became Plains' assistant chief.

know what that means. You have to love it, and you have to accept it or you can't live in one. If you want to shop, you have to do it during the day, there's no 7-11 around here. If you want to go out to eat, you go to Albany or Columbus. It sounds funny to people who haven't lived that kind of life and are used to city life, but it's what we love," Walters said.

It's also a life with commitments.

"That's right, you can't just sit back and wait for someone else to do it, you have to do it yourself. You don't just join the Lions Club and enjoy their swimming pool. You have to take your turn cleaning the pool and policing the area. You're a part of things," he said.

And so he is. He serves as fire chief of the volunteer fire department, and it was the commitment of Walters and his men that kept an explosion at Billy Carter's Service Station from turning into a disaster and also kept a fire at Hugh Carter's antique warehouse from spreading into the downtown block of stores. That's commitment.

Apparently many people still savor that kind of life, for during the campaign Plains became a symbol for more than just Jimmy Carter. To many it was Small Town, U.S.A. When people looked at Plains, they thought of a life that used to be. They saw that despite their own hectic, frantic world, an untouched, leisurely world was still alive.

The town is still the town that spawned a President. Miss Julia's school is still there, although the paint is peeling and the grounds are bare from softball games between the press and the Secret Service, with Jimmy and Billy doing the pitching. The church bells still ring at the Plains Baptist Church, even though ropes now section off the churchyard to allow members freedom from Sunday morning tourists. Billy Carter's Service Station still has its Saturday afternoon barbecues with an occasional President dropping in to eat, although not so often. Hugh Carter's Worm Farm is still mailing out brochures on how you, too, can farm red wigglers.

For some, life is still the same.

What isn't the same is the pace of life. Tourists swarm into town daily, leaving behind a few dollars but a lot of troubles. Phone books are to be guarded. If a tourist spots one, he sees in it more than a way to find the number of Turner's Store, he sees a souvenir. The one and one-half pages of local listings include several Carters, although most of them have been forced to change their numbers. There's even a listing for Jimmy Carter, although the time when he or Rosalynn would answer that number is long past.

Army of reporters who followed Carter put Plains on six o'clock news.

Alton Carter knew things had changed when a lady browsing through Carter's Antique Store coveted a sign that hung over the auction area. "Ladies Rest Room Up Street in Worm Farm Office," the sign read. She offered the 88-year-old Carter a dollar for it. He took it, too.

Local merchants—who once depended on their former stock for a living instead of souvenirs—now complain that their regular customers can't find parking places and don't enjoy being ogled by tourists who gloat over discovering a native. "You mean you really know Jimmy and Miss Lillian?" they'll ask. Many fear that the town will be turned into a neon village with plastic people.

"I think we can pretty well regulate what's built here and how it looks," explains an optimistic Boze Godwin, the town's mayor pro-tem and a third-generation druggist in Plains. He points to action taken by the local government after a group visited Johnson City, Texas, to see what effect the Lyndon Johnson presidency had on his hometown.

"We've enacted strict zoning restrictions, adopted the Southern Building Code, established a Historic Zone along Church Street (Highway 280), and new public rest rooms have been built in the roadside park. We think the state and federal people will be willing to give us any help we need," Godwin said.

Others are not so optimistic, or else are greedy.

Property values went up every time Carter scored another victory. When he was elected President they zoomed off the graph.

A December 1976 classified ad in the *New York Times* advertised some Plains property, complete with a lake, just off Highway 45. The owner, W. O. Cochran, said his town now was "like an Air Force base or a traveling circus." He offered his land for sale in a publicized auction in March 1977. A vacant lot next door to Alton Carter and facing Jimmy's home on Woodland Drive sold for $22,500. All because a Toronto man "wanted to be a neighbor of the President."

Godwin had a realtor call him, suddenly wanting to buy his house. The price was tempting. "I don't know why they called us. Our house hadn't been on the market," the druggist joked, adding that his next-door neighbor happens to be Mrs. Lillian Carter.

Walters thinks Plains will survive.

"We don't like chrome and plastic in this town. And we don't aspire to get real big. We take things one day at a time in Plains. I don't know whether people understand this or not, but we all made a living here before this all happened, and we'll make a living when it's all over," the grocer said.

The reason it will survive is its people. Early in the campaign author Richard Reeves said Plains looked like a Hollywood set, that you expect to walk behind the storefronts and see nothing but props. Well, the people of

When Jimmy was elected, property values went up and so did signs.

the town are not something out of Central Casting. They're real people. Most of them voted for Jimmy Carter and would fight the first person who said something bad about Miss Lillian's oldest boy. But they think for themselves. They're not puppets on a Carter string.

Writing about the creaking steeple when the bell tolled at Fourth of July Bicentennial Services at the Plains Baptist Church seemed to be the thing to do at the time, but members disagreed with the local newsman.

Even Jimmy Carter got into the act. He mentioned it to me one morning in front of his house. "Understand you've been writing bad things about my church. Hear folks around town are a little mad at you," he said.

That's the way the people of Plains are. They speak their mind, even if it costs their neighbor a vote. If it does, that's the way the peanut shells.

James Earl Carter, III, known to folks at home as Chip, is the President's 26-year-old son. He was born in Plains but went away to college while his father was governor of Georgia. He came back to live in a mobile home, a few doors down Main Street from the train depot.

Chip and Caron Carter worked in the campaign for two years. Now they're living with his parents on Pennsylvania Avenue while Chip works for the Democratic National Committee and helps Caron care for their White House-born son, James Earl Carter, IV.

When Chip came back to Plains, he wasn't just another young person. He was Jimmy's son. He had been away and had developed a new way of thinking. It didn't take long for that difference to be evident.

Refurbished train station a symbol of campaign back home in Plains.

"I like the pace here, and I like the people. In Atlanta I was always around people who were just like me and who thought just like me. You can get stagnant in an atmosphere like that. It's sure not that way in Plains," he said.

He pointed across the railroad tracks, toward his Uncle Billy's service station.

"I can go in there and probably be the most liberal thinker in the place. But I can talk or argue with anybody, or question anything anybody else might say. We get loud, but we never stop listening to each other. They listen, and I listen to them. We're friends despite the fact that we disagree. To me that's healthy," Chip Carter believes.

So it is. However, there are those who still do not believe that all of this is real; they think that Plains was the creation of some press agent on Carter's staff. Take the tourist who drove into town one afternoon and cornered Mrs. Maxine Reese.

"Okay, I want an answer. I've been reading and hearing what a small town this is supposed to be. I was driving into town and I looked up on that water tower and saw the population—31780. Now, who's kidding who?"

She just smiled. "That's the zip code, you old fool."

Whatever the population it's where Jimmy Carter feels at home. It's where the people are who still think of him as Mr. Earl and Miss Lillian's boy, where folks aren't bashful about walking up to him and telling him how much they disagree with something he might have said. It's the place where he can eat grilled steak with the boys at Billy's station and have the guys call him Jimmy instead of Mr. President. It's the place where he can be close to those he loves.

Long ago he explained what Plains is to him.

"It's as far away from politics as a South Seas island. I put on my work clothes and nobody defers to me. All through the campaign, when I'd hurry home to Plains on the weekends, people would want to know why I wasn't going to Sea Island, Miami, or some other fancy resort.

"I'd tell them this is where I can relax. This is where my roots are. I can come home, take off my suit, put on my blue jeans and some old work boots, and walk these fields. That's where I can clear my mind of all my problems, whatever they may be."

His feelings can be squeezed into three final words.

"This," says Jimmy Carter, "is home."

Tourists once took leaves from the Carters' lawn for souvenirs, but now Secret Service outposts keep visitors at a secure distance.

The Carter Clan

Miss Lillian:
She's Everybody's Mother

The church was cold—not air-conditioning cold, but wintertime cold. The organ was quiet—no one knew how to play "The Wedding March." There was no rice—or even grits—to throw at the bride and groom. Wedding guests included a few tourists and two newsmen.

The occasion was the wedding of the former Mrs. Emma Cushton of Springfield, Illinois, now of Homestead, Florida, and Charles Pierce MacDonald of Bay City, Michigan, now of Homestead.

Giving the bride away was Tom Pollock, a sunglasses salesman from Atlanta. Her matron of honor was Mrs. Lillian Carter of Plains.

Performing the brief Baptist ceremony was the Reverend Bruce Edwards, then the pastor of the Plains Baptist Church, which was opened especially for the afternoon services that December 1, 1976.

It might have been any wedding, anywhere, except for the unusual cast of characters, unusual setting, and unusual circumstances that brought them together in the historic old church.

"I told Em to choose a special place, somewhere that meant something to both of us. You see, we met in a mobile-home park in Homestead. We don't really have any ties there," the groom said, accepting congratulations from the strange assortment of guests in the congregation.

"We had both worked real hard in Carter's campaign in Florida. We were really involved. So when I said I wanted to come to Plains for the services, he agreed," the new Mrs. MacDonald said.

The couple had arrived in Plains two days before the ceremony, not really knowing just where they might be married. The next day they were touring the refurbished train depot. There, greeting visitors in her favorite rocking chair, was Miss Lillian. They stood in line to meet her.

"Em told her what we were here for, and Mrs. Carter got all excited. She wanted to know when we were planning to have the ceremony. We told

Miss Lillian as matron of honor for Plains wedding of Charles and Emma MacDonald.

her that afternoon. 'You can't do that, I can't get ready that fast,' she said. She told us to wait until today and that she'd talk to her pastor and arrange things. So here we are," MacDonald said.

Services were arranged for 2 p.m. that Wednesday afternoon, and Miss Lillian was scurrying around the depot making last-minute arrangements when a reporter and photographer from Columbus wandered in.

"You ARE coming to the wedding, aren't you?" When Miss Lillian puts things in that tone, you know you'd best say yes. She was looking for any familiar face she saw to join them at the church. When the entourage arrived at the church, tourists were in the churchyard taking pictures.

"Why don't you go to the wedding?" Miss Lillian called to them, heading toward the door.

"Is there really going to be a wedding?" a skeptical woman asked. Told there indeed was, she hurried her husband back to their well-packed station wagon for their camera. The Reverend Edwards arrived and produced a key. He directed the guests into the sanctuary and led the happy couple toward his study in the rear of the church for some last-minute counseling.

"Does anybody know how to play 'The Wedding March'?" Miss Lillian asked. No one did. Nor did anyone know how to turn on the heat in the sanctuary. The only salvation was the December sunshine peeking through the stained-glass windows.

Pollock explained how he came to be a part of the wedding party. It turned out that he, too, was an indirect product of Miss Lillian's recruiting talents. He was recruited by Judy Pearl, also of Atlanta.

"I met Mrs. Carter at a department store in Columbus last summer, before the convention," Miss Pearl said. "I was there, calling on the store and she was there signing autographs of Jimmy's book. We met, had lunch together, and I gave her some big, round sunglasses she wore to New York. We were passing through Plains this afternoon, and I stopped in to see her. She introduced us to the people who're getting married and asked Tom if he'd give away the bride. We had never met either of them before."

At last, the happy couple, followed by the minister, came through one of the side doors. Joined by Pollock and Miss Lillian, the bride and groom stood in front of the Reverend Edwards, who repeated the familiar vows.

Autographing Jimmy's and Ruth's books was one of Miss Lillian's campaign contributions.

Throughout the ceremony the new Mrs. MacDonald held tightly to Miss Lillian's hand, sometimes looking down and smiling at her. When the pronouncement had been made and she had been kissed by her new husband, the bride turned and kissed her newfound friend.

Flashbulbs were exploding as Mrs. MacDonald talked about her fast-paced stay in Georgia.

"You know, Mrs. Carter is really something. This morning, I was at a dress shop she had recommended in Americus, buying this coat I have on. Who should walk in but Mrs. Carter. I was worried. Somebody had told us we couldn't get married this quickly by law. Before I knew it, she had the girl in the store on the phone, calling somebody at the courthouse to see what the law was. In a few minutes the salesgirl was able to explain everything," she said.

Soon the couple were heading toward their overstocked car, ready for a honeymoon and a return to their Florida home. They said private good-byes to Miss Lillian.

"I feel," Mrs. MacDonald said, "like she's my mother."

Mrs. Lillian Carter's that way. Her face is a map of experience. Her smile comes easily and often. Her voice is strong, and her tongue is quick and honest, not afraid to say what's on her active mind. She's 78 going on 21. Like the lady said, she is almost like your mother.

During her son Jimmy's amazing rise to the White House, Mrs. Carter—known to one and all as Miss Lillian—became a darling to the liberal sector and to the Geritol set. She is a heroine to the liberal thinkers because even her son admits she's always been his liberal conscience, especially on Civil Rights. The Geritol addicts love her because she doesn't let age stand in the way of being active and getting involved.

Active she certainly is. That was evident long ago when a reporter, who had been unable to reach Miss Lillian at home, called the local campaign headquarters, hoping someone there could get a message to her.

"Carter headquarters," the person said.

"I'm trying to reach Mrs. Maxine Reese."

"She's out right now," the female voice answered.

"When do you expect her back?"

"I'm not sure. Maybe I can help you. I'm Jimmy's mother."

She must have thought the call had been disconnected because she heard nothing but silence. That couldn't be Miss Lillian, Jimmy's mother. Not answering the phone.

"Really, this is Lillian Carter. Can't I help you?"

That she could. She also explained her presence there. "I try to come down for a while every day, to do what I can. Jimmy and Rosalynn can't be here and Billy's at work. People coming through want to see one of the family, so I guess I'm elected," she said.

Word soon would spread. Visitors dropping in at the depot would ask first thing, "Where's Miss Lillian?" They wanted to meet her, to talk to her, to have their picture taken with her. Few were disappointed. She would drive in, squeeze into a parking place, and get out of her car looking weary and cross. All of that was forgotten when people crowded around her. If you'll keep a secret, it seems as if she enjoys it as much as the thousands who have filed past her since her oldest son burst onto the presidential scene.

She has a love of life and of people that not even 78 years of living has diminished. Her steel-blue eyes still dance and twinkle when she talks, and her laughter can fill a room. Her will is as strong today as when she was a girl in Richland, 18 miles from Plains.

She was Bessie Lillian Gordy then, one of five daughters and four sons of James Jackson Gordy and Mary Nicholson Gordy. Her father was one of those courthouse fixtures who always had a political job. A disciple of Populist leader Tom Watson, Jim Jack Gordy was a proponent of rural free delivery and was postmaster in Richland for many years. When he died in 1948, he was keeper of the door for the Georgia House, and godfather to any candidate seeking political blessing in Stewart County.

As a girl in Richland, her ambitions ranged far beyond the county lines. At a time when girls were not expected to want education, Lillian Gordy wanted to be a nurse. The compassion welling inside her had to come out.

"I wanted to go overseas in World War I. My folks didn't want me to, but I was determined. The army was begging for nurses, and I volunteered. I was finally accepted on the day the war ended," she says.

She finally began her nursing studies at the Wise Clinic in nearby Plains. Five brothers operated the clinic there, which served as a hospital for the surrounding counties. She was a willing student, quick to learn. It didn't take her long to absorb all that she could learn there. She departed for Grady Memorial Hospital in Atlanta to complete her studies.

Meanwhile, she had met James Earl Carter, a friendly, hard-working store owner in Plains. They kept in touch while she was in Atlanta. He mailed her engagement ring while she was in Atlanta, and they were married in 1923, moving into a small, upstairs apartment on Church Street in Plains, in sight of the store her new husband operated on Main Street.

"I can remember going up there and playing with Aunt Lillian. They didn't have any kids then, and she used to ask me up there all the time. She had specialized in children's diseases and was great with kids. I always looked forward to visiting with them," remembers Hugh Carter.

Earl was involved in an assortment of businesses. He operated his dry goods store, sold insurance and farming equipment, bottled syrup, had a dry-cleaning store and was a farmer. He was a member of the local board of

Miss Lillian shows off her first child, one-year-old James Earl.

education and served on various agricultural commissions.

There were to be four children in the Carter clan: Jimmy, Gloria, Ruth, and later Billy. Discipline was the rule and love the byword in this country home. "I love you goodest," was their favorite saying.

Earl was dollar minded—"You can't spend yourself rich," he often said—but business was left at the store and never discussed in front of the children. At home Lillian was in charge, although her nursing career was abandoned because "Earl wanted his wife to stay at home." Music often lilted through their clapboard house, usually Tommy Dorsey, Glenn Miller, or some other "Big Band" number, which was Earl's favorite kind of music. He attempted to pass on his love of music to his children. Gloria and Ruth each took piano lessons, but he forbade them to practice at home because "none of us had a dab of talent," according to Gloria Carter Spann.

Earl was a lover of parties, and he and Lillian were often off to weekend dances at Magnolia Springs, a nearby pavilion. Saturday night was date night for them and reserved for only them. The children would be left with a baby-sitter, and their parents would head to the nearest dance. "My father was a good dancer, and my mother was one of the best dancers ever," Gloria says. At other times activities would be scheduled involving the whole family. But Saturdays belonged to Earl and Lillian.

While Earl was absorbed in his varied business ventures, Lillian had interests of her own. Although she had given up nursing as a profession, she was on-call for those in need. "She was sometimes the only doctor we had," an old black woman in Plains remembers. "Whenever we called, she'd be there." It wasn't for money, but because she cared. As a child, she had seen her father go to a restaurant in Richland to buy food for blacks who could not eat there. She had seen blacks shuffling to the back door of a house when the front door was closer. Long ago she had decided she was going to be different, an attitude her children inherited. Her other activities were more typical—playing bridge, going to the literary guild, ladies missionary society, PTA. These things she did alone, without her husband.

Her children were taught the same respect for others that Miss Lillian had. "I've always been for the underdog," she explains. "I'm very compassionate, and I have seen so much mistreatment in the South all my life. My one aim has been to get a better life for blacks, for them to be equal to us. And at last I think we're getting that way."

It wasn't always that way, however. Jimmy Carter remembers how it used to be, in the days when Archery and a strict racial code were alive.

"In those days," he recalls, "Archery society was built around Bishop William Johnson, a black leader who was bishop of the African-Methodist Episcopal Church for five or six states. He was undoubtedly the most prestigious person in the community. Alvan, one of the Johnson sons, lived and

Jimmy, Gloria, and Billy bring kids to visit their grandmother.

was educated in the North, in Boston, I believe. He became a very good friend of my mother and we children. He was used to the ways of the North and would come to our front door. He was the only black man who ever did. Whenever we heard Alvan was home, there was a quiet nervousness around our house. We would wait in a combination of anticipation and trepidation until we finally heard the knock on our front door."

When the knock would come, his father would pretend he had not heard it and slip quietly out the back door. Lillian would answer the door. Alvan and the rest of the Carter family would sit in the living room, talking, while Earl worked or walked in the back yard. Somehow he seemed to believe that if he didn't see what was going on, it wasn't really happening. He still lived by the old standards, as did Bishop Johnson, who would park out front and wait for Mr. Earl to step outside to see him. After he was elected President, Carter invited Alvan and his sister to join him for services at the Plains Baptist Church, showing that racial bars were broken.

Miss Lillian and Jimmy today point out that Earl Carter was only a mirror of his time. They cite his kindness to both black and white as reason to think that he would have mellowed in time, as did many other Southerners. Gloria remembers days in the family store that paint a similar picture. "If a child—white or black—came in on a Saturday, he'd leave with a piece of candy. You could depend on it. That's the kind of heart Daddy had," she says. After his death, it was found that candy in his desk drawer was the reason local children always stopped by on their way home from school.

From the local school board, Earl had moved into politics. He was serving his second term in the Georgia House in 1953 when doctors told the family that he had cancer in its advanced stages. Jimmy, away in the navy, came home to be with his daddy in his final weeks. At 59, Earl Carter died.

There was talk that Lillian Carter would be his successor in the House. She was well-known, well-respected, and, despite her liberal ways, well-liked. "She was always the politician in the family anyway," Earl's brother Alton still says. But politics were far from her mind then. She was bitter, disillusioned, and alone. Jimmy came home to save the business, but Billy, her youngest, stayed around only long enough to pick up his high school diploma before joining the Marine Corps. Lillian Carter's once-orderly life was a shambles. She searched for a new interest.

Auburn University became that new interest. A friend told her that Kappa Alpha Fraternity was looking for a housemother. Miss Lillian jumped at the chance. It was the ideal job for her embittered situation. She was mother and friend to a houseful of partying students who soon treated her almost like one of the guys. When they were going out for a pizza, Miss Lillian was sure to be included. It was easy to think young and stay young in that atmosphere. Yet, when her 68th birthday came, Miss Lillian was back in Plains, technically retired, but still looking for a new challenge. For a time she had operated a nursing home in Blakely, but that wasn't the challenge she was seeking.

That challenge came one evening during the "Tonight Show." An announcement urged interested people to consider the Peace Corps as a way of fulfilling a dreary life. The kicker was one phrase—"Age is no barrier." Age is no barrier? Could a person 68 years of age qualify? That was what Miss Lillian intended to find out. She wrote away for information, and it wasn't long before she had been invited to Chicago for screening interviews. Her remaining hurdle was her family.

"Do you love me?" she asked Jimmy and Billy, together in the warehouse office. This signaled them something was up. Jimmy responded with a tender, "Of course, we do, Mama," but Billy got to the point. "What in the hell are you up to now?" he wanted to know. She told them about the Peace Corps, about her interviews, about wanting to go to India. A while later she told Gloria of her plans. "But who'll go fishing with me?" she said. Long distance, she told Ruth. "Bombay? I'll come visit you." By that time in their lives, Jimmy, Billy, Gloria, and Ruth all knew better than to try to talk their

Ruth, Jimmy, Billy, and Gloria strike family pose with mother.

headstrong mother out of anything. If she was looking for them to change her mind, she was out of luck.

Months of testing followed. Then refresher courses in nursing along with a crash program in the Indian language and dialects. She was assigned to a family-planning program in Vikhroli, a small Indian village just north of Bombay. When she arrived she thought she was ready for what was ahead. But classrooms and lectures did little to prepare her for the poverty, disease, and starvation she saw firsthand. And the leprosy. How could anyone prepare for lepers, those afflicted with that disease that man has turned his back on for centuries? "Unclean," people had once cried.

"After I had been there for about four months, a man came into the clinic one day with his 11-year-old daughter slung over his shoulder like a sack of flour. She had infectious leprosy and couldn't have weighed more than 30 pounds. 'Oh, God, I can't touch her,' I thought, and when I went into the doctor's office, I told him the same thing. He said that leprosy isn't transmitted by touching. 'Try and treat her. If you can't, I'll come and do it for you.'

"I made up my mind to try. But after the injection, I washed my hands over and over. Then I put alcohol on them, and I was feeling so ashamed. I had told them to come back the next day. When she came that next day, I washed my hands like normal. I learned to love her, and after a few weeks she began to get better. We got her into a leprosarium, and six months later she came back to see me. She put her arms around my neck and kissed me. I thought only about how happy I was," Miss Lillian now says.

After her son's inauguration, she went to India to represent him. It was a tearful reunion with those she had grown to love.

Returning to Plains after two years in India was a shock to her. She still loved the life there, but inside she was different. She had fed that gnawing

Returning from the Peace Corps, Miss Lillian became popular speaker.

Rosalynn and Miss Lillian answered gubernatorial questions at Columbus College.

feeling she had felt since her youth to help others. She had lived in a world not controlled by whites and knew firsthand what blacks must have been feeling in her homeland for centuries. All of it only intensified that outspoken liberal side of her that had always been there—not liberal in the academic sense, but liberal in the Old South tradition that dubbed you a liberal if you let a black person ride in the front seat with you or call you by your first name. She was Sumter County liberal.

India was now thousands of miles away. Atlanta wasn't so far. Jimmy Carter wanted to move there. He wanted to be governor of Georgia. Joining the rest of the family, she began to campaign for him again, just as she had done four years before when he came in a surprising yet disappointing third in the Democratic Primary. "This time it was different. In 1966 when he lost, Jimmy wasn't ready to be governor. But he was ready when he won in 1970," she says.

He was ready, and he won.

During his four years living in Georgia's governor's mansion, Miss Lillian stayed behind in Plains, visiting her son from time to time. Near the end of his term she was in Atlanta, recovering from a broken shoulder that still pains her today. He came into her room at the mansion one night to see how she was feeling. Sitting on the edge of her bed, he dropped a bombshell into a casual conversation.

"Mama, I'm going to run for President."

"President of what?" his startled mother gasped.

"President of the United States."

Was he serious? It took a mother to know for sure. "I looked at him closely. I could tell by his face that he wasn't kidding. And I never doubted him for an instant. When he says he is going to do something, he usually does it," she says. That was in 1973. There were to be years of work and preparation ahead for all of them.

Some of that work was behind them in the summer of 1976 when a reporter searched for Miss Lillian's Pond House. This was her retreat. Her children had built the light-filled house by the small lake for her as a surprise when she returned from India. A few miles from Plains, she now came here to escape the sightseers and news personnel who would badger her if she stayed at her home.

You needed an appointment to see her, and driving between the pine trees that surrounded the house, you could see why. Miss Lillian was sitting in a chair outside. Her daughter Gloria was there, watching and listening. Between them was a man with a tape recorder, carefully recording Miss Lillian's words. He was from *U.S. News & World Report.* Apologizing for taking too long, he excused himself.

Interviewers found Miss Lillian so relaxed that soon she asked the questions.

Going inside the modernistic but rustic house, Miss Lillian looked weary. Not just tired, but drained. She was keeping a rigorous schedule of interviews and had little time of her own. She had little leisure to use the fishing rods sitting idle outside and little time to relax in the hammock strung between the trees. "This is really a lovely setting out here," the visitor said, looking out over the peaceful pond.

"It's my favorite spot," Miss Lillian replied. "But I'm afraid people may start bothering me out here, too. A reporter from Atlanta gave explicit directions how to get here in a story in the paper the other day. I don't know why he had to do that."

Fixing herself a Coke, she sat down on the well-stuffed couch, casually hanging her legs over the arm. She patiently listened while the reporter asked her the familiar questions about Jimmy's life. He apologized, telling her he was sure she had heard them all before. She said she didn't mind, and in a few minutes the twinkling of her eyes made the weariness forgotten. They moved quickly through the years ("he was an ordinary, country boy"), tracing her oldest son's life through the navy ("I thought he'd be chief of staff"), through the governor's office, and on to the campaign trail. The reporter soon forgot he was the interviewer. It was Miss Lillian who was asking the questions.

"What do you think (Frank) Church's after?" she asked. It would not have been surprising for her to produce a notebook and pen. It became a conversation instead of a serious interview, and the conversation soon returned to Jimmy. She talked about a recent visit home when she had driven over to his house one evening and found Jimmy, Amy, and the neighborhood children in the street throwing a frisbee. "It was the most relaxed I had seen him in a long time. Later on I told him how tired he was looking, that he had better start taking care of himself. He looked at me real serious and said, 'Don't worry, Mama, I'm doing just what I want to do.' I thought to myself how I couldn't figure why anybody would want to go through all of that."

Between the words, there were the telltale signs of motherly concern and motherly pride. To her, Jimmy was still her red-haired little boy. She shows this same kind of love when you ask her about her other children.

"Here's Ruth's book. Have you read it?" she asked, retrieving a book from the well-stocked shelf. Its title is *The Gift of Inner Healing*, and in it Ruth Carter Stapleton explains her psycho-religious teachings. However, her mother admits, "I don't understand everything in it." It was Ruth—Jimmy's younger sister—who introduced him to Rosalynn, and it was she who walked with him through the fields one day in 1966, consoling him after his gubernatorial defeat and leading him toward a spiritual reawakening. The wife of Dr. Robert Stapleton, a Fayetteville, North Carolina, veterinarian, she travels the world as an evangelist and faith healer. Early in his campaign Jimmy Carter discovered that in some circles, he was known as Ruth Stapleton's brother.

Gloria Carter Spann is the one her mother looks to in a crisis and the smartest of her children, Miss Lillian has claimed. It is Gloria who may be most like her outspoken mother, for this wife of a Plains peanut farmer is one who will quickly tell you what she thinks, often offering an opinion even before you've asked for it. Like the rest of the family, she has a smile that is contagious. "I quit smiling when visitors in town would ask me a question. That always gave away who I was," she says. Although she preferred to spend her time fishing instead of campaigning during her brother's presidential campaign, it was Gloria who ran his office in Plains when he was elected governor. She lives the most private life of any of the Carters, content to ride her motorcycle with her husband Walter, sit on the river bank, or dabble in art. Even though her brother is President, she intends to stay where she is. "My life is perfect. Why change?" she says.

As for Billy, his mother is quick to point out that her son the beer drinker hardly lives up to the image he sometimes portrays. "Billy's just like the rest of my children, he loves to read. I don't think he's ever without a book or something to read. They were always that way, even at the dinner table. He just drinks too much beer and cusses," his mother said.

Daughter Gloria has her mother's outgoing personality and smile.

First grandmothers Lillian Carter and Allie Smith shake voters' hands.

But when Miss Lillian talks about nine-year-old Amy Carter, she sends a different kind of message. This is a grandmother talking now, a grandmother who would go to war for her Huckleberry Finn of a granddaughter. When she talks about freckle-faced Amy, her dancing eyes move doubletime. "She's my heart. My job, from the beginning of the campaign, was to keep her. She's been my joy," Miss Lillian said. Now that the campaign is history, Amy has moved to Washington, sadly leaving her grandmother behind in Plains. There are other grandchildren there for her to pamper, but her house and her hours are quiet without Amy.

Keeping Amy hardly was a job for a loving grandmother, but it was hardly Miss Lillian's only contribution to her son's lengthy, uphill campaign. Her still-painful shoulder kept her off the road full-time, but she talked about what she saw her role in Plains to be. "I don't have to do it, but I think people ought to be able to see someone in Jimmy's family if they care enough to come to Plains. That's why I stayed down at the depot. It was my way of helping," she said.

Television and newspaper stories made her rocking-chair appearances at the train station known across the country, and sightseers soon came to expect an opportunity to see Miss Lillian. They wanted to snap her picture, beg her for inside information on the campaign, or just talk about the hot Georgia weather. "Miss Lillian's down there, just talked to her," tourists would say, spreading the word. Some expected more. "Mrs. Carter, I'm just back from Korea. I want to talk to you about the situation there," the man in Bermuda shorts told her. "Jimmy should know," he continued, ignoring her pleas that she didn't talk policy with her son the candidate. Others would tell her how they had met her years before, here or there. Somehow, she would make most of them believe she remembered.

Yet, her honesty still seeped through.

"Hello, Miss Lillian. You probably don't remember me. I was at Auburn when you were a housemother there. I dated some of the boys in the fraternity," the smiling, attractive woman said.

"I remember you. And I remember that I never did like you either," Miss Lillian said flatly.

As the campaigning summer grew hotter, Miss Lillian became more and more involved. Her stays in the depot grew longer. She even made short trips out of town to campaign for Jimmy. She continued to have a line of reporters waiting to ask her the predictable questions. Her face became almost as recognizable as her son's. Around the country, travelers were showing off pictures of Miss Lillian. "We took it right out there on that loading dock at the train station," they'd tell their friends. One summer-of-1976 visitor even said that "If Miss Lillian was doing the campaigning, this thing would already be over."

By the time convention time came, she was a celebrity, Plains' No. 1 tourist attraction. She cast the same shadow when she arrived in New York. She told Walter Cronkite on CBS that Joe Namath was her favorite football player, and he surprised her with an autographed picture of the New York Jets quarterback. The next night she told NBC's Tom Snyder that her biggest thrill in New York had been visiting with Walter Cronkite. She sent a daily column back to the *Columbus Enquirer* so that folks back home could read what she thought about the convention. When Jimmy wanted to know what she was writing, she all but told him he'd have to buy a paper to find out.

It wasn't her first Democratic Convention, however; that had come in 1964. A Georgia delegate had become ill and Gov. Carl Sanders—the man her boy Jimmy was to defeat for governor six years later—invited Miss Lillian to join the Georgia delegation in Chicago. She had been an outspoken campaigner for Lyndon Johnson, which in Sumter County was like injecting yourself with the plague. Sanders knew this and thought she would be a welcome addition to the Georgia delegation. She still talks about having dinner with the late Mayor Richard Daley of Chicago and of being in the hall the night the late Robert Kennedy gave a moving speech about his assassinated brother John. "You could have heard a pin drop," she says. But the excitement of Chicago was nothing like New York.

Months before, when her son was in a struggle against the multitude of Democrats who wanted the nomination, she had said she might not even go to New York. "I don't know if I could bear to go all that way and have him lose. I couldn't take it," she would say. But the events of that June solved the problem. Jimmy went to New York as the Democrat's Conquering Hero, their Prodigal Son. She, of course, went along, and shared his moment in the nation's spotlight.

It was that time in the spotlight that was to cause more problems when she returned to Plains. If she was ever just another mother of just another candidate, she certainly was not that when they returned home. He wasn't just another candidate—he was the Democratic nominee. Within four months he was the President-elect. The effect that all of this had on Plains and on Miss Lillian took its toll.

She continued to hold court in her familiar rocking chair near the exit in the crowded depot. Now there were longer lines, waiting for a chance to seal a friendship that usually had begun when they saw her on television or read something provocative she might have said to a newspaper reporter. The dancing eyes grew tired, but still they came, and so did she. Her friends and family tried to get her to stay at home, but you could set your watch by her arrival every day.

"Be patient. You'll get your time in just a minute," one of her friends would tell visitors who looked over merchandise at the souvenir counter while they waited. The counter was packed with memorabilia about Plains and the President. "Jimmy items," Miss Lillian calls them.

"When you get up to her, don't shake her hands, they're hurting her," the friend told tourists, who nodded their heads as if they heard, only to forget when their turn came.

Mrs. Maxine Reese had taken notice of the visitors' actions. "They want to pump her hand, squeeze it hard, hug her, trying to be nice. They don't know what they're doing to her. She can hardly get her coat on by herself most of the time. It's that shoulder she broke and her arthritis. She tells people not to touch her, but they won't listen. They just think she's being cute. We try to get her to stay away, to rest, but she won't listen," Mrs. Reese, said, shaking her head.

Even Miss Lillian had to admit the pace was tiring. "I'm getting irritable. I'm going to have to taper off. I have to tell them, please don't touch. But the time to worry is when they stop coming. All these people, the majority of them, voted for Jimmy. I want to have a good rapport with them. I want them to vote for him again," she said.

Not even a bout with arthritis kept Miss Lillian from her appointments.

Finally, she was forced to taper off. Three days before Christmas her doctor put her in a hospital in Americus. There she was to spend Christmas 1976, her family crowding into her private room, bringing armloads of presents. Her doctor called it exhaustion and complications from arthritis. It was also the only way to keep her away from the depot.

When she returned home after the New Year was ushered in and only three weeks before Jimmy's inauguration, people were to learn just how much she had been trying to do. Not only had she been serving time in the rocker, but she had been going through mountains of mail that daily flooded into the tiny Plains office, some of it addressed only to "Miss Lillian," some to "Jimmy Carter's Mother," one having only her picture on the envelope. Now her sister, Mrs. Sissy Dolvin, and Miss Lillian's daughter Gloria were there trying to help her sort through the messages of congratulations and the cards ordering her to "get well." "I don't know how she's done it," Aunt Sissy said.

No longer was Miss Lillian driving her familiar blue Chevrolet to the depot every day. She was refusing all interviews and visitors until her strength returned. That was doctor's orders. But she placed an order of her own. She wanted a visitor, not just any visitor, but a masked visitor. Contacting Fred Ward, a wrestling promoter in Columbus, Gloria Spann put in the request. One January Friday, it was filled.

The visitor, hailing from parts unknown, was Mr. Wrestling No. 2, a masked man who is one of wrestling's "good guys." His mask stands for truth, justice, and the American way. And he happens to be Miss Lillian's favorite wrestler. Mr. Wrestling No. 2 (yes, Virginia, there is a No. 1) arrived that morning, wearing a black-and-white mask and a black-and-white sports coat. He soon found that Miss Lillian disliked Abdullah the Butcher and some of the other villains more than she disdained Republicans.

"Are you good looking under that mask?" she asked him.

"Well, I don't know. My wife and family seem to think so," the masked man said, showing modesty unbecoming a wrestler.

"What do you think?" she persisted.

"Yes, I guess I am," he admitted, a smile showing through the slit in his mask. But not even the First Mother was to know for sure. "But she said she was sure I didn't have a mustache or a goatee because she had seen some wrestler get my mask halfway up my face on TV one Saturday," he said afterwards.

Miss Lillian, you see, is a fan—Wrestling Fan of the Year, one magazine called her. Down South this doesn't mean polite clapping or football cheers. This means cursing the bad guys. screaming at the hapless referee, throwing kisses at the good guys. All of this Miss Lillian enjoys. For many years she was a regular at the Wednesday night matches in Columbus. Every Saturday

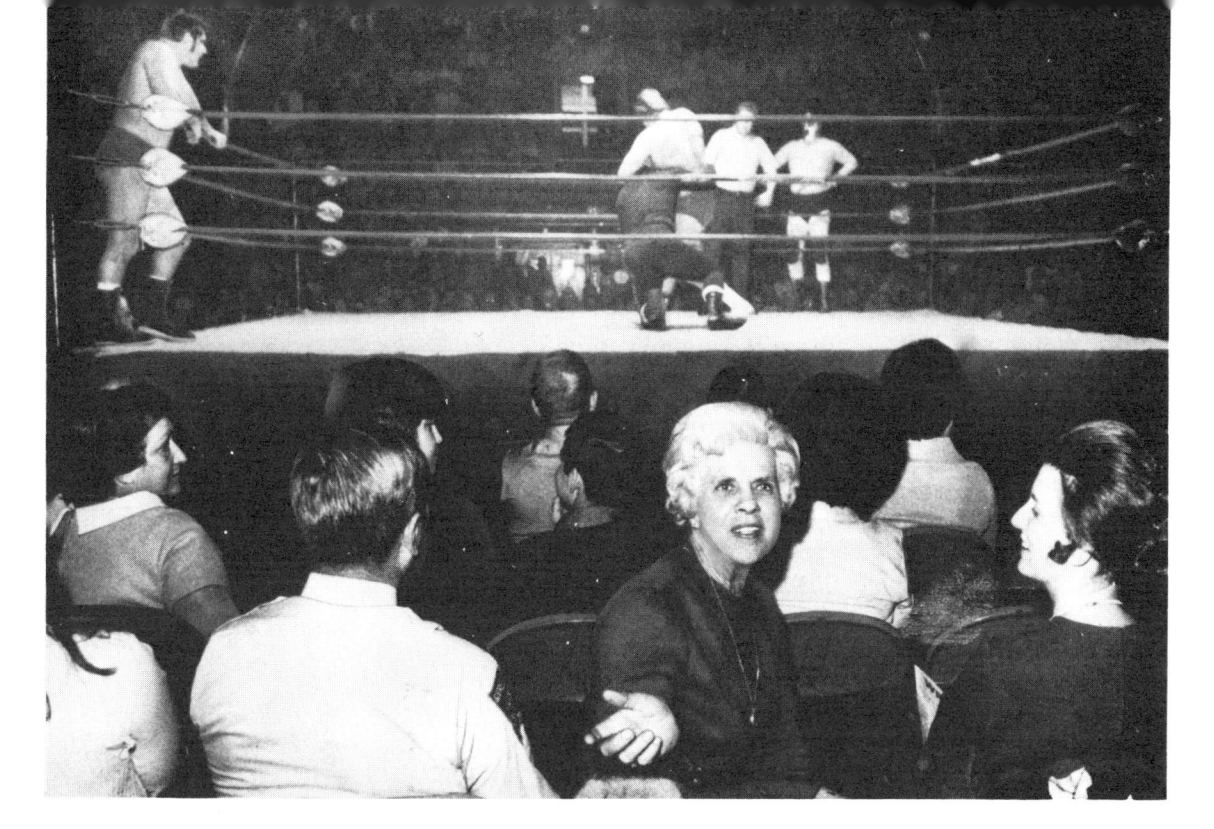

A rabid sports fan, Miss Lillian has followed wrestling 25 years.

she is glued to her television set to view the bouts. A visitor once advised her that if she had cable TV, she could see five hours of wrestling every Saturday. "Five hours?" she said, a smile taking over her face. "I'd better look into that." That would really make life hard on her friends and neighbors, who already know better than to disturb her while she's watching her wrestling, which she views as regularly as her daily soap operas.

"She's a real fan," the masked man said, driving down the highway with his mask still in place. "She talked about a feud I had with my partner a few years ago, about matches I've had, and about my shoulder I hurt one time. They had to put a pin in it, and she said she could sympathize with me because they had to put one in her wrist after she broke it and she knew how that hurt. She wanted to know why I didn't run Abdullah and some of the others out of town."

Ward quickly found that Miss Lillian was no wrestling-come-lately fan. "She wasn't sure when she first started coming, but by matches she talked about, I know she's been coming since 1951 or 1952. She could remember them a lot better than I could, I know that. Her husband took her to her first match, but after that she said she took him. She could even tell me where she always sat," the veteran promoter said.

When her son was running for governor in 1966 and 1970, she would go to the Columbus City Auditorium and urge her fellow wrestling fans to vote for him. Carter himself visited the arena early in his presidential push. That

Carter had a headlock on Mr. Wrestling II and his opponents.

night Secret Service agents were openly nervous when that same Mr. Wrestling No. 2 grabbed the candidate in a headlock, for the benefit of the cameramen. Had they been there years before when the masked man lifted Carter up above his head, they would have likely turned in their badges and their earpieces. Miss Lillian also went to the matches during the presidential campaign, and she vows it was her last visit.

"A man from Americus took me. I made him promise we wouldn't sit down front. I wanted to sit up where I knew people. I just wanted to enjoy myself. Anyway, we got there and our seats were right up front. They introduced me and everything. Well, once the matches got started, I started getting excited. I was up on my feet, screaming at the referee, louder and louder. All of a sudden, I felt like everyone was looking right at me—they all knew me—thinking what was the mother of a presidential candidate doing acting like that. I'm never going to go again," she claims.

The afternoon after he visited her, Mr. Wrestling No. 2 was on television—sans sport coat—easily taking care of some overbloated opponent. What would a wrestling show be without an interview? So after straightening his mask, he was at the microphone. First No. 2 sent a get-well message to his No. 1 fan in Plains, telling the fans he wished they all could meet her. Before a shouted promise to run some bully named Dick Slater out of town, he offered this message to Jimmy Carter. "Mr. Carter, I hope you hold on to that mama of yours for as long as you can," the wrestler said.

So does everyone else. She has brought to presidential politics a combination never before seen in our history. She loves her son. She loves people. She loves attention. She loves to be the center of attention. Yet, she's no doting mother, content to be proud, content to smile on cue, content to say only the right things, content to stay in the background. At times she has even been irreverent about her son the President.

Miss Lillian is a remarkable, headstrong woman, out of a mold that the South once turned out regularly but that is becoming extinct today. She's of a breed that would deny knowing the definition of liberation but could wield influence like few Southern gentlemen. Pleading helplessness, she might flutter her eyes and reach for her handkerchief one minute, then grab the reins the next. She's from a stock of woman that was bred at a time when women had to be strong, for a generation of Southern men were either buried in some Northern cemetery or shell-shocked to find their lives had been set afire by a pillaging army.

Forgetting all of this, however, Miss Lillian is just Miss Lillian. At a time when most of her contemporaries were checking into the nearest rest home, she was packing her bags for India. Still ahead for her was an active, frontline role in her son's campaign for first, the highest position in his state, and then in his nation. All after the calendar alleged she was growing old. To the young, she was a revelation—an old person who had not forgotten how to live, to laugh, and to think. To the older generation, she was proof positive that Social Security can be a beginning instead of an end.

As Emma MacDonald put it, "I feel like she's my mother."

Billy Carter:
Baron Of The Beer Cooler

It was a Saturday night gathering of the boys, the Good Old Boys. There was a lot of laughter and a lot of fizzing when the top was popped on another cold one. One of the guys was in the middle of another tall tale when all hell broke loose. Men were tripping over each other, running for cover. Some sought protection behind a nearby pickup truck. A few ducked behind the drink machines. The only guy who didn't move seemed calm about it all, leaning against one of the Amoco pumps, sipping on his Blue Ribbon.

The cause of the commotion was a speeding car that roared off of Highway 280 into the dusty lot, screeching to a halt next to the gas pumps. This driver didn't want gas, however. She was hot enough without adding any more fuel to her fire. "What do you think you're doing, just standing down here?" the woman shrieked, quickly establishing eyeball-to-eyeball contact with a man at the gas pump. "You've got a sick young 'un at home. I told you that two hours ago, and you're still here. You better get yourself to that house."

Her finger continued to shake, and her tongue continued to quiver. No one stirred until her husband sheepishly walked away from her and wandered casually inside the service station toward one of the beer coolers. All that listening had made him thirsty. That seemed to break the ice. Things began to return to Saturday night normal.

"See, that wasn't the first time she had been down here tonight," Billy Carter explained, grinding a burned-out Pall Mall into the dirt with his shoe. "She had come down here once before and told him he ought to get himself home. He had been duly warned."

Another regular around the station explained what was happening. "That fellow ain't going home with her right now. She's embarrassed him in front of the other guys. He'll go on home in a little bit. But not right now,"

Billy's service station is a study in red-neck architecture.

he correctly predicted.

That's the code around Billy Carter's Service Station. It's been that way since long before Billy bought it, back when Mil Jenning owned the place. And Billy hasn't changed a thing. "Before Mil died, he must have had 25 bids on the station. He sold it to me because he knew I'd keep it just the way it was," says Carter.

The way it is is Early Southern Gothic. The lot is paved with a layer of red Georgia clay. A shed covers the gas pumps and shades the front of the station, where a row of soft drink-machines stands guard. Inside are chairs, well-worn from daily use. There's an easy chair and a row of seats from a now-deceased school bus. You can tell the pecking order by who sits and who stands. Coolers form an "L" around the walls, which are lined with fan belts and with pinups that promise a different female body whenever a new month arrives. Nobody has to ask where his favorite beer is cooled. He knows. Around Billy's, it is serve yourself.

Long about dark the regulars begin to drift in. It's the same bunch, day after day. No one needs any introductions. As the guys arrive, one-by-one, the talk gets louder and the lies get taller. They solve the problems of the world and try to outdo their buddy's tall tale. Supper can wait and so can their wives.

"Shoot, when you can't find your husband, you just call the station. Most times he'll either come to the phone, or somebody will say he ain't there. But usually, in a few minutes, he'll mysteriously appear at home," one knowing wife said. Around Plains there has always been a service station where the men could drink their beer and buy a little gas. The station is one of those human melting pots that somehow blend together the work-weary old farmers with the younger generation who put in an eight-to-five day at a factory in Americus. The common denominator there is the pop top.

Weekends, the smell of gas and beer and the aroma of sizzling steaks are joined together. One of the fellows heats up the grill next to the station, plops on some steaks, and in a few minutes all are munching on beef between sips of beer. "For as long as I can remember, the men have been gathering up there and cooking on Saturday afternoons. You couldn't get them to cook a lick at home, but they enjoy it up there," a local housewife said.

Inside, among the fan belts, rows of chewing tobacco, flashlight batteries, redhots, crackers, and girly pinups, Billy Carter is The Boss. Baron of the Beer Cooler, one reporter dubbed him. When he arrives, all conversation gravitates around him. He directs his friends like a philharmonic.

Carl Unger is one of Billy's favorite targets. Unger and his wife moved to Plains from Minnesota so he could become a cattle farmer. They are Billy's neighbors. Unger's Polish heritage and laughing good nature make him a popular target when the words turn into needles.

"Say, Polack, who let you in?" Billy belched.

"I sneaked in the back door," Unger fired back.

The exchanges go on and on. You haven't been accepted until you've been kidded. If you're thin-skinned, you'd best not venture inside. Newsmen are first on the guys' lists. A press card and a dime won't get you a cup of coffee with the guys at Billy's station.

"Mr. Jack, that's the fellow who wrote bad things about your peanuts," Billy said, pointing out a visiting reporter.

"That him?" the old boy wanted to know, reaching for the nearest Coke bottle.

But if you're with Billy, you're safe. Hopefully.

The press has long been a favorite target for the President's kid brother—Billy's 40 and the father of four girls and two boys—since the campaign cranked up. Watching the newsmen and women invade his town in their Gucci shoes and blue jeans, he started to laugh. He hasn't stopped laughing yet.

"I've gotten to the point to where I don't believe a damn thing I read in the papers or hear on the television. I used to read six papers every day, from cover to cover. Now I look at the headlines, glance at the editorial pages, and that's about it. It takes me 15 minutes to read all of them," he claims, breaking out into that staccato laugh of his.

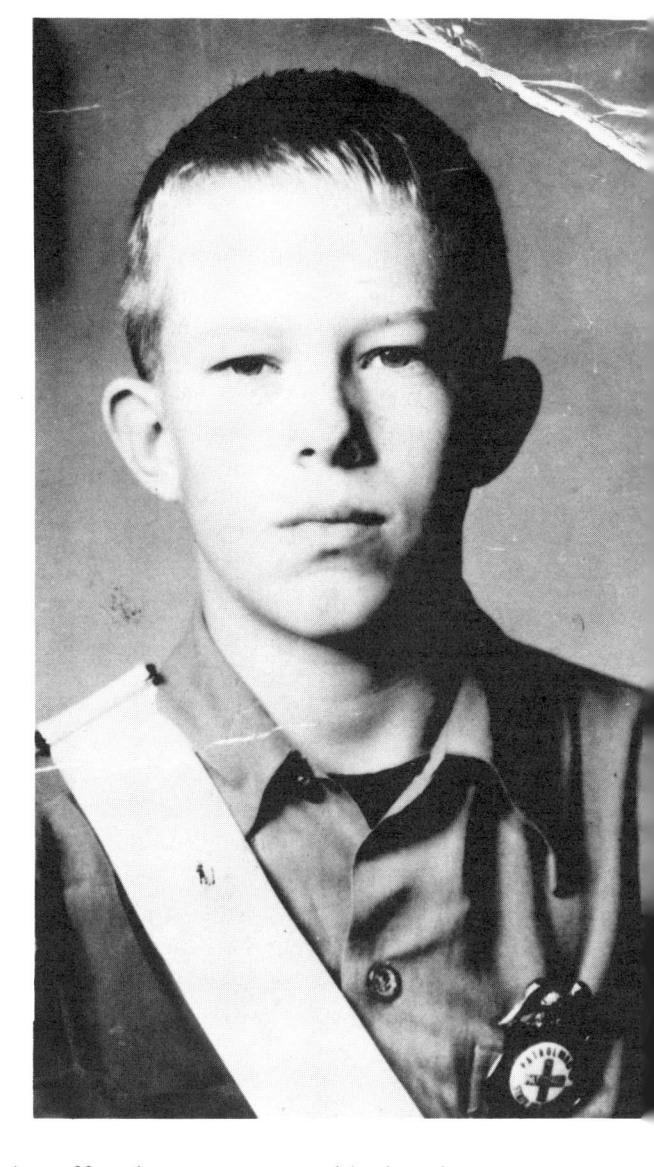

Billy proudly wore the belt of a safety patrolman in 1950.

After seeing newsmen close up, he offered one reporter this description: "It's a good thing you're a reporter because 95 percent of you would be on welfare if you weren't reporters. I've seen so many of them who can't write a damn story for themselves. They get all their stories off the Associated Press wire. There's been so many lies come out of Plains that it's changed the weather around here."

That's Billy Carter. Was. Is. Will be. Through the glamor and pageantry of seeing his brother elected President of the United States, Billy Carter has remained Billy Carter. He still drinks his beer—although his input is often exaggerated. He still puffs on his filterless Pall Malls—often lighting up seven packs on a particularly nervous day. He still speaks his mind—often salting his sentences with words that don't make print in a family publication. His mother can't tame him, his patient wife Sybil apparently has quit trying, and one of Billy's friends thinks Jimmy can't either. "I've got faith in Jimmy," the fellow said. "He can solve our problems with the Russians, get us oil from the Arabs, and put some folks back to work here at home. But I'll tell you one thing he'll never tame, and that's Billy."

Through it all, we've seen Billy Carter through the eyes of a story in the newspaper or through the perspective of a TV camera. We've seen him the way he wanted to be seen. Is this really Billy Carter? The answer is probably a little bit of yes and little bit of no. His mind belongs to only him. He loves his family as much as anyone can. He loves his beer as much as anybody in Milwaukee. He loves to work, wrapping 15 to 18 hours of work around four or five hours of sleep every day. He says "yes ma'am" and "no ma'am," and most of the time he won't curse in front of a lady. He loves his town and is proud of it. These are the positives. Only Billy Carter can really add the negatives. He lives life by a code all his own.

It has been popular to describe him as the epitome of the Good Old Boy, that vanishing breed of Southern manhood that once reigned supreme away down South in Dixie. Author Paul Hemphill, a native Alabamian and former newspaper columnist, wrote a book entitled, *The Good Old Boys*. In it Hemphill offered this definition of this Dixie genre:

"...He could be a mean S.O.B., half-educated, vengeful, regressive, sadistic, and by all means, a racist. He could kill a dozen people with bad moonshine, then come out against fluoridation as a Commie plot to poison the water. He could teach his kids hymns on Sunday morning ('Red and yellow, black and white, they are precious in His sight....') and string up the church janitor that Wednesday after prayer meeting."

There is not that much of Billy in Hemphill's definition. He is not openly vengeful or sadistic and does not appear to be a racist, carefully saying "black" and never "nigger." He likes his beer, and he might even drink some moonshine if someone offered it, but he's not mean. He would like to save the good things in his hometown, but he's not regressive. He surely doesn't cling to religion, saying Jimmy is the born-again Carter.

Author Tom Wolfe offers another definition. To him, a Good Old Boy "has a good sense of humor and enjoys ironic jokes, is tolerant and easygoing enough to get along in long conversations at places on the corner and has a reasonable amount of physical courage."

That's getting closer to Billy Carter.

His sense of humor is right out on the surface for anyone to see. He enjoys jokes, and his rapid-fire laugh is highly contagious. He's tolerant, even of the tourist who wants "just one more quick picture." He can carry on a conversation for as long as it interests him. His courage is another story.

Softball became an escape for the people who followed Jimmy Carter's hop-scotching around the country for headlines. When all were gathered in Plains, it was the press versus the Secret Service, with Jimmy pitching for one side and Billy the other. They all would gather at the diamond in front of the old school every evening. Winning wasn't important—it was everything. How you played the game mattered little.

This particular Saturday afternoon came at the peak of the competition. Consumer activist Ralph Nader had been imported to umpire—who would be fairer than he? Action was so fast that a newsman had pulled a hamstring muscle, and the biggest question was where to put him so the game might continue. All of that was forgotten when they heard a deafening explosion. It sounded as if it came from Billy's service station. Everyone began to run toward it, even Jimmy Carter, who quickly was tackled and driven away by Secret Service agents. Everyone ran except the injured correspondent, who was still lying on the dusty field.

When the crowd reached the highway, flames were burning the sky. Smoke was everywhere. A spark from a drink machine at the station had ignited fumes. Gasoline was still coming out of the tanker truck that was there refilling the underground tanks. Everyone seemed content to stand and watch, except Murray Smith and Randy Coleman. Smith, Rosalynn Carter's younger brother, shut off the gas from the tanker, and Coleman, an employee of Carter's Warehouse, jumped in the cab. He had never seen that many gears before, but he knew he had to get that truck out of there so he faked it. The truck soon was moved, and the volunteer fire department quickly had the fire under control.

But not before Billy Carter had his picture taken.

When Billy arrived on the scene he saw the flames, but he didn't see his teenaged son Buddy, who was pumping gas there earlier that afternoon. Billy panicked. Where was Buddy? Photographers were taking his picture, which Billy liked not one bit. He wanted to go inside to see if Buddy might be there, and he wanted to tangle with the photographers who apparently were more interested in getting a picture than in finding his son or helping put out the fire. Photographs of Billy being held back from a magazine photographer by Jimmy's press aides Jody Powell and Rex Grannum were on the front pages of newspapers across the country. Billy became a hero to Spiro Agnew fans, who hated the media. But few really knew the reason he was upset. He was his usual self once he found that Buddy was not inside the station.

You can get another glimpse at Billy Carter if you go back to the summer of 1976 when his brother was at the peak of his campaigning. One Wednesday morning Billy's nephew, Chip Carter, burst into the warehouse with a message from his daddy. "He wants to drain the pond so we can have a fish fry," Chip said, pulling a piece of paper out of his pocket. "He drew out these plans. Said if we followed them, we could pull the plug in the pond."

"Hell, he knows I never could read blueprints," Billy said. "After all, I didn't go to Georgia Tech." But looking at Jimmy's diagram, he said he thought they could handle it. Friday afternoon they all were at work, up to

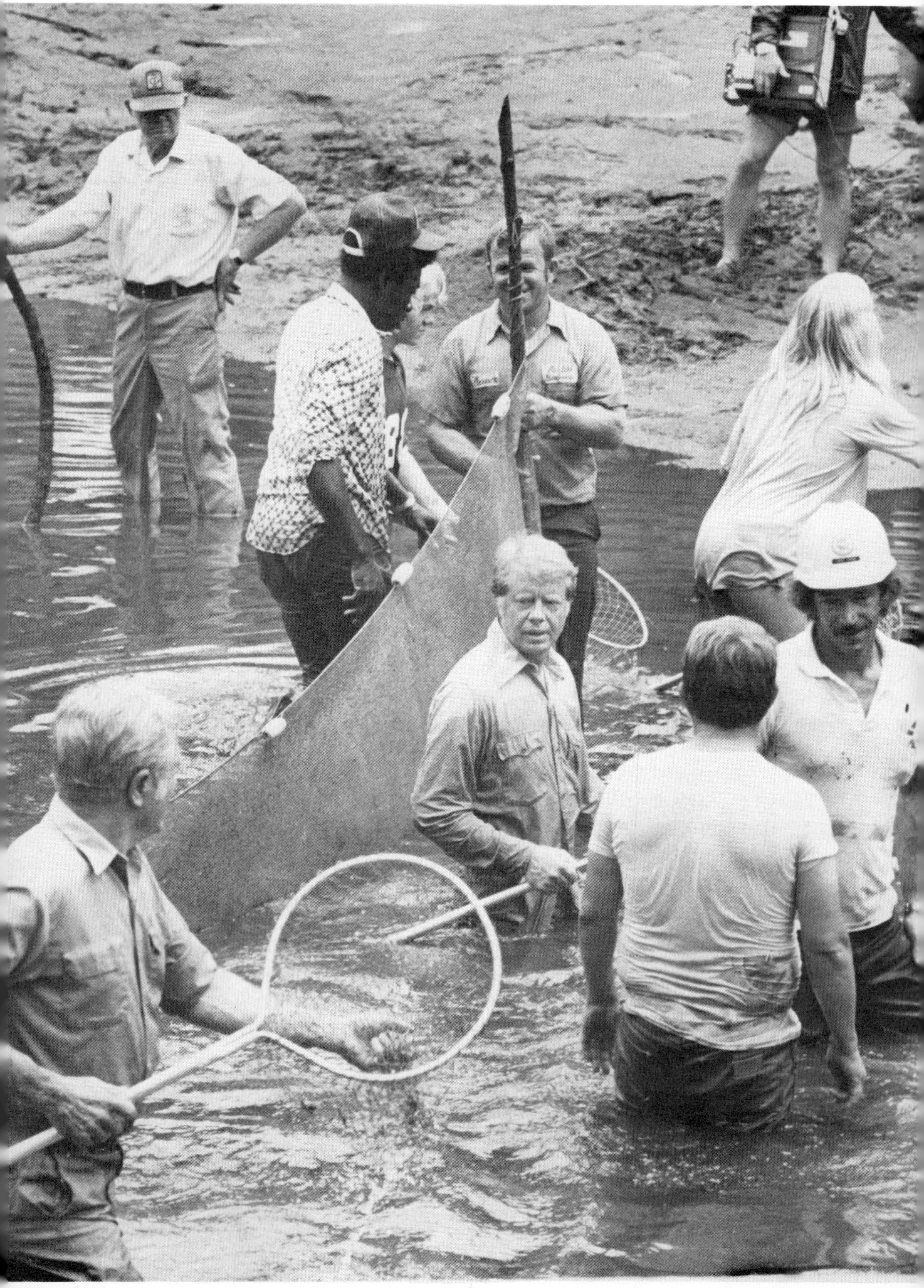

their necks in muddy, slimy water. Beside them was Jimmy. Somehow, even with the water tickling his chin, Billy was able to keep his Blue Ribbon from becoming contaminated. The water was not going down fast, so Billy kept up a lively round of chatter.

"Jimmy, those guys sure aren't taking good care of you. How can they protect you standing up there on the bank?" he asked, pointing up toward the Secret Service men who circled the pond.

Then he turned on the press.

"Look at 'em up there. They can't get a story from up there. They oughta be in here with us." Spotting a local reporter he knew, Billy whispered something to his brother the candidate.

"Richard, come on in here."

But the cityfied reporter didn't budge.

"Jimmy says if you'll come in here, he'll tell you who he's gonna pick as his Vice President."

I faced a tough choice. Billy's daughter Jana made the decision for me when she screamed something about a snake. The sighting of a water moccasin sent Billy—who doesn't even know how to swim—heading for the bank and the safety of his cooler.

Later they were to find out that the snake did more than just swim by. Larry Jones, a construction worker from Albany in town to tear down Plains' old water tower, discovered that—the hard way. "He was sitting at the dinner table that night when his wife noticed he couldn't hit his mouth with the fork. They took him to the hospital and found out he had gotten bit on the shoulder," Billy was to say, roaring with laughter.

The events of that day as they drained the pond—for ecological reasons, it was explained—and the fish fry the following noon became symbolic of a side of Jimmy's appeal. In muddy, cut-off jeans, he wasn't something created by Madison Avenue—he was real. Although, certainly, both days were partially done for the benefit of the all-seeing media.

Saturday morning everyone showed up at Miss Lillian's Pond House for a down-home fish fry. One reporter had spelled the fish they scooped out of the pond as "brim," but local folks were quick to point out that they were "bream." However, when someone took a head count of how many people had been invited to lunch, a secret visit to an Americus fish market was arranged, so there were some foreign fish on the red-hot grills.

It was a Southern gourmet's delight—fried fish (fried, naturally, in pea-

Billy Carter, with back to the camera, keeps up lively chatter as brother Jimmy, up to his waist in water and mud, directs the pond draining. Perhaps no fishing venture has received such publicity since some fishermen "cast their nets on the other side" approximately two thousand years earlier.

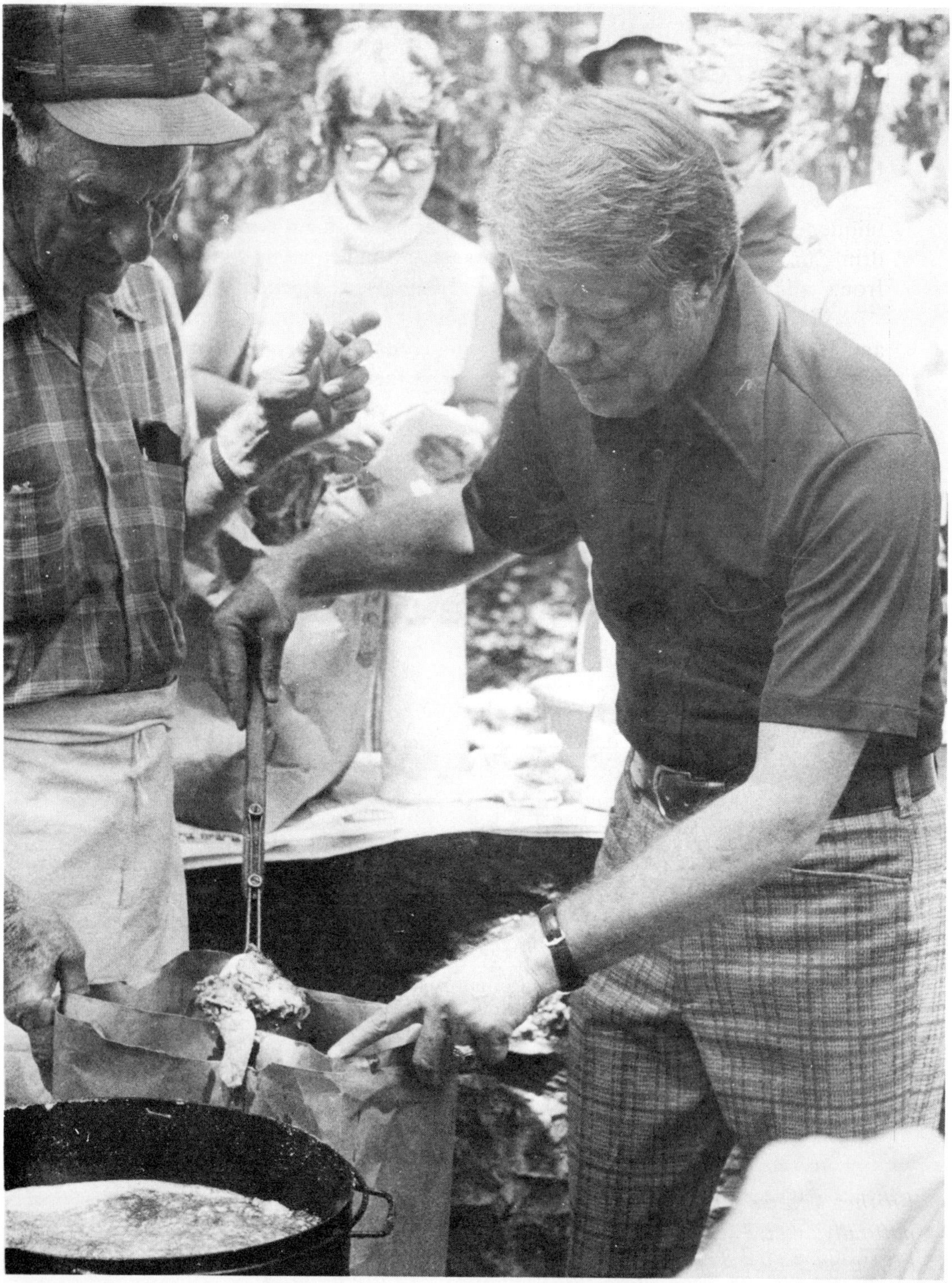

nut oil), hushpuppies, french-fried potatoes, and, if you were nice to Billy, some of those midget cans of Pabst Blue Ribbon from his personal cooler. Norman Murray and Robert Paul did the cooking, and Jimmy explained that he had been eating their cooking all his life. "I hate to tell you what all I've eaten that Norman has cooked...coon, chitlins, possum...he can cook anything," Jimmy said, sampling the still-sizzling fish.

But it is Billy who is the one in the family with the reputation for an unquenchable appetite. He can eat and drink with no end in sight. "I can drink anything anybody mixes," he brags. Around town he's known as "Cast Iron," and that is also his CB "handle." His feats are legendary.

Maybe all of this can be traced back to his beginnings. Jimmy, Gloria, and Ruth were well on their way to being teenagers when William Alton Carter—named for his grandfather—was welcomed into the home. His father said he had raised the others the "right" way. "I'm going to enjoy Billy," Earl said. As soon as Billy was old enough, Earl bought him a hunting outfit just like his. Like he said, he was enjoying Billy.

By the time Billy was ready for school, Jimmy was away earning his bars at the Naval Academy. Wherever the younger Carter would go, he faced comparison with brother Jimmy. When Jimmy was growing up the house was alive with children; for Billy it was adult quiet. He was 16 when it became even quieter. Earl Carter, at 59, was dead. Billy, everyone agreed, was too young to run the family business. Big Brother was coming home from the navy to do that. And Billy hardly knew Big Brother.

That, it appeared, was more than Billy could take. He stayed around Plains long enough to pick up his high school diploma, then joined the Marine Corps. He was not to come home to live for nine years, although he did come back long enough to marry Sybil Spires. He was 18 and in his marine uniform when he married 16-year-old Sybil, his hometown sweetheart. Billy spent four years as a marine, then attended Emory University in Atlanta until English got the better of him. "I flunked it four times," he says. But the fact that he was accepted at an academic-minded institution like Emory shows that Billy Carter is hardly the bumpkin he sometimes portrays. A lot more goes on inside his tousled-hair head than he lets on.

He did construction work and sold paint in Macon before finally returning to Plains to work with his brother in the family's peanut warehouse. Today he's in control of that multi-million-dollar family enterprise which has grown larger since he assumed full control in 1970, when his brother was

Brother Jimmy is left to make sure that the fish is cooked in peanut oil, naturally, while across the yard Billy is just out of camera range proving that his stomach deserves the title "Cast Iron," Billy's CB handle.

Earl Carter said he was going to enjoy his youngest son.

Jimmy was a big brother Billy grew up hardly knowing.

Coming home from the marines, Billy married sweetheart Sybil Spires.

elected governor of Georgia. However, he will laugh and tell you very quickly that it is his wife Sybil who holds the business together. His gregarious, friendly wife manages the warehouse office and somehow manages to care for their six children.

But don't joke with Billy about business. He treats it seriously. He's a crafty businessman (much like his late father) who can talk seriously with you about modern agriculture and who knows peanuts from the rich Georgia soil all the way into the peanut butter jar on the pantry shelf, although, strangely, he claims to be allergic to peanuts himself. In season he will stay on duty as long as there are peanuts to be weighed and stored. He usually sleeps only three or four hours a night, and a normal working day finds him unlocking the doors at 5:30 a.m.

First thing he does is to check to see if his newspapers are on time. If they aren't, he will ride down the highway and meet the carrier. He subscribes to five daily newspapers, and don't believe it when he says he doesn't read them all anymore. He is quick to jump a reporter about something insignificant near the end of a story. Like the others in his family, he grew up with something to read in his hands. He still reads four or five novels a week, sometimes having two or three going at once.

Billy Carter became the folk hero of the Merle Haggard set when newsmen first invaded this side-road hamlet. He didn't sound like the usual politician's brother who chooses his words ever so carefully. He says the first thing that pops into his head ("I liked Mondale from the first—he drinks beer"). He would load the big-city reporters into his blue Blazer truck and take them on rides they would not soon forget, not missing a bump on the dusty farm roads, showing them sights they would never see from the main road or read about in the tourist guides.

When the Closet Red Necks emerged after the Carter bandwagon picked up speed, Billy was the guy they patterned themselves after, although he says he doesn't even know what a Red Neck is. Billy was a hero, to some at least. But it was about this time that he began to sour on the whole affair. He didn't like what was happening around him. Oh, he went to New York to see his brother duly nominated and was a big hit in the Big City, even though he griped about the price of beer from the moment he arrived. He made friends there, too. When his son Earl Gordy was born in October 1976, shortly before the election, Shirley MacLaine—whom Billy had met in New York—sent along a gift for Earl—diapers monogrammed with tiny Pabst emblems.

One thing Billy said in New York was prophetic. Somebody asked what was happening back home. He moaned about the state of affairs and said, "If things don't get better, I may have to move to Preston (in Webster County, nine miles from Plains)." As the campaign progressed, tourism became a local industry. Everybody was trying to get into the act. Billy stood to gain as much as the next guy, probably more. His gas sales were suddenly rivaling his beer sales. He owned acres of choice land around town, and property values were sure to rise. Still, it bothered him. After the votes were counted, he said he would have voted for George Wallace had he known this was going

If there's anything Billy's serious about, it is peanuts.

to happen to Plains. He didn't like what Plains was becoming. It wasn't that he didn't like money. He is, after all, his father's son. He just happened to like Plains, too. It took a lot of persuading for him to consent to putting up a large sign identifying his service station. He is, simply, one of those people who enjoy progress but just don't enjoy some of the things that go along with it.

His only concession to the invasion of souvenir hunters was putting his liquor in a paper cup or wrapping a Coke label around his beer can. He continued to pose for tourists' pictures, smiling for every shutterbug who would tell him, "I drove a hundred miles out of the way, just to see you." Finally,

A well-dressed Billy talks politics with State Rep. Ward Edwards.

he had to hang a "No Admittance" sign outside the warehouse office—not that it stopped all of them. Visitors had proven too often that they had no compunction about interrupting the business by marching in and demanding to see Billy.

Really, it was some of his own neighbors who rankled Billy most. He didn't like the counters of souvenirs that were lining most of the stores in Plains. He didn't like the image that his was a town with its hand out. "I'm glad Plains is popular for the reason it is, but I'm still sad that it is....I wish Jimmy had lived in Atlanta when he announced. Atlanta is so damn fouled up already that you couldn't have hurt it. Folks said it would get bad, but I couldn't picture it this bad," he says.

When election night finally came and Jimmy was finally an uncrowned President, television interviewers back home in Plains looked for Billy, by then well fortified with his favorite brew. Dan Akens, an Atlanta newsman, asked him what he thought all of this was going to mean to Plains. "It's going straight to hell," was his plain and simple answer to the interviewer and the network viewers.

Since 1970 Billy has run family's multi-million-dollar business.

Friends then took him back to his house, where a party was in full swing. It was mainly the fellows from the station, just home folks, although a few reporters did wander in. There were a couple of kegs of beer iced down on the porch and plenty of food on the table. Three TV sets were tuned in, checking up on each of the networks. Pulling up a seat on the floor, Billy sank down and turned to Carl Unger, his favorite Polack. "You know, now that Jimmy's President, you guys can't call me Billy anymore. From now on, it's MISTER Carter," he laughed.

Gas pumpers at his station publicized Billy's unsuccessful mayoral campaign.

Somehow Billy survived that hard day's night. He was waiting at the train station when Jimmy Carter came home from his all-night vigil in Atlanta. They hugged, and Jimmy went to the microphone to speak to the waiting crowd. "It's good to see all of you here...especially, MISTER Carter," he said, gesturing toward his sleepy-eyed brother.

Mr. Carter didn't seem to fit well, but it wasn't long after his brother's presidential election that Billy began to think MAYOR Carter would. He had run for mayor the last election two years ago, losing by either two or four votes—depending on who tells the story—to A. L. Blanton, the barber in Plains and an air-traffic controller at the airport in Albany.

"First Brother" decided to try again.

It was a campaign typical of Billy. He told the gullible national press that Leon Johnson was his campaign manager when Johnson didn't even live in Plains. He said the only reason he was running was that somebody went down and paid the $15 filing fee for him. He was serious, however, about one plank in his platform. "I don't want to see Plains turned into a complete tourist trap and junk shop—which it is fast doing. I'm interested in seeing it stay as much like it was as humanly possible," he said. He also pledged removal of a plastic Christmas tree the town had decorated, saying it was too artificial. Someone did that for him, dragging it away by night. Billy was quick to point out that he was en route to New York at the time.

His gas pumpers were decked out in "Billy for Mayor" T-shirts, and many of his friends wore "Billy Buttons," but Billy himself did little actual campaigning. "You don't politick in a town this size," he explained. So he didn't...and he lost. Blanton, the incumbent, received 90 votes to Billy's 71.

Around the service station on election night, you couldn't tell the difference. A party had been scheduled—win or lose—and it was going strong until late that night. One guest who showed up took the blame for Billy's defeat. "He would have made a good mayor. I probably cost him the election. Folks already have elected a Carter to the White House and have a Carter in the state senate. They probably didn't want another Carter to be mayor," his brother said, analyzing the outcome.

The political experts searched for other, deeper reasons. No one had a profile of the typical voter in Plains. Gallup wasn't there to give his side of it. No one could give you a precinct-by-precinct breakdown. When you lose in a town as small as Plains, you just lose. The next day it is business as usual. So it was for Billy Carter.

On the more philosophical side, it will never again really be business as usual for Billy Carter, or for Plains for that matter. The day his brother turned over the keys to the warehouse office to him and went off to Atlanta to be governor, Billy's life was changed, though nothing like the change that was to be when Jimmy went off to Washington to be President.

Miss Lillian and Billy show that smiles run in family after Jimmy's election.

From now on, there will be newspeople looking for a funny line, an off-beat angle. Tired of the usual string of political cliches, they will come looking for Brother Billy. There will always be tourists wanting him to move just a little to the right so they can have better light for their pictures. There will always be hard-shell Baptists warning him that his soul is doomed to burn in that fiery lake forever. As Billy himself put it, "I'm the token Red Neck." As Alabama governor George Wallace, a Southern symbol himself, put it, "Jimmy Carter actually was my third choice for President. Naturally, I was my first choice. Billy Carter was second," a statement Billy brags about.

Billy Carter is the comic relief, and that is not meant as a personal put-down, not meant to say he's a joke. It's just that the Billy Carters in this world simply don't give in to the temptation most of us do to take life—or themselves—too seriously. At the most serious, tedious moment, Billy is there to lighten up life.

Even Jimmy recognizes this quality. At a time when he was embroiled in the tedious task of selecting a Cabinet, he was facing the press at the University of Georgia Agricultural Field Office, just outside Plains. Carter had announced his choice of native Georgian Griffin Bell as Attorney General, a selection that even before becoming official had felt heat from some Civil Rights leaders. A questioner had asked about the Bell appointment. "I know that John Kennedy named his brother Robert to this position, and I would have named my brother Billy except that he's not a lawyer. I'm naming Griffin Bell until Billy meets the qualifications," Jimmy Carter joked.

Billy's most quoted remark of the campaign concerns his personal description of his family. It goes something like this: "I've got a mother who joined the Peace Corps and went to India when she was 68. I've got a sister who races motorcycles and another sister who's a Holy Roller preacher. I've got a brother who says he wants to be President of the United States. I'm the only sane one in the whole family," he says.

Billy Carter hasn't spent his life searching for some slice of pie in the sky. Nor has he had to travel the world looking for his own little niche. At some point in the past, he found that niche.

Still, you wonder just who this Billy Carter is. Is he the side you see in the media, a side even he says is a "Frankenstein monster"? Or is he the private side, shut out from public inspection when he slams the door on his home? Part of the puzzle is his family, which he worships. Another piece is his hometown, which he is fighting to preserve. Another is his work, which he relishes. And another one is his friends, the guys at the station, who share his beer and his stories. Put all of this together and you may have Billy Carter.

After Billy's defeat in the mayoral election, columnist John Keasler—with tongue in cheek—offered him this advice, aimed at getting him elected the next time around.

"...Wear a little flag in your coat lapel, join the Elks, and whenever possible, haul off and sing something sacred. They like that," suggested Keasler.

Don't do it, Billy.

Stay like you are.

Meantime, pass me another beer.

Amy Carter: Lemonade And Freckles

Amy Carter was a nine-year-old with big-girl problems. Sitting there among her fourth-grade classmates at the Plains Elementary School, she could feel the hook loosen on her body stocking and the zipper begin to creep down. Something, Amy knew, had to be done.

"Mrs. Williams, may I be excused?" she asked her teacher, discreetly explaining the delicate situation. The understanding teacher gave her permission, and Amy started toward the door, either forgetting or ignoring another hurdle.

"Where are you going?" her personal Secret Service agent demanded to know.

"You're not supposed to ask questions, you're just supposed to follow," said Amy.

Amy Carter may have been only nine and the daughter of a President-elect only a short time, but she did know what a bodyguard is supposed to do. For most of her life Amy Carter has lived in a goldfish bowl. She was only a toddler when her father was elected governor of Georgia and she moved into the governor's mansion. Since then she has had an escort to school, a state trooper to drive her wherever she wanted to go, aides to dote over her, and a public to watch her every misbehavior.

Life for Amy can hardly be termed normal, not by the usual standards. She had two parents in their forties and grateful she arrived, two grandmothers who just wanted to be grandmothers, three brothers who treated her like a playhouse doll, and a state that proudly watched her grow up in their house. Overnight, when her father became America's 39th President, she inherited a nation that wanted to share in her exploration of the White House, a place usually reserved for adults.

Given those nine years, it would be easy to think of Amy as a hopeless, pig-tailed brat. Dee Bryant of the *Columbus Ledger* explored this issue quite

Amy stole the show when her daddy was sworn in as governor of Georgia.

well. She spent an afternoon with the youngest of the Carters and came away with this impression:

"In most discussions of Amy Carter...the term 'spoiled' is frequently mentioned. Some less-understanding folks even throw 'brat' into the conversation. Who can expect her not to be? A child who was thrown into the limelight of the governor's mansion when she was a toddler, who lived under the constant eye of gubernatorial aides, driven about by a state trooper, given private swimming lessons in an affluent section of Northwest Atlanta. But, to call Amy spoiled is to do her an injustice. Precocious, yes. Determined, yes. Exceptionally bright and inquisitive, yes. But spoiled or bratty, certainly not," wrote Mrs. Bryant.

Amy Lynn moved into the Carter household on October 19, 1967. During her father's presidential campaign, he explained her arrival this way: "My wife and I had an argument for 14 years...and I finally won." That was a lighthearted way to look at it. The serious side was that Rosalynn Carter had a large tumor removed from her uterus. Doctors said she might have another child, and Jimmy and Rosalynn prayed for a daughter. And when their prayers were answered, they called her Amy.

From that first day they brought her home, Amy was the dominant figure in the Carter clan. She was introduced to Jack, Chip, and Jeff—three teenaged brothers who were to fight over who held her. "Amy," her father said, "made us young again"— which was good, because her parents were picking up the pieces of a 1966 defeat for governor and plotting a return bout in 1970. They needed to be young.

Amy was the new kid in the house of a trio of boys who were born with seawater in their veins. Each one of her brothers had been born in a different place while their father was serving in the navy. Amy was born closer to home—in Americus—but when she was three, she was packed up for Atlanta and her new home in the governor's mansion. She grew up a petted, tow-headed child in a grownup world.

Rosalynn Carter lights up when she talks about her daughter. "I'm proud of Amy. She has always been a special child. She is really a good, well-adjusted child, and bright. She's getting independent, too. Maybe it's because she has grown up in a world of adults," her mother says.

That world was to change in 1975 when her parents' lease on their

Little girls do get tired, and bean bags offer welcome relief.

Atlanta home expired. Jimmy Carter was going out of one office but was going after another. The Carters moved their belongings back to Plains, and Jimmy Carter moved into the world of presidential politics. Instead of an adult world, she was in Plains, close to her cousins and lots of old-but-new friends. It didn't take her long to become a bona-fide country girl.

"I can't keep shoes on her feet. She just won't wear them. I send her to school wearing them, but she takes them off as soon as she gets there. About once a week, I have to drive up there, gather up her shoes, and bring them back home. I don't know what I'm going to do with her," grandmother Lillian Carter said. Not only was she going barefoot, but she was also into "clogging," a spirited form of square dancing. She even danced on the Grand Ole Opry.

Plains made her feel at home. She could climb trees, catch snakes, run through fields, ride her bicycle with little fear of traffic, have a general run of the town. And there was Miss Lillian, "Grandmama" to Amy. Grandmama was her stand-in mother and full-time friend. While Jimmy and Rosalynn searched the country for votes, Miss Lillian searched for things that she and Amy could do. It might be fishing at the Pond House. It might be finding a new book to explore. It might be just sitting and talking. There was always something for them to do.

The peaceful life began to end early in 1976. Until then no one really believed that Amy's daddy would ever be President. But that January and February he made some believers. On February 24 he won the New Hampshire presidential primary. Back home in Plains, her grandmother went into Amy's room to tell her the exciting news. "I'm sleepy," was her reply. It all seemed so far away, like something she had read about in her books. Maybe then it was, but slowly it grew closer to her and Plains.

Tourists began to disturb her town, her friends, and even Amy. They wanted to see everything in town. They wanted to go everywhere. Her playhouse was disturbed. Traffic made her quit riding her bicycle everywhere. Outside, in the pines where she had roamed free, were Secret Service agents. They were nice to her, but they got in the way of childish games. Life was changing. Amy decided to take advantage of these changes.

Consulting with her neighbors, John Gnann, 9, and Sidney Gnann, 7, they formed a business partnership that was to reap them up to $23 a day until the Secret Service closed them down in late July. Putting together an old crate and painting a sign on the front, they went into the lemonade business. They set up on a vacant area between their two houses. Tourists traveling Woodland Drive for a look at the Carter home were hailed down and offered service in their car. Most, however, wanted to come up to the counter, especially if Amy and her partners would consent to a picture or small talk.

Lemonade was only ten cents when John Gnann and Amy opened up.

Some of her best customers were the hordes of newsmen who invaded Plains that summer, especially when Amy's father was in town. When he was home newsmen would stand guard outside, hoping for an interview or a few words of wisdom from the candidate. Newsmen have this built-in mistrust of one another. As long as one of them stays, they all stay, no matter how thirsty or hungry they may become. This was made to order for a budding lemonade salesperson. Amy, with an eye for profits, took advantage of it.

The street that particular July afternoon was lined with cars, most rented on the expense accounts of news agencies from around the world. Their drivers lounged around on the ground, sat on the car hoods, or played cards on the curb. Inside the house was John Glenn in the morning and Walter Mondale in the afternoon. They were in town to be auditioned by Carter for vice-presidential roles. This attracted even more newsmen than usual and a stream of tourists as well. The July sun was heating up, and the gnats were out in force. People were wiping away perspiration and swatting at the bugs. Most of them had visions of lunch and a cold drink when Amy set up shop.

By then her price had gone from a nickel a cup to a dime a cup, but suddenly the price shot up to fifteen cents or a quarter. Of course, either she or John or Sidney would deliver, and she did have some larger cups, but mainly she was smart enough to know she had the only stand on the block.

"Say, Amy, we like your lemonade, but we're getting hungry. How about something to eat?" ABC correspondent Sam Donaldson asked her. Huddling with her partners, they soon disappeared into the house. In a few minutes they were back with a platter of sandwiches. Naturally their specialty was peanut butter, but if you didn't relish the thought of peanut butter sticking to the roof of your mouth while you asked the candidate (should he venture outside) a question, they also had pimento cheese. Their sandwiches sold for fifty cents apiece—for the time being.

Business was brisk, and if you were going to eat you had to drink, so the lemonade was moving fast, too. The trio returned with more sandwiches. "We've got tuna fish, too, a dollar each," Sidney advertised. "Why so high?" somebody asked. " 'Cause meat's more expensive," the young businessman retorted. As the sandwiches sold, the prices rose. Soon peanut butter and pimento cheese were selling for a dollar and—Sorry, Charlie—tuna was up to a dollar and a half.

While Amy was bringing in the money, her frisbee was lying idle, and a CBS cameraman wanted to borrow it. Anything to make the time pass.

Some customers got personal delivery service on their lemonade.

"That'll be a quarter an hour," Amy told him. He laughed, said OK, and found himself a partner. Meanwhile, Amy disappeared into the Carter house, returning with her mother's kitchen timer. Not to time eggs, but frisbees. She knew from experience that throwing a frisbee works up a thirst, and by that time the price on lemonade was rising, too.

The following morning I wrote a front-page story for my newspaper in Columbus charting the business acumen of this budding entrepreneur. It began like this: "At the sight of newsmen, Amy Carter's eyes light up in tiny little dollar signs. Has she got a deal for you?" The rest of the story chronicled her business success from the previous day. That story and a picture of Amy in her new glasses were headlined in Friday's *Enquirer* that was delivered to the Carters that morning. Amy didn't like what she read. So with the help of her next-door partners, she issued this statement through the offices of her daddy's press secretary, Jody Powell. It read:

"We don't charge too much for lemonade. The first day we had a pasteboard box and sold lemonade for five cents a cup. We found it cost more than five cents for lemons, cups, sugar and ice. The next day we fixed a wooden box stand that would not (as Daddy says) melt in the rain and put a price of ten cents, which is still what we charge. Tips are okay.

"P.S. When we sell sandwiches, our parents have to help and we charge fifty cents each. We don't make anyone buy lemonade or sandwiches even reporters who want free interviews while we serve our customers."

What can you say when you've been upstaged by an eight-year-old? What do you say to a 78-year-old grandmother who slaps you on the wrist for picking on her granddaughter? These are things they don't teach you in journalism school. But it was not the press that shut down Amy's business, thus ending that light-hearted hope that she might franchise lemonade stands across the country. That hard-hearted chore was left to the Secret Service. While Amy and her folks were away in New York for her daddy to be officially nominated by the Democratic Party, barricades were put up at each end of Woodland Avenue. They were designed to keep out sightseers and to improve security. What they did was keep out Amy's customers. The closed sign was hung.

When she was in New York, I brooded about that press release she issued, and so I wrote her a letter that was published on page 1 of my newspaper the day she returned from New York. Here's what it said:

Dear Amy,
It must be nice to be home. There weren't too many trees to climb in New York, were there? And even though that's a mighty big place, there's not much room to play when you have to stay inside a hotel room all the time. Guess that's why you didn't stay around long enough

Arriving in New York, Amy was armed with stuffed animals and books.

to have your picture taken Friday when all those folks came out to welcome your folks home. You were more interested in finding your friends and catching up on your playing. Besides, you had your picture taken enough up in New York, didn't you?

It must have been a surprise for you when you first went home and found they had put up those barricades so people couldn't get to the front of your house. That's going to make it real hard for your lemonade business to survive, even though thousands of people are going to be coming to Plains to see where you live. They would have bought lots and lots of lemonade, too.

I only hope that all of this doesn't keep you from having a good time. When you're eight years old, it's hard to know why they put up fences and have Secret Service men around all the time. But I guess you're used to it by now.

Before you left, you got upset at something I wrote. Remember? The story about how the price on your lemonade was going up and how you were selling sandwiches and renting out your Frisbee. I wasn't in Plains that next day, but I heard you wrote out a press release saying you "didn't charge too much for lemonade," and that you "even gave free interviews while you served your customers." Your grandmother said reporters were taking advantage of you.

I've been thinking about that and I guess you were right in a way. It's not overcharging when you're the only stand in town and the customers are willing to pay, which we were. Anyway, you come by that naturally because I've heard your Daddy tell folks about how he sold ice cream on the streets of Plains when he was a kid. He sold it for a nickel a scoop, and I bet folks complained about his prices, too.

As for us taking advantage of you, maybe we did. You see, most of us come up to you and ask you the same questions we would ask a grownup. Like that person in New York who asked you if you had a message for the kids of America. That shrug of the shoulders you gave was the best answer you could have given. Although some people claim we write with the intelligence of an eight-year-old, it's hard for us to

Amy soon branched off from lemonade into renting frisbees.

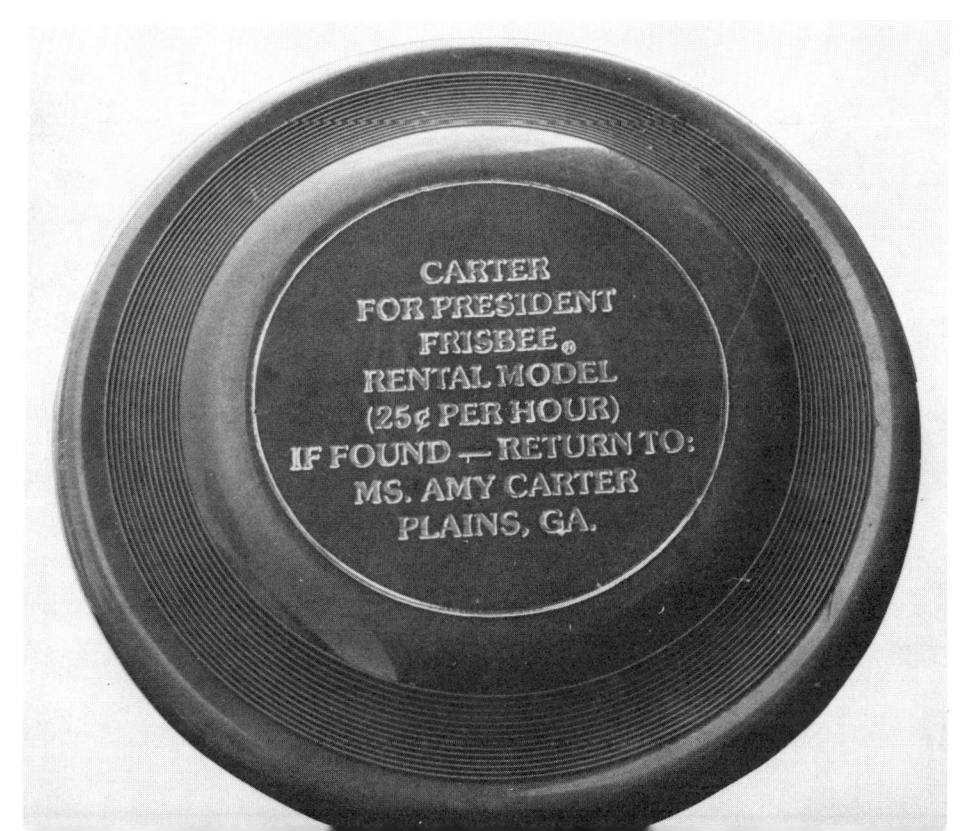

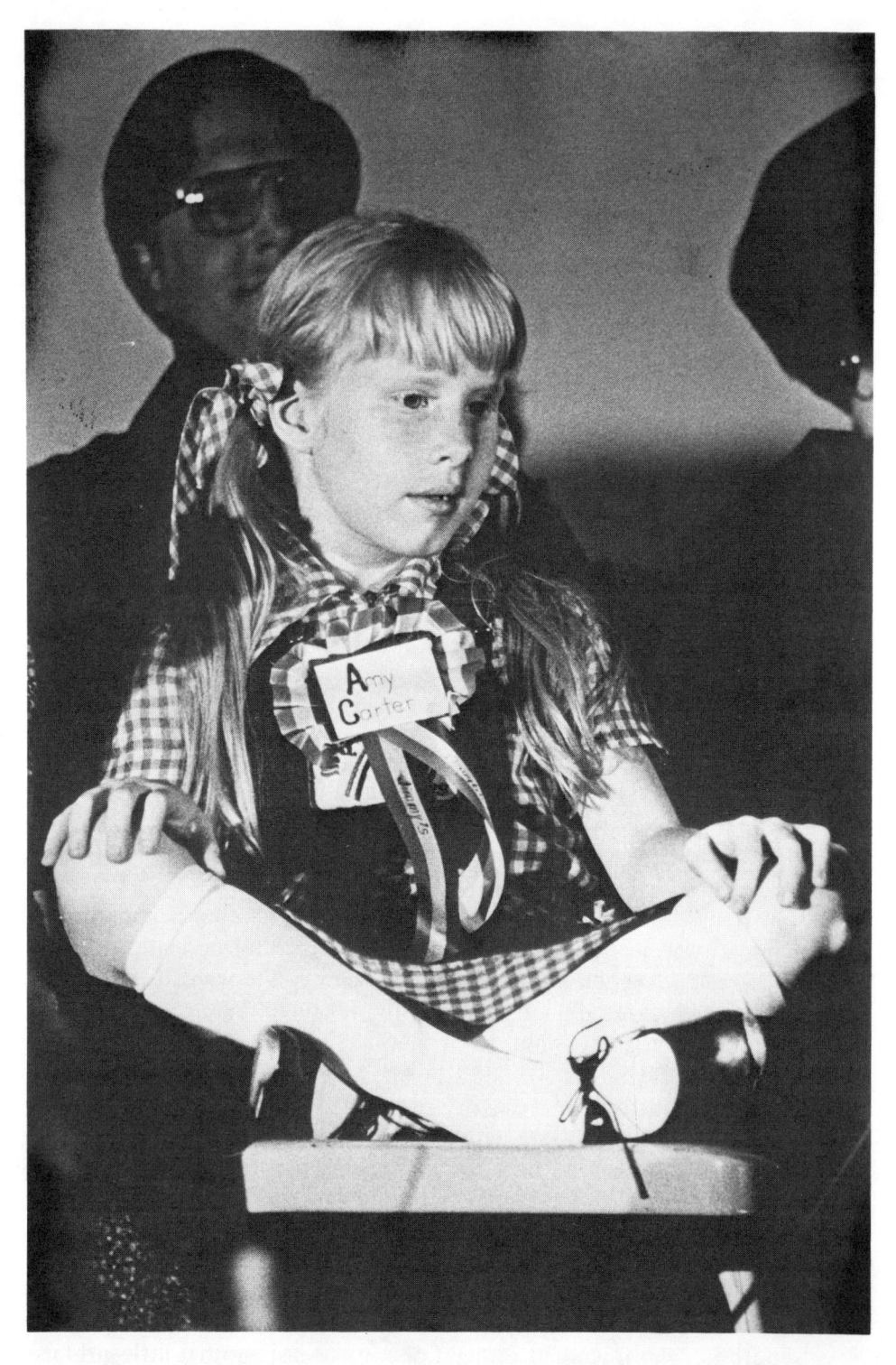

Red, white, and blue tag identifies Amy as "Jimmy's daughter."

talk to one sometimes.

It really bothered me when I rode into town the other day and saw those barricades around your street. It's going to be hard on all of your family, but I thought of you. You're going to be shut in and shut off, and so's your father, at a time when he said he wanted to stay close to the people.

But then, when I got to town the day your folks were getting back from New York, I saw your cousins out in the grassy area next to the railroad tracks throwing around a Frisbee with some newsmen from CBS. They had some Frisbees like I had never seen before, a special rental model, inscribed with "If found—return to Ms. Amy Carter, Plains, Ga."

They're called "Carter for President Frisbees," and a copyright is pending. Somebody up in New York made them up and they are flying all over town. But it won't seem right throwing them around without you and your little friends there keeping an eye on your mother's kitchen timer. Somehow, it won't be the same.

Best regards,
Richard Hyatt

It wasn't the same for the visitors, and it wasn't the same for Amy either. Her father was still going out on the road, and when he was home there was usually a steady stream of strangers filing in and out of the house. There was always a mob of newsmen following wherever they went. Secret Service agents were their shadows. Not even school was the same.

Ann Helms, a math consultant for the Muscogee County School System in Columbus, was serving on a state committee monitoring math programs around Georgia when she visited the Plains School. She wanted to see what school life was like for Amy Carter while she was there.

"When we started to walk down the hall," Helms said, "the principal, Claude Frazier, told us we wouldn't be allowed in Amy's classroom unless we were accompanied by him or Amy's teacher," and when she saw the burly Secret Service agent sitting outside the door, she knew well what he meant. "He was just sitting there reading a thick paperback book," but the principal told her not to be misled. "He knows you are here and is watching your every move," Frazier said. Amy's favorite subject is reading—as was her father's. She also is fond of catching wildlife and bringing them to school, including "the heads of water moccasins and copperheads we put in a jar of alcohol."

Reporters, who once had thought of Amy as just another little-girl face to be photographed, began to look for profound statements from her. "Out of the mouths of babes," as the verse goes. Many seemed irritated when some of her answers sounded as if they were coming from a little girl, which she is, even though she has lived for so long in a public, adult family.

Dee Bryant discovered that when she interviewed the precocious Carter offspring: "Armed with Life Savers, barbecued corn chips, a package of chewing gum and soft drinks (Amy was to make hers into a 'slushee') and a stack of books, the gangling child was ready to go....She declared she prefers quiet Plains, to Atlanta, her home for half of her life. 'It's the country and I like that. I can ride my bike anywhere here. Did you know school's out Friday?' she neatly changed the subject. 'I'm going to swim all summer. Didja see where the pool is? The road there curves like this....'"

Her other summertime plans included reading: "I like books by Beverly Cleary....You've never heard of her? She's an author for kids. She writes funny books. Not COMIC books, funny books." Cooking: "Here's 'No-Cook Dandy Candy,'" she said, reading from a cookbook for children, adding that she's an excellent cook—"Fudge brownies—from a box. Frozen pizza. Chocolate. Slushees. Banana floats and all that junk. And, oh yes, grits." But her favorite food wasn't on that list. "I loovvee fried eggplant," she says. As for hobbies, she likes to fish. "Who doesn't?" she demands to know. She catches bass, bream, and water moccasins...water moccasins? "Sure, I cut off their heads and take them to Miss Shields in the library at school where everybody can see them," Amy told Mrs. Bryant.

Usually her interviews were brief. "Are you finished?" she would ask, rolling her eyes in childish boredom. She would let the interviewer know she had better things to do, not adult things but important things, like playing. Politics bores her. It means you get to go to some neat places, but it also means your mama and daddy are away from home a lot. And it means you're going to have to leave Plains and grandmama.

On Election Day 1976, that boredom showed through as she held her mother's hand going toward a platform set up in the middle of Main Street. There their friends were going to tell them good-bye. Amy and her parents were going to Atlanta to wait while they counted votes. She had a poutish look on her face until she looked into the crowd and saw Rusty Robinson. She waved. He waved. They made faces at each other and mouthed out words as Jimmy Carter spoke to her friends. When the words had all been spoken, Amy wanted to jump off the front of the platform and see Rusty, but someone stopped her. She did, however, have time to yell a message to her friend, sitting on top of a barrel they were using to keep away the crowds. "Tell Mrs. Williams, I'll be late for school in the morning," she screamed.

Her father was in every headline around the world. Millions were going into the voting booths to pull the lever by his name. By morning, he would

Railroad tracks are there, and little girls find use for them.

Her grandmother was a friend and playmate to Amy while Jimmy and Rosalynn were away from Plains campaigning.

Even in a quiet moment, Amy can't escape reminders of spotlight.

be recognized leader of the Free World. But to Amy, he was just her daddy. She was more interested in getting all of this over and getting back to Rusty, her other classmates, and Mrs. Williams. With them, in school, she was just another fourth-grader, although her teachers privately say her parents should tell everybody just how bright Amy really is. There were Secret Service men around, but they were her pals. She could pull off her shoes—if it was warm enough—read her books, whatever she wanted to do, without being the center of attention. That was to remain her routine until January, when she said tearful good-byes to her pals, packed up Misty and Sausage (her two cats), and went to Washington to make new friends at the Thaddeus Stevens School—a public, not private, school.

A few weeks before she moved to the town, the *Washington Post* listed Amy among "The Biggest Bores of 1976," saying she wasn't witty enough. Those are pretty harsh words to describe a nine-year-old who has been on center stage since she was old enough to crawl. The *Post* was guilty of the same mistake many have made in describing this Carter with the freckles. What, you wonder, do they expect?

Amy may be impatient, but what child isn't? She may give short answers, but what child doesn't? She may prefer jeans to frilly dresses, but what child doesn't? She may prefer riding her bike to giving interviews, but what child wouldn't? She may enjoy filling her mouth with a fistful of bubble gum, but what child doesn't? She may turn up her lip and whine when she doesn't get her way, but is that so different from other nine-year-olds?

Amy Carter may be a little spoiled. Sometimes she may let a little of the brat that is inside most children creep out. Sometimes she may not act like a little lady. But what people are forgetting is that she isn't a little lady—she's a surprisingly ordinary nine-year-old who, despite her spotlighted attention, has managed in many ways to escape being a miniature adult. She's an active, bubbly girl who may be spoiled, but it's the same kind of spoiling you see in houses down the street, not the kind you might expect from a celebrity household. She likes to bounce in somebody's lap. She likes to be with her grandmama. She likes to play little-girl games with her friends, instead of being imprisoned inside the house. Amy Carter, in short, is just another little girl. Only she happens to live on Pennsylvania Avenue.

Maybe she'll be able to liven up a White House that has been turned into a mausoleum instead of a place where somebody lives. Maybe she'll open the windows and let those ghosts out and some sunlight inside. Maybe the sounds of children playing will echo down halls where it's been quiet too long.

If anybody can do these things, a nine-year-old can.

And that's what Amy Carter is.

Rosalynn Carter:
A Wife And A Partner

The visitors could see the house, but suddenly it seemed so far away. Between them and the front door were 15 minutes of having people check under the hood, look into the trunk, eyeball the glove compartment and inside the photographer's bags and cameras. A tight-lipped Secret Service agent was at every stop, even pointing the guests to a certain parking place along the sparsely traveled street, now used only by official cars on official business.

Leaves had deserted the trees and taken up on the lawn, now brown from winter and the constant patrolling of the watchful agents. The driveway was unpaved, and the only way to keep from taking mud along with you was to dodge the puddles in the drive, then use the granite stones that formed a walkway toward the front door. Madeline McBean, an officious but pleasant aide, met the guests at the door, quickly spelling out that they had only about 30 minutes of interview time left. Passing inspection outside had insured that.

While the guests were arranging themselves in the staid, formal living room, the door from the rear of the house opened, and Rosalynn Carter came in, apparently surprised that her visitors were there. "What time is it anyway? I took off my watch when I was washing dishes this morning and forgot to put it back on. I haven't known what time it was since," she said.

It took a moment for her words to sink in...she had been washing dishes. Behind this wall of security, this layer of insulated aides, and this newfound celebrity status, life was still going on as usual. We were there to probe and pick, a photographer from Atlanta was setting up lighting in the kitchen, and a TV crew from Atlanta would be arriving as we departed. It was funny and yet it was reassuring to know that less than a week before Jimmy and Rosalynn Carter became the First Family of the World, she was scraping and rinsing dirty dishes. "I'm going to have to tell my wife about you washing dishes," I said. She laughed and added, "Well, so does Jimmy." That, I told her, I'd just as soon keep a secret back home.

Looking at her, you can't believe those writers who have dubbed her "Sister Rosalynn, the First Female Vice President," or those who call her the "Steel Magnolia." She's too delicate, having a face carved out of fine china and a body too fragile to be steel. Her voice is soft and lyrical, not sugary Southern, but still quiet and controlled. Her soft, stylish clothes are not designer originals, yet she wears them as if they were from no rack other than her own.

Yet, there's another side to this demure Southern lady.

"I don't know why he didn't tell them about Kennedy," Rosalynn Carter told a friend after her husband's first news conference as President-elect. Reporters had jabbed at Jimmy Carter about his narrow victory. His so-called mandate. Carter had been content to talk about 1976 and his own election. Rosalynn wanted him to talk about 1960, too. "Jimmy got more votes and a better majority than John Kennedy. I don't know why he didn't tell them that," she second-guessed, hardly being a background wife who only smiles and nods and echoes her husband the President.

No, Rosalynn Smith Carter, this daughter of a mechanic father and seamstress-postmistress mother, long ago learned that she had to work and think for herself if the world was ever to stop long enough to let her on. She is not the back-biting, win-at-any-cost type, yet she does believe in winning. She is a unique blend of motherly, wifely love and ambitious single-mindedness, wrapped up together in an attractive package that contradicts her status as a two-time grandmother.

Like her husband, she is a product of Plains, born on August 18, 1927, to W. Edgar and Allie Murray Smith. The Carters were among the landed semi-elite, but the Smiths were hardly from the other side of the tracks, as some have indicated. Her mother's family, the Murrays, were among the early arrivals in the area, settling in Botsford, and it was there on the family farm that Rosalynn was born. But when Edgar Smith died in 1940 at the age of 44, hard times were ahead for the wife and four children he left behind. As the eldest, at 13 Rosalynn became a stand-in mother for her brothers and sister while Miss Allie went to work both as a seamstress for the women of Plains and in the local post office. Somehow she was able to make her family's a life in which they might want, but would seldom go in need.

Like her daughter, Mrs. Allie Smith is quiet. Through all of the campaign noise, she has moved quietly in the background. While Miss Lillian was posing for the pictures, Miss Allie was content to answer the phone at the local Carter headquarters and seldom be recognized by the fawning tourists who filed through. She's a small, gray-haired first edition of Rosalynn, even to the prominent cheekbones. The most outgoing member of her clan is Mur-

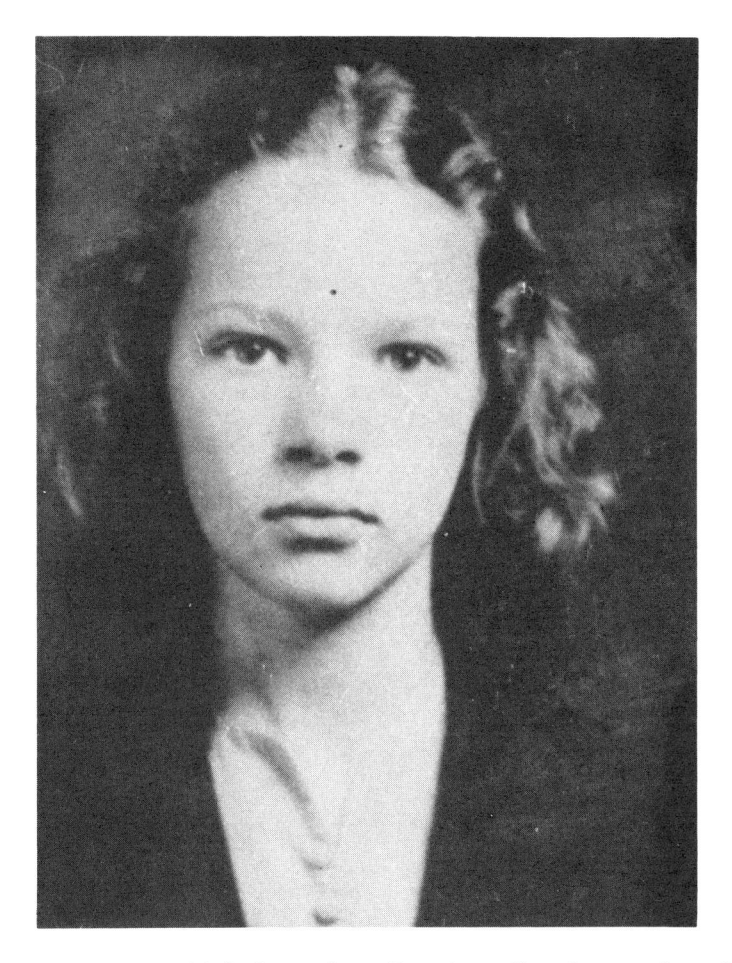

Other mothers couldn't figure how Rosalynn Smith stayed so clean.

ray, a tall, angular, athletic type who once coached the high school basketball team in Plains but now teaches at a high school in a neighboring county. These days he also drives a tour bus part-time, circling around Plains hourly. To the mustachioed Murray, Rosalynn is "Sister," the sometimes-mother who danced to every tune that came on the radio and kept the rest of them from going astray while their mother worked.

    Her childhood in Plains wasn't much different from that of any other youngster growing up in a see-all, know-all country town. Summers were spent at her grandfather's farm in Botsford. The rest of the time was spent in Plains, going to school during the week, playing with the other kids on Saturday, and going to the Methodist church on Sunday. Her neatness was a legend among the mothers of Plains, who never could understand how little Rosalynn could stay so neat and clean while their children came home muddy and soiled. Growing up wasn't easy, but it was fun.

Rosalynn Smith's best friend was Ruth Carter. They were classmates learning their multiplication tables together and friends learning to dance together. When Edgar Smith was dying of leukemia, it was Ruth's mother, a registered nurse, who cared for him. When he died, it was Miss Lillian who took Rosalynn home to be with her and Ruth. Ruth's older brother Jimmy was usually around, but like most boys, he seemed not to notice that either his sister or her friends were there. All of them were together at school or around the Carter house, but they might as well have been miles apart for all brother Jimmy noticed.

But Rosalynn noticed, especially when he came home from Annapolis in his white navy uniform. He had always been around. She knew him oh, so well. Yet, he seemed different. There was the uniform, but there was more. Ruth's brother Jimmy was now a man of the world. He had seen that world that existed outside of Sumter County. And he could take Rosalynn to see it, too. "I guess I always idolized him. He was older and so good-looking. But I don't know what made me fall in love with him. I just did," she says.

Their first date came two days before he was to go back to Annapolis for his senior year. What followed was a long-distance courtship with letters and phone calls instead of Saturday night dates. That Christmas he proposed. She said no. But by February they were engaged, and he gave her a ring at a Washington's Birthday dance at Annapolis. On July 7, 1946, they walked the aisle at the Plains Methodist Church. As they left Plains, both of them thought they were leaving for good. He was a navy officer, and his ambition was to be an admiral; hers was to be a good navy wife.

It was at this time that the foundation was laid for their partnership. This is what has caused observers to call her the President's No. 1 advisor or the Vice President. Rosalynn Carter doesn't see it quite that way. To her there is nothing unusual about a man and wife talking over his problems, his decisions, and his professional life. Jimmy and Rosalynn have always been that way.

"It started when we were first married. We were so young and were really away on our own for the first time in our lives. We talked about everything together. We were all we had. When we came back home and took over the business, it was the same way. I kept the books, and if Jimmy wanted to buy something he had to come to me to see if we could afford it. If he wanted to buy corn he'd come to me to see if we made money on it. It was a partnership. We are still that way. I sat in on all of the vice-presidential interviews and the Cabinet discussions. We talk about things. Jimmy listens to what I have to say. But he doesn't always do what I say," she says.

There was evidence of this early in the campaign when columnists Evans and Novak criticized Carter for spreading misconceptions about him-

Rosalynn was a smiling bride when she and Jimmy were married in 1946.

self. One of them concerned his membership in Common Cause. Carter, they said, had never been a member, although they conceded that his wife was. "Ever since we've been married, Rosalynn has written the checks and handled the money. She still does," Carter said, between bites on a quick campaign lunch break in New Hampshire. "She wrote that check for me to Common Cause just like she's written all of the others." Her young-girl love of arithmetic was paying off.

But all of that was in a faraway future when Jimmy and Rosalynn left Plains that hot July evening in 1946. She had been there with him when he was graduated from the academy. Now she was with him as he began what they thought would be a lifetime in the navy. Their first assignment was in Pensacola, Florida, where Jimmy—to his chagrin—was trained in blimps. Then it was on to Portsmouth, Virginia. Here their family was to begin to grow.

John William Carter—now known as Jack—was born in Portsmouth in 1947. James Earl Carter III—now called Chip—was born in Oahu, Hawaii, in

1950. Donnel Jeffrey Carter was born in New London, Connecticut, in 1952. The Carters had seawater in their veins. Their sons were navy born and bred. So almost was their mother, who by now was enjoying the life of a navy wife. She enjoyed the independence, the freedom, the demands that were placed on her as the wife of an ambitious young officer. Plains was only a faraway memory, a place to visit on holidays and leaves. Home was where the navy sent them next. Their roots were shallow and could grow in any soil.

They were to be reminded of Plains in 1953 when Jimmy received an urgent call from home. Earl Carter was dying. Cancer, in its advanced stages, dictated that he had only a few months to live. Making the long trip to Georgia from Schenectady, New York, Jimmy and Rosalynn returned to Plains. The months to come were trying ones. Jimmy, nearing 30, didn't know where to turn. He had his navy career, the thing he had dreamed about since he was a boy. He had his own growing family. He had the promise of an exciting future in the navy.

But there was another side that he hadn't bargained for. There was Plains, his mother, his father's business—responsibilities that are not easily ignored or forgotten. A decision had to be made. Jimmy could turn his back on his family and see Earl's business go under with no one to guide it, or he could turn his back on his own dreams and his own career and come back to this almost-forgotten home. Jimmy knew what he had to do. Rosalynn knew what she wanted him to do. And that was the conflict.

They argued bitterly. Rosalynn had visions of coming home and having life be the way it was before—or worse, the way she thought it might be. Both of their widowed mothers were there with their well-meaning influences. Although she and Miss Lillian may never have been the warring women that some have depicted, their relationship might well be described as a peaceful coexistence. In reality, the two are much alike, which may be the problem. Each has an iron will. Each has her own ambitions and her own dreams for Jimmy. They are two irresistible forces. With three young sons, Rosalynn wasn't sure she wanted to come back home and have them partially taken away from her, along with her own freedom. But she came. In 1953 Jimmy resigned his commission and returned home to Plains. They lived in a cramped public housing project and despite their hard work made only $187 that first year.

Though the deed might not have made it official, Rosalynn soon was a partner in the business. As Miss Lillian told one reporter, "Rosalynn was co-partner in everything Jimmy has ever owned. My husband owned the business, and I was just his wife." Taking a crash course in bookkeeping, she took over the business side of the peanut warehouse, leaving the other side of the operation to her husband, who was trying desperately to learn all he could about peanuts. He had picked them, bagged them, and sold them as a boy, but that meant as much now as a peanut butter and jelly sandwich. Slowly he learned and slowly business began to improve.

So did their life in Plains. There were dances at the Americus Country Club or the American Legion in Albany. Rosalynn's feet had loved to dance since she was a girl. Now she was keeping them busy. Jimmy was busy, too. The business was expanding. He was active in the church. He was a leader in the Lions Club, spearheading an effort to build a swimming pool in Plains. And their marriage, like their business, was a partnership.

By 1962 Jimmy had other ambitions. Maybe by design, maybe by accident, one by one Jimmy had taken on his late father's responsibilities. The business, the school board, the community...all that was left was politics. Nine years after their return to Plains, Jimmy was running for the state senate. His election gave Rosalynn added responsibilities in their ever-growing business. By now she had four sets of books to keep, but she was enjoying herself. "To make all those books balance....I liked it more than anything I've ever done," she says.

Four years later Jimmy had new ambitions, deciding to run for governor. He consulted Rosalynn, and she encouraged him. This thrust the shy, retiring Rosalynn into new roles. She had new responsibilities, new demands. She believed her husband was the best candidate, and now she was being asked to convince others. It was a frightening experience for her. However, joining the rest of the family, she took to the winding Georgia roads to campaign for her favorite candidate. But even all their efforts couldn't overcome

In 1966 Rosalynn, Jack, and Chip helped Jimmy campaign for governor.

his newness to the Georgia voters. He came in third, but by the next day Jimmy was telling people he would try again in 1970.

While 1966 had its disappointments, 1967 was to be a year of fulfillment, fulfillment of something Jimmy had been wanting for so long. It had been years since a baby had brightened their house, but a cyst was keeping Rosalynn from becoming pregnant, and they decided to have it removed. On October 19 Amy Lynn Carter arrived. "She made us young again," Jimmy and Rosalynn agree. "She has given us such joy," her mother says. Amy's perky smile was a welcome addition to the male-dominated household.

And, living up to his word, Jimmy Carter again ran **for** governor in 1970. With Rosalynn at his side they traveled Georgia from the mountains to the sea, shaking every hand that was offered, some 600,000, they estimated. This time it paid off. In January 1971 the Carters moved into the sprawling, walled-in governor's mansion in Atlanta. Ahead were new challenges for Jimmy and new fears for Rosalynn.

"Oh, I guess I ought to sit right," Rosalynn Carter said, shifting her legs. In 1976, days before Jimmy would take the presidential oath of office, she could laugh at such things, but six years ago she might have cried. Some

Americus welcomed Carters home after his gubernatorial election in 1970.

have said that those first days as Georgia's First Lady were traumatic for her—a description she denies—but they were difficult—that she will readily admit.

"I've read where people say it was traumatic for me when I went to Atlanta, that my hair was wrong, my clothes were wrong, everything was wrong, that I didn't know what to do. That never happened to me. I did worry the first few months we were there. I thought I had to be dressed up just perfect all the time to meet guests at the mansion or to conduct tours. I thought Amy had to be just perfect," the First Lady said, thinking back on those early years in Atlanta.

It may not have been traumatic, but it was a time of growing. The shyness had to be overcome. Her fear of public speaking was conquered when she found projects and causes in which she was truly interested. She became a spokeswoman for mental health in the state. She became a proponent of women's rights, speaking out for the Equal Rights Amendment, a cause she still champions. She became a person in her own right, not just an extension of her chief-executive husband with whom she still was close.

These were the major things she faced. It might have been the minor things that caused the most trouble. "I remember the first time I went in the kitchen at the mansion. All the pots were this big around," she said, extending her arms in a large circle. "You had to cook for 25 or more people every meal. That can be frustrating. You don't mind it if it's for a party, when you plan ahead for it. But not every meal." She learned quickly to leave the cooking to the cooks, although when they are at home she still enjoys cooking. "I doubt if I'll do much in the White House, but there is a small kitchen upstairs."

Her life was taking on new dimensions daily. Her sons were no longer boys. Jack was a lawyer. A graduate of Georgia Tech, he married Judy Langford of Calhoun, Georgia, in 1971. The daughter of a state senator, she and Jack gave Jimmy and Rosalynn their first grandchild, Jason, in 1975. Jason was to make his television debut at the Democratic Convention in 1976, bouncing on his grandfather's knee while grandpa was being nominated for President. Chip was married to Caron Griffin of Hawkinsville, Georgia in 1973. Their first child, James Earl Carter, IV, was born February 20, 1977. It was a White House baby, as Chip and Caron had moved to Washington from Plains with the Carters. Jeff, their youngest son, married Annette Davis of Arlington, Georgia, in 1975. He, too, is living in the White House and plans to attend college in Washington.

What would Rosalynn Carter do if one of her sons decided to enter politics? "I wouldn't be surprised if Jack does some day. He's just that way. Chip probably will. He has already run for the city council in Plains and had to resign when he started to campaign for Jimmy. I don't think Jeffrey ever

Rosalynn overcame early shyness to become a bubbling campaigner.

will, although he's gotten much more interested in it recently. I wouldn't try to change their minds. I learned long ago that you have to let them live their own lives." For Amy her ambitions are different. "I only hope Amy can grow up and do what she wants to do without being held back by prejudice."

The Carter children were exposed to people from all walks of life while their father was governor, and so were their parents. For the first time in their lives, they were seeing world leaders eye to eye instead of from a distance. They met presidents and would-be presidents. All of it made them realize that these persons were human beings with human weaknesses and faults: Their thinking was sometimes shallow and narrow; they drank too much; they talked too much. The Carters' first-hand look at what the political parties had to offer made it easy for Rosalynn to understand when Jimmy told her he was considering running for the presidency. She not only understood, she encouraged. As he left the Georgia governor's office, he was ready to make public his intentions. By December 1974 the world knew—although the world apparently did not care.

Arming herself with a compact wardrobe of washable items, she prepared to join Jimmy on the road. She would set her own schedules, make her own speeches. He would do the same. "I was scared to death all over again, but you develop confidence after you start doing things on your own," she recalls. Weekends they would be home, catching up on their correspondence, washing their clothes, being together, and being with Amy.

Again it was a partnership. His picture was on the poster, but she was as much a part of the campaign as he was. Too often she found herself on the

Since their marriage, Jimmy and Rosalynn have been partners.

defensive, but she never slipped or faltered, something even her husband was to be guilty of doing on a few occasions. She was speaking for herself, not mouthing some puppeteer's words. At 49 she was still growing.

When they were home, life was changing, too. Coming down the church steps one Sunday morning, she laughed as a horde of newsmen trampled over one another scrambling to the other door where Jimmy was exiting unexpectedly. "He had to vote on some new deacons," she said, enjoying the peaceful stroll while the cameramen shoved and shouted across the churchyard. "I can never get used to all of that."

Until barricades were constructed in July, the press waited like vultures outside their home. If it wasn't the press, it was tourists, wanting a glimpse of where this man Carter lived. Some wanted more than a glimpse, as one Secret Service agent recalled. "The woman said all she wanted was some leaves from his yard to take home with her," he said, shaking his head.

All of this made Rosalynn Carter change some of her everyday habits. "I couldn't go outside to tell Amy it was time for lunch without getting dressed up, combing my hair, and allowing 20 minutes to meet and greet people," she says. No longer could she drive her car to the store and expect to push her buggy around Walters' Grocery. "C. L. has to deliver now," she said.

Through it all, she somehow kept her composure, even maintaining her friendly manner toward visitors to her church. "You look like you need help," she told my wife one Sunday morning. "I sure do, but I never expected I'd be guided to my class by you," a surprised Peggy Hyatt said.

By November 1976 she had been campaigning nearly two years. But that first Tuesday made the exhaustion worthwhile. Jimmy Carter was the choice of 51 percent of the American voters. Election night was spent at an all-night vigil in Atlanta, but by dawn the Carters were home. As he spoke to a weary but enthusiastic group at the train station, tears came easier than words for Jimmy. He didn't have to speak to Rosalynn, she understood. With tears streaming down their faces, they embraced. He had won. They had won.

Now the security thickened, the layer of insulation around the Carters was increased. Looking around their livable home, however, you could hardly tell it. On one wall of the living room, a portrait of Amy still hung. A similar one of Amy and her mother was going to the White House, probably to the Oval Office. The kitchen, despite the glare of photographers' lights, still looked as if it were used. The family room in the rear looked lived in. Books lined two of the walls, and another wall was dotted with photos chronicling the past. In the sunlit Florida room were a row of plants and a large dollhouse, left behind when Amy went to school but soon to be carted away to Washington. On the inside, you could tell that a family lived there.

Campaign trips often took Rosalynn away from nine-year-old Amy.

On the outside, the bleakness of the day was intensified by the dreary security men, making the house seem like a fortified castle.

The new First Lady looked at the security pragmatically. "After the primaries we had so many cars and visitors coming down this street that we had to put ropes around the yard. Now we don't have to do that," she said. Another side came out as she continued. "We had campaigned so hard with people across the country, and after we won we wanted to share it with them. That first week we had 18,000 or 20,000 letters to come in, but they all went to Atlanta. I had nothing. I finally said I wanted to see some of them. They sent down a stack of telegrams, and I went through them. And you know, I only knew two people out of all of them. So you are sort of cut off. I can see how you can get isolated. That part of it is kind of sad," she said.

You had to wonder if this feeling of sad isolationism would only fester once they were in the White House and after the welcoming parties were over and the guests had all gone home. But Rosalynn said she was looking forward to the move. "I'll just be glad to get settled. We moved from the mansion in January of 1975, and I started campaigning that April. We've hardly had time to be at home since," she explained.

Amy, however, was another matter completely. She didn't want to go to her new home. But a playful physical education teacher and the promise that two of her playmates from Plains—John and Sidney Gnann—would visit her at the White House during the inauguration were apparently soothing the hurt.

School was ahead for Amy, but what was ahead for her mother? Many were comparing her to Eleanor Roosevelt even before she moved into the White House. One pundit said, "Jimmy has Eleanor's teeth and Rosalynn has Eleanor's brain." That she might instantly turn into an active, full-time First Lady like the wife of FDR was a lot to ask, but Jimmy Carter makes it clear that she will be an important member of his administration. One reporter asked the President if there is anyone on his staff who feels free to say "you're wrong." "Some say your wife performs this function at times," the questioner said. "She does," Carter answered, "and you can leave off 'at times.'"

Rosalynn Carter will be a leader in seeking improvements in mental health care, just as she was as Georgia's First Lady. She already has spoken out for the Equal Rights Amendment in Georgia, although her efforts have failed thus far. She will be an ambassador to foreign countries at times. She will be the President's partner. But an Eleanor Roosevelt? Rosalynn's not sure.

"I believe all of this started when I spoke at a benefit performance of *Eleanor* in Los Angeles. I admire Mrs. Roosevelt greatly, but I don't know if I can emulate her or would want to. I've read that Mrs. Roosevelt never once

Jimmy and Rosalynn share Bicentennial surrey ride in Lumpkin, Georgia.

had lunch alone, or just with her family, at the White House. For her, lunch was a time for one more meeting, one more function. I really can't imagine doing that," she admitted.

She won't be an Eleanor Roosevelt. She won't be a Jackie Kennedy. She won't be a Lady Bird Johnson. She'll just be herself, a self which she comes to know better almost every day. Rosalynn Carter has her own ideas and her own ideals, some new, some old. She has an unquenchable thirst to learn new things, yet she clings to the past. On her left hand is the Annapolis ring that Jimmy gave her 30 years ago. "...And he gave me this row of tiny diamonds for our 25th anniversary," she explained.

Clasped hands and peaceful expressions leave no doubt this is a family.

On inauguration night in Washington, she wore the same gown she had worn when he was inaugurated as governor. "It's a lucky dress for me and a pretty dress," she said when some eyebrows were raised. She enjoys fine things and being waited on at times, but she still buys her clothes from a retailer in Americus and still enjoys cooking for her family. When a story reported she was taking a 185-piece wardrobe to Washington, she laughed, "I haven't bought that many new clothes in my life." And when designers were describing the clothes they had fashioned for her, she candidly said, "I've never talked to them, or even heard of them. I bought the dresses in Americus." As First Lady, Rosalynn hopes to cling to old ideas and old ties. "We're going to have old friends, just regular people, at state dinners."

Years ago, when he was dying, Edgar Smith told his daughter that he wanted her "to have a better position in life." It was his dream, and she turned it into a reality. She married her first love, mothered four children, has two grandchildren, and now is America's First Lady. But, perhaps more importantly, she has improved herself. Some of her self-improvements may have been designed to help her husband and to strengthen their partnership, but in the end they have also helped Rosalynn Carter. Her life has a purpose. She has her own goals. She is confident that she has the abilities to reach these goals herself.

Rosalynn Carter is hardly the fragile rose she looks. Yet she is far from being the steel-nerved, pushy wife some would have you believe. She's a Southern blend of resourcefulness and helplessness. That's why she needs Jimmy and why Jimmy needs her. There again is that business of a partnership. He must have felt it that night long ago when he told Miss Lillian he had just gone out with the girl he was going to marry. Rosalynn apparently sensed it even before he did. They are very much alike—low-key, under absolute control, warm, and yet detached. Thirty years, four children, and two grandchildren later, they still are known to act like high school sweethearts, grabbing the other's hand whenever they're near.

It's a long way from Botsford to Pennsylvania Avenue, but Rosalynn Smith Carter has traveled the road, some of it holding on to her husband's hand, some of it holding on to herself. How much further can they go? Time holds that answer. What is certain is that they'll go together.

Gloria Carter Spann: At Home In Plains

The night was young and so were the convention results, but already the celebrating had begun. A rock band was tuning up in front of the bank. Television cables were turning Main Street into an obstacle course, their lights turning night into noon. Everybody seemed to be wearing a button or banner supporting Jimmy Carter. Those who did not support him surely would not have been in Plains that particular evening.

Gloria Spann was lost in the revelers. It would be hours before the Democrats would have themselves a nominee for President, and she was visiting the crowded railroad station to say hello to friends. The rest of her family was with her famous brother in New York, where in a few hours the throng at Madison Square Garden would crown him their nominee. The spillover crowd was here in Plains, enjoying a party that would not end until the wee hours. Among them, for now at least, was Gloria Carter Spann.

"This is where I belong," she explained, before returning to her house for a quiet party. "This is home." Throughout her brother's rise to the White House, this was where she chose to stay. She shied away from the bright lights of New York during the convention, staying close to her favorite fishing hole. She didn't join the Peanut Brigade when her friends and neighbors were packing their bags for faraway states to campaign for her brother, deciding to stay home where she could escape on her motorcycle or help her mother look after a restless Amy.

While other members of the Carter Clan were on the talk-show circuit and on the covers of the national magazines, Gloria and Walter Spann were going about their own business as if they didn't know who this Jimmy Carter was. Well, almost, anyway. Their lives had been touched by his campaign just as everyone close to him had been affected by this overnight burst of attention. But perhaps no one survived better than Gloria Spann.

Her unpretentious home is a monument to her stubborn desire not to let the spotlight shine on her. Hidden on a sleepy state road surrounded by acres of farmland, her white frame house has a homey look to it, complete with large shade trees, which are home for families of squirrels, and a friendly front porch. There are no signs warning visitors to keep away, but then how many even know whose home this is? When a car full of unannounced guests drove into her driveway one evening, they were welcomed in by a barefoot, denim-clad hostess sipping on a glass of iced tea. She seemed unaware of the public relations demands or the image the sister of a would-be President should maintain. She remained Gloria. Her only concession was on trips around town. "I've had to stop smiling," she explained. "When I smile they know I'm a Carter."

She does have that family smile. Like the others, her eyes take on a dancing sparkle which peeps through the wrinkles that take over the corners of her eyes when she breaks into a wide grin. She enjoys a good laugh and likes to kid her friends, which leads you to believe she was practicing this art long ago when her brother—two years older than his little sister—shot her in the backside with a BB gun. But all of this is a private side that she shows reporters only on her own terms. She has remained a private person with her own life to lead.

Some of this may result from problems with her 30-year-old son William, who is serving time in a California prison for armed robbery committed under the influence of drugs. This is not his first time behind bars. His life has been a burden on Gloria for many years, although folks around Plains remember Willie as a cute little boy, hardly an indication of the heartache that was to come. Gloria has refused to comment on her son, although she did author a first-person story for *Good Housekeeping* in January 1977, an article she described as "my first and last public statement about my son." It is a story oft-repeated by parents today.

"My story," she wrote in the magazine, "is not one of symptoms and solutions. It is simply a record of how I, as a mother, learned to face the reality of helplessness in my son's situation and to release the heartbreak and embarrassment that engulfed my husband and me so that we could find joy in our own lives. But most of all, I am writing this piece to find fulfillment in sharing with others our failures and triumphs in rearing a child who, in spite of great charm and intelligence, continues to live at odds with the world."

It is a story of strength, strength gained through years of failures with doctors, public and private schools, and learning to say no. Perhaps in this you can understand this friendly but private person. "Each time my son was granted parole we gave him money and encouragement for a 'new start.' When we learned that the money we sent him was going for drugs, I reminded myself again, as I have over and over through the years, that God has my son in His hands. And thinking this, I finally found the strength to

While her family was on the talk-show circuit, Gloria Carter Spann preferred to stay close to home.

tell William, 'I will never send you another cent.' Within a few days he was back in prison again, and when his imprisonment was announced to the world, I affirmed, 'This is God's business, and He is working on it.'"

Saying no was a test of strength, and when William's story made headlines during the campaign, she was to find her strength renewed by the support she found forthcoming from parents who had experienced the same type of heartache. "The first letter I opened," she wrote, "said 'God bless you. I know what you are going through. Don't lose your head. My son is a duplicate of your son.'"

Whatever her reasons, Gloria Spann stayed in her personal shell—unlike her brother Billy and sister Ruth—until the inauguration, when she accompanied the rest of her family to celebrate in Washington. The day after her older brother had been sworn in as President, I was walking through the White House along with other visitors from Georgia when I felt a hand on my arm. I turned to see a familiar face. It was Gloria in a long, flowing gown on the arm of a military escort. She had exchanged her embroidered blue jeans for a floor-length dress. For the first time since I had known her, she was wearing a touch of makeup. But she was wearing the same smile. "You didn't recognize me," she said—which was almost true. "See you back in Plains," letting me know her heart was still back home and that she soon would be, too.

All that most people know about her is that she enjoys the out-of-doors—fishing and motorcycling—that she enjoys sewing—turning blue jeans into works of art—that she has a natural flare for other art forms—painting primarily outdoor scenes—and that she is an outspoken voice for motorcycle safety. But there is much more to this complex person. She is an accomplished accountant, still doing books for many long-time customers around Plains. She is, like her brothers and sister, a full-time reader. She is deeply religious, finding solace in her sister Ruth's belief in inner peace, and is a frequent speaker to religious groups throughout the area. She also is a writer, compiling letters from her mother for publication in late 1977.

Of all of Lillian Carter's children, Gloria Carter Spann may be the one most like her mother. Her tongue is sharp and quick to react. She is compassionate, especially when the person needing help is her mother, as she showed when Miss Lillian's health waned after the election and Gloria became her constant companion, shielding her from the constant demands. She's tolerant. When the Plains Baptist Church closed its door on blacks in 1965, she left the church, showing a streak of Carter stubbornness as well.

This is Gloria Spann. She hasn't needed the limelight or the headlines, doesn't enjoy seeing herself on the six o'clock news, and has an ego with a small appetite. She's content with life the way it was. All she needs are her husband and the things she enjoys.

Which may be the best life after all.

Cousin Hugh And Uncle Buddy: Worms And Antiques

It was easy to separate the curious from the customers. The curious were in line to sample the churns of homemade peach ice cream or the steaming barbecue, while the customers were running educated fingers over seasoned wood or thumbing glassware so their ears could estimate if it was worth a bid. The walls were lined with antiques, and soon Hugh Carter would be climbing the steps toward the podium to open the bidding.

Inside the crowded room, people were searching for the cardboard fans that once were regular accessories inside any Southern church—usually donated by the local funeral director—to combat the July heat and the gnats which go along with a warm Georgia evening. Those not lucky enough to have a fan of their own were using the bolo paddles which Hugh Carter decorates with numbers to make it easier to recognize bidders when the buying heats up the already-sultry room.

Finding a vacant folding chair was impossible. The regulars at a Hugh Carter auction were used to putting up with those who come to browse and bid for fun and not necessarily profit. Now they were being joined by invaders with strange license plates on their bug-speckled cars, armed with flashbulbs and shopping bags which they wanted to fill with the souvenirs of this small town that suddenly was hogging the world's headlines.

A smiling Hugh Carter had these newcomers in mind as he sipped on a soft drink and watched the customers weave in and out of the antique obstacles in the dusty aisles. "See that old armchair over there," he said, a grin creasing his freckled face. "Wonder what I could get if I told the people that that old chair was Jimmy's favorite, that he sits in it whenever he stops in?" But that night, Jimmy wouldn't drop in nor would Cousin Hugh put his favorite overstuffed chair on the auction block. Instead, he would sell an unlikely grouping of items ranging from a wicker bird basket—sans bird—to rusting Coke signs to priceless pieces of furniture and glassware. There would be something for each of them—the curious and the connoisseur. Between blinks of his camera, a photographer from *Newsweek* even got into the bidding, finally writing a check for a large upright chest.

This was one side of Hugh Carter's life. His antique store is a fixture on Main Street, and so are the Carters. There's been a Carter open for business there almost since there's been a Plains—first, Hugh's father Alton, still, at 88, in partnership with his son, then Alton's brother Earl, who was to diversify his interests, resulting in the peanut business his son Jimmy was to inherit. When he opened the antique store Hugh turned a hobby into a bustling business which is well-known around Georgia. But these days the antiques have been pushed away from the front door to make room for a booming trade in "Jimmy Items," which folks around Plains call the souvenirs that either bear the President's smiling face or his now-familiar name.

Hugh's store was one of the first along Main Street to stock a full line of souvenirs. Carter anticipated what was ahead and created his own buttons, banners, and bumper stickers and anything else the wily merchant thought would sell. Those who know him best say that Hugh has a better nose for the dollar than anyone in the Carter clan, and he has lived up to that description since he and Jimmy sold peanuts and hot dogs on the streets of Plains 40 years ago. And antiques aren't his only ways to earn.

Down the street from the antique store is the office of the Carter Worm Farm, a farm that grows just what its name implies. "His house was built with worms," Alton Carter jokes, alluding to his son's expansive home on the edge of town. In reality it is no joke. Started in 1945, the Carter Worm Farm is one of the largest in the country, "second to one in Denver," claims Alton. Hugh can send you a case of wigglers or he can sell you books he has written telling you how to grow your own. His business—even before the Jimmy boom hit Plains—was great enough for his mail alone to require a better grade of post office than a town the size of Plains normally would demand. Business really began to boom nearly 20 years ago when Tom Sellers, then a newsman in Columbus, did an article on Hugh's worms for *Life*. During Jimmy's campaign his cousin's business was boosted again when Hugh and his worms were pictured in *Newsweek*. "I didn't think the orders would ever quit," Hugh said. "I couldn't have bought a better ad."

When he's not hearing the bell on his cash register ring, Hugh Carter is probably talking politics. When Jimmy ran for the state senate in 1962, his older cousin was his campaign manager, a job he also was to hold eight years later when Jimmy was elected governor of Georgia. It wasn't family ties that caused Jimmy to select him, either. Hugh Carter is a throwback to a vanishing breed of Georgia politicians who practice ward politics on the county level. He knows everybody and everybody knows him. And it was this talent that made Hugh a shoo-in to succeed Jimmy as the 14th District state sen-

Alton Carter, 88—Uncle Buddy to the family—is a source of history on the Carters and Plains.

ator, a position he still holds, with little opposition. While Jimmy was governor Hugh became a valuable ally in the senate chambers, where the influence of Lt. Gov. Lester Maddox was so prevalent.

Underneath his low-key covering, Hugh is similar to his cousin. Each can be stubborn—a trait Alton Carter traces back through the Carter generations. Each drives a hard bargain when he sets his mind on something. Each has an easy, relaxed manner dealing with people one-on-one. Each has been successful at anything he tried. Neither is used to losing—which is why Hugh's only political regret still brings a wistful conversation as he describes why his cousin did not appoint him to the U.S. Senate when the late Richard B. Russell died. "I'd have made a good Senator, too," he still says.

That same boastful side shows in Alton Carter's words when he talks about his sons. "You must know my son Don," he'll say, reaching for a picture of him that sits on his desk in the rear of the store. "He's a vice president for Knight Newspapers. He used to be with the *Wall Street Journal*," he'll tell you, showing typical fatherly pride in describing his son's successful career in the newspaper business. "All of us Carters have been leaders in whatever we did. I was mayor of Plains 27 years. Hugh's a state senator. Don's done well. Earl, Jimmy's daddy, was a member of the Georgia House. It's the way we are." Hugh Carter, Jr., has now added his name to the list.

Hugh Carter was a proud father when Hugh, Jr., (left) joined Cousin Jimmy's White House staff.

He's a White House aide in charge of removing the pomp and frills.

At 88, Alton Carter still drives his well-worn car to the store every day, neatly dressed, with a hat usually covering his white hair. "Uncle Buddy" to the family, he's a walking history book for Plains and the county, and he knows every branch on the Carter Family Tree. Driving you around the countryside, he can tell you the history of seemingly every house and every plot of land. But the proud point on his tour is when he drives you toward Ellaville and shows you the Carter Family Cemetery. "I fixed all this up myself a couple of years ago, " he says. Every grave is clearly marked, and there's a fence around the outside. His love of family history made Alton a popular source for reporters who sought folklore on the Carters of Plains. On one occasion one of the visiting reporters from the *Miami Herald* took Alton Carter's tour and when she returned home wrote a story that had Hugh Carter bristling. She had quoted Alton's liberal use of the word "nigguh," a word that rolls off old Southern tongues with regularity. After nearly nine decades you just don't teach new words to someone who's been using the old ones all of his life. But it didn't faze Alton Carter. He wasn't about to change just because of one story. When the next reporter showed up he was ready to get out his old map of Georgia, tell stories about the early days of Plains of Dura, or put on his hat and take the newsman on a dusty-road tour of Sumter County.

It is difficult to read between the lines on Hugh Carter and understand how he stands on Civil Rights. He is a practical man, and he professes to be a Christian man. As he describes it, "Jimmy and me's first remembrances are of going to church." As a church deacon, he originally voted not to allow the Reverend Clennon King, a black minister from Albany, Georgia, membership in the all-white Plains Baptist Church. Yet it was Hugh who stood behind the Reverend Bruce Edwards and tried to correct him as the minister mistakenly told a Sunday morning press conference that the church bylaws contained the word "nigger," a claim that in a few days the pastor corrected. And it was Hugh Carter who vainly fought to keep the church from firing Edwards three months later in February 1977. He called that Sunday "the darkest day in the history of the church." Later he led an unsuccessful move to reinstate Edwards.

His church is a big part of Hugh Carter's life. As church clerk, he can instantly produce written record of any birth, death, marriage, or religious decision in the history of the church. It's right there in his vault. When I asked him about Jimmy, he thumbed through a ledger and reported that "Jimmy was saved in 1935." He also is the church music director, leading the congregational singing every Sunday morning. On the Sunday morning after his auction, however, he was too hoarse to do much talking, much less singing. But sitting in the Sunday School room overrun with members of the press, his voice was strong enough to lead the prayer and later to joke that "since the press was on expense accounts they should fill up the collection basket."

By the next day his voice had returned to normal, and he stood with Alton demonstrating to a reporter how their hand-operated elevator worked. "Way back, this was a furniture store. They'd load the elevator full of heavy furniture, but one man could pull it up to the top floor," Alton said.

They were proud of history. It surrounded them. Also around them was tomorrow's history, being made right there in Plains. They were taking advantage of it, too, stocking the store with items to catch the tourist's hungry eyes. In them, you could see the embodiment of what Plains is all about these days. Yet, none of it has seemed to shock Alton Carter. When you talk to him about Jimmy and ask if all of this has surprised him, he just turns his mouth up in that half smile of his and shakes his head no. Why should it?

"He's a Carter, ain't he?"

A Time For "Amazing Grace"

A High-Priced Cameraman

Joe Newton's mother didn't send a dummy to Washington to meet the President. All the time he had been snaking through the White House waiting to shake Jimmy Carter's hand, he had been pondering a problem. Problem was, he had his trusty Instamatic—complete with one of those magical cubes that provide instant light—but he could not figure how he was going to get a picture of both himself and his wife when time came for them to be welcomed to the Carters' new home on Pennsylvania Avenue.

While the Newtons waited, they met Lee and Aletia Wall of Ellenwood, Georgia. The Walls were relative old-timers. By then, Mrs. Wall's sister, Rosalynn Carter, had lived at the 1600 address for nearly 30 hours. Lee Wall said he would help Newton, a friendly Waycross attorney. The plan seemed foolproof. The Newtons were going to step up beside the President, then Lee Wall was going to step back and snap. Well, it didn't work quite that way. Wall snapped, but all that flashed was his wife Aletia's face, which turned an instant shade of red. Help was needed and help arrived—from a high-priced cameraman.

"Let's see what's wrong with that," Jimmy Carter said, stepping out of the receiving line. He toyed with it for a moment, handed the repaired camera back to his brother-in-law, and with the flash of a cube, Joe Newton had an instant memory.

So did 2,000 other Georgians who filed through the White House that afternoon. "Y'all come," Jimmy had said. And come they did, sampling cake and punch, sharing old memories and making new ones they will talk about for years to come. By then, Jimmy Carter's inaugural was in the history books. He was officially our 39th President. But was he? Was all of this over? Had the dreams come true? Making their way through the East Room, the Green Room, the Blue Room, the Red Room, the State Dining Room, and into the reception hall, it was still hard for the guests to realize that Jimmy

Americus (Georgia) High School students spent free time touring capitol with Rep. Jack Brinkley.

and Rosalynn were now the master and mistress of this hallowed old place.

Half a block away, within those same tightly secured walls, Press Secretary Jody Powell's slow, syrupy voice was bouncing off the solemn walls of the White House Press Office. The Carter Administration was still in diapers, but already it faced some full-grown problems. Reporters pried open an eyelid, tuned in an ear, and waited for a message. "Governor Carter will have a statement on the energy question within the hour," Powell said, following habits of years past. By the time his words had echoed through the suddenly revived room, he had seen the error of his still-new ways. "President Carter also will have a statement," he said. Like his Georgia neighbors, reality had not yet caught up with Jody Powell, formerly of Vienna, Georgia, now of Washington.

Washington during inaugural week was hardly a week to grab hold of reality. It was a fairytale week of receptions, parties, and balls. A person merely went from one line to another, one coat check to another, one cash bar to another. There was a Jaycee smile on every face, a firm hand waiting to grasp you and yours at every turn. Hands not waiting to be shaken were waiting for a tip. It was billed as a "People's Inaugural," and although people did come—real people, the folks next door—so did the seers and the beseeners, hopefully to gain mention in the society columns and definitely to drop some important names into the conversation, whatever the subject might be.

The town may have belonged to the Carters, but the week belonged to the Georgians and the thousands of other tourists who came to Washington to see Jimmy Carter take the 188-year-old oath. There were free concerts in the snowy parks, art shows, poetry readings, horse shows, dance festivals, and even films of inaugurations past ("Inaugural Recollections from McKinley to Coolidge"). There were puppet shows. There was a young Jimmy Cagney yankee-doodling it through some vintage George M. Cohan. There was King Tut, holding court at the Smithsonian to a turn-away group of would-be constituents. There was bluegrass music or string ensembles. There were cloggers or ethnic folk dancers. There were the conventional tours giving you a brief and patriotic glimpse at the historic sights. There were the more modern ones, swings through town, offering a look at the Watergate Apartments, the Tidal Basin, and even Amy Carter's new school. There was something for everybody, even those who did not arrive by Brink's Truck, because many of the activities were free.

Georgia had begun its invasion the weekend before the Thursday noon ceremony. They came by car—those who were brave enough to test the horn-blowing traffic—by bus, by plane, even by train. One of the trains was put together by Mrs. Maxine Reese of Plains, who gleefully celebrated its departure from the historic old station in Carter's hometown, only to curse its arrival in Washington where she discovered there was not enough room at the inn or if there was room, there was no heat for many of the travel-weary, drink-weary passengers. By the time they were tucked into their hotel, they must have felt like a congregation because they had been preached to at every turn. "When you're crossing the street," warned the shuttle-bus driver, "beware, especially of diplomats. If they hit you, you can't do a thing about it. If you see a car with a tag beginning in DPL, look out—those folks can't drive." They were told not to go out alone at night, not to ride elevators alone, to be wary of unauthorized tour guides. Most of the advice was received like a Sunday morning sermon...going in one pew and out the other.

It was the folks from back home who were the guests of honor around the capital city. Sharing scarce cabs, the ice-breaking question usually began something like, "Are you from Georgia?" Both the listenee and the listener were more often than not perplexed to find that both of them were from Jimmy Country. The sprawling Sheraton-Park Hotel became Georgia-Away-From-Home. It offered reruns of Atlanta TV news on a special channel and even listed grits on the breakfast menu. Gawking Georgians walked the lobby 24 hours a day hoping for a glimpse of a celebrity but were rewarded mostly with faces from back home.

Jimmy Carter and his family had been preparing for that week for a long time but like most folks discovered that you can't prepare for the unexpected. The unexpected arrival in Plains of some arctic air had left some pipes frozen in his garage, and the President-elect directed the repairs. There

The inauguration trip was like a continual party aboard the "Peanut Special."

Sheraton-Park ballroom was wall-to-wall with folks from Georgia.

were business papers to be signed, friends to be called, cats to be inoculated, clothes to be packed. There were quail hunts, though no quail cooperated. Back in Plains, Jimmy and Rosalynn had methodically gone about these inescapable getaway chores, trying to avoid the pains of saying good-bye. Sunday came, and so did church time. In Sunday School, teacher Clarence Dodson said that "all Christians and especially those labeled Baptists will share in the spotlight that shines on Jimmy and Rosalynn." As the group came to their feet for a closing prayer, Dodson said: "We want to pray for President-elect Carter. We want to pray for our nation, pray for our world, pray for your church and for your pastor, and for yourself so that you may be a Christian citizen." Moving from Sunday School into the sanctuary, there were more tears and more hugs. Plains was saying good-bye to one of its own.

Monday and Tuesday were full of everyday things. Last-minute errands. Last-minute chores. Last-minute good-byes. It was time to close the door on Plains and open the door on Washington. Yet, there still was time for per-

The old station was busy once again as people lined the sleepy tracks.

sonal, stolen moments. Lillian Carter, the matriarch of the clan, was visiting with her youngest grandson, Earl Gordy Carter—Billy and Sybil's youngest son—when Jimmy unexpectedly arrived for a Tuesday afternoon visit. This wasn't a time for tape recorders, notebooks, or glaring lights. This was mother–son talk, quiet talk, talk they knew would be difficult to have once he had moved into his new home, thousands of miles from Plains. "All of it hit me for the first time," Miss Lillian said afterwards. "He wanted to come and talk. He knows we won't be seeing each other often now."

The following morning Carter drove the four blocks to the railroad station to say good-bye to his neighbors who were shoving off on Maxine Reese's train.

"It's a new day, a new beginning, a new spirit for our country," he told the festive Wednesday crowd that gathered on Main Street. "You're my friends and you helped me get elected....I'm going to try to do a good job for you." However, he made it clear their friendship went only so far. "If you get in trouble in Washington...don't call me—I'll have my hands full."

Before boarding for Washington, some old friends came to say good-bye.

By that afternoon the Carters were in the air, on a chartered jet departing Albany, Georgia, for Washington—loaded to the brim with Carters. The President-elect had carried his own bag aboard, just as he had helped the movers load some of their precious cargo the day before. Another Washington-bound charter had left Albany earlier that day. It was loaded with beer and Brother Billy's army of friends—the Filling Station Mafia. "I'm not going to get into anything wild. I promise I won't get locked up. I promise you that," Billy pledged. Washington—ready or not—was about to be invaded by Carters and by most of the state of Georgia.

The Washington that greeted the Carters was freezing, familiar, and family. Temperatures were in the twenties. Familiar faces were everywhere. Members of the Democratic family now outnumbered the Republican clan that had held the majority in the capital city for the past eight years. The airport arrival was hectic, so hectic that Mrs. Gloria Carter Spann—having trouble locating her wayward luggage—was left behind. Redfaced, an aide was sent back to retrieve the First Sister. The other Carters aboard were hustled to the Blair House, where they had only a short time to refresh themselves before it was time for an exclusive gala at the Kennedy Center.

This was Hollywood's turn to turn the tables on the rest of the country. Instead of being gawked at, Hollywood was gawking at Plains. It began with soulful Georgian Dobie Grey's version of "The Star-Spangled Banner," then moved on to excerpts from Shirley MacLaine's Las Vegas review. From there the evening turned into an assembly line of talent that included Paul Newman, Redd Foxx, Linda Ronstadt, Joanne Woodward, Paul Simon, Loretta Lynn, Freddie Prinze (who would be dead within two weeks from a self-inflicted bullet wound), Muhammad Ali, and Hank Aaron. After an intermission when the President-elect left briefly to sign some official papers, there was Chevy Chase and Dan Aykroyd—doing a Carter takeoff straight from "Saturday Night Live"—Jack Albertson, Beverly Sills, Bette Davis, poet James Dickey, and Aretha Franklin. Even John Wayne showed up, a Republican pledging himself a member of the "loyal opposition," with the emphasis on the "loyal."

At the party afterwards, everyone took turns fawning over one another. A high school volunteer almost turned over a punch bowl when she looked up from her heavily laden table and gasped, "Cher." Her co-workers almost fainted. John Lennon and Yoko Ono were there, and when a commotion surrounding Jimmy Carter erupted across the room, the former Beatle said, "Oh, Elton John must have arrived." Miss Lillian was surrounded by men all evening, not ordinary men but the kind of men moviegoers swoon over. "We must get something started," Paul Newman joked with her. However, the plain-spoken First Mother later confided that her favorite was not the blue-eyed Newman but Warren Beatty. That evening she could choose among those two and dozens of others. The Carters' youngest son Jeff was burdened with his camera and with a program on which he was collecting autographs at a rapid pace. "This was Dad's camera. He gave it to me about four years ago, and I think he's forgotten. I'm not going to remind him whose it is, either," Jeff smiled. The ill-fated Freddie Prinze was the apple of the eye of a group of Howard University chorus members. "Seeing Freddie is just the biggest thrill for me," one of them gushed. Looking around, Chevy Chase looked tall, Jimmy Carter looked shorter than most had thought. Everybody else just looked and looked and looked.

While the stars were shining at the Kennedy Center, Georgians were turning the rest of Washington into a dressed-up version of a Down Home shindig. The Georgia Society, an organization composed of Georgians now transplanted into residents of the District, was having a party on Capitol Hill honoring the newly arrived visitors from back home. Many of those visitors, however, would overnight become membership prospects for the Society, as soon as they were confirmed as members of the still-forming Carter Team.

That was not the only Georgia Party going on that night. Across town at the Sheraton-Park, Governor and Mrs. George Busbee cordially invited anyone from Georgia to a not-so-intimate party they were giving in the ballroom. The only invitation needed was some type of identification card showing you were a Georgian. At the door, people were flashing outdated Georgia driver's licenses, well-worn ID's from days gone by at a Georgia university, old charge cards from Rich's (Atlanta's best-known department store), and anything else that might convince the man on the door that they had either lived in, passed through, or even heard about Georgia. The ballroom soon was wall-to-wall Georgians. Dancing was out of the question. So was breathing. The cash bars scattered around the walls could have done a brisker business had guests been able to reach the bartenders. The topic of conversation, naturally, was a Georgian who was not there—Jimmy Carter.

"If we had lost in Sumter County (Carter's home county), I'd have left the country," county campaign chief Langdon Sheffield told someone. "I bet the editor of the paper back in LaGrange we'd win. He still owes me the $2, too," City Councilman Glenn Robertson was saying. "All of this gives me new hope," said A. J. McClung, the black mayor pro-tem of Columbus. "I was telling folks about Jimmy Carter eight years ago, but I never thought we'd end up here," said Atlanta sportscaster Al Ciraldo. But perhaps the most revealing comment of them all came from Rep. Bobby Hill, a legislator from Savannah who happens to be black: "If a Georgia peanut farmer can be elected President—maybe I can, too."

This was the theme of the evening, even for Busbee, once he had pushed and pried his way through the mass of handshakes. His was a simple

*It took flying wedge of state patrolmen to get Gov. **George Busbee to stage**.*

Walter Mondale was 24 hours away from taking oath when he greeted guests at reception.

"Welcome!" but State Democratic Chairman Marge Thurman summed up the attitude of every Democrat in town when she said she was happy to be there. "I haven't been invited, you see, for the past eight years," she said to knowing laughter.

    Like restaurants all over Washington, the dining room at the Sheraton-Park was serving until it finally had to lock the doors if it expected to be cleaned up in time to serve breakfast the following morning. Thursday was to be a day for Georgians to remember, but Wednesday night they were acting like they wanted that to be a night to remember. The lobby of the Sheraton saw a steady stream of well-heeled visitors parading through until the wee hours.

    Jimmy Carter? He was in his bed at the Blair House as soon as he could excuse himself from the glad-handers at the Kennedy Center. He was one Georgian who was confident he would have four years to enjoy the sights and sounds of the town that had been making history for 200 years.

    Another chapter would be written on Thursday.

The Impossible Dream Comes True

"I pray Heaven to bestow the best of blessings on this house and all that hereafter inhabit it. May none but wise and honest men ever rule under this roof."—John Adams.

A new spirit was mixing in with the winter cold that blanketed that January morning. At high noon on January 20, the Constitution dictates, a new President should be given the oath. The Constitution says nothing about the weather, but somewhere it surely must have been written that this day shall be beyond comfort. This January 20 in 1977 was wintertime cold, yet it was warmed by a sun that was cooperating with the visitors from Georgia who invaded the capital city expecting the worst that a Washington winter could offer. All of this blended to make this a day of expectation and celebration.

Nowhere were rows of hecklers waiting for a glimpse at the newly proclaimed President. Nowhere were there signs ridiculing the new Chief Executive and sometimes committing blasphemy against the nation he led. This was an Inauguration Day beginning in prayer. Nearly 10,000 were huddled together in the early-morning cold at the Lincoln Monument to offer prayers for Jimmy Carter. The Carter and Mondale families joined together for services of their own at the First Baptist Church of Washington. It was a spirit that was to pervade throughout the day.

You could feel it at the Lincoln Memorial when a felt-hatted Dr. Martin Luther King, Sr.—standing on the spot where his late son 14 years before had proclaimed he had "been to the mountain tops" and now "I have a dream"—talked of his son's preoccupation with feeding God's sheep.

"The sheep must be fed, that's what it's all about...that the least of these never be forgotten, and that's why the President-elect is here, because he believes in helping the downtrodden. God grant that our President will always remember the least of these, for there always will be more of the least of these than the rest," extolled the white-haired old man, affectionately known as "Daddy King."

A 400-voice choir reverently echoed "Amazing Grace" across the quiet morning. ("How sweet the sound, that saved a wretch like me.") Mrs. Ruth Carter Stapleton, Jimmy's preacher-sister, read from the Old Testament, choosing a passage where the young King Solomon was asking for God's wisdom before he began his rule. The Reverend Bruce Edwards, then the pastor of Carter's church back in Plains, closed the service by reading a "prayer for the President." "Bless, oh, Lord, Jimmy Carter, who by the people's choice is now our leader," it began.

Soon after Edwards' prayer had been offered, the Carters—blocks away at the Blair House—left for a 45-minute private prayer service at the First Baptist Church of Washington. The church's pastor, Dr. Charles Trentham; an old friend of Carter's, the Reverend Nelson Price of Marietta, Georgia; and Vice President Walter Mondale's father-in-law, the Reverend John Maxwell Adams, participated in the services, which sent up additional prayers for the new leadership which in a few hours would take control of America's future.

The Reverend Price, who pastors the Roswell Street Baptist Church in Marietta, had known Carter for three and one-half years. The two of them were speaking to a Jaycee convention in Marietta, and afterward the minister was invited to the Georgia governor's mansion. "I've been thinking of running for President," Carter told him. "Dear Brother, you'd better get prepared because the Lord may have a hand on your life," the minister admonished. They then got down on their knees and prayed. Now standing in the pulpit of the old stone church only blocks away from the White House, Price was fulfilling his pledge to continue to pray for his friend.

"Let the spirit of heaven guide the new spirit of Washington to a new commitment to personal purity, prolific prayer, and proper principles," Price told the congregation, which included members of the Carter and Mondale families and Carter's staff and Cabinet. He also quoted President John Adams, using a prayer which is inscribed above the White House mantel. "I pray heaven to bestow the best of blessings on this house and all that hereafter inhabit it. May none but wise and honest men ever rule under this roof." Paraphrasing Thomas Jefferson, Price said, "Our generation needs persons with hearts like unto that of James Monroe, who was so honest that if you turned his soul inside out, there would not be a spot on it."

Not long after the simple services, Jimmy and Rosalynn left the Blair House again, this time to join the Gerald Fords and Nelson Rockefellers for coffee at the White House. The traditional inaugural day was beginning. They exchanged words of advice, then Gerald Ford—still President—and Jim-

Flags were proudly waving as people arrived for the inauguration.

my Carter—soon to become President—got in a White House limousine for the up-hill ride toward the Capitol.

Long before the Fords and Carters started their trip toward the Hill, the icy Capitol grounds were filling with people, some arriving by dawn. Early that morning an honor guard of soldiers snapped to "parade rest" on the outer boundaries of the grounds, forming a cordon which was remindful that the man who would soon take the historic oath would be our Commander-in-Chief. Souvenir hawkers already were open for business, offering "Jimmy items" of all shapes and sizes. A smiling group of young people were giving out souvenir leaflets that bore pictures of Carter and Walter Mondale along with brief biographies of the running mates. At closer inspection the leaflets turned out to be religious tracts, indicating Bible verses that would be appropriate for that day.

Police whistled pedestrians toward the faraway corner of the grounds, where other officers, taking a quick glance at the tickets, would direct guests toward the correct gate. Most of the entrances were a human wall. One of the gates turned the waiting crowd into an overstuffed sandwich, pushing people aside so an ambulance could exit. Everyone had to have a ticket. Everyone had to wait his turn. Those who sought shortcuts were sent back to the line.

Already in place in the shadow of the Capitol were the familiar faces of government...the Muskies, Bayhs, Udalls, Jacksons, men who had dreamed of this being their day. Members of the House were to the left of the podium, Senators to the right. Many of them peered through the crowd, looking for old friends' faces or hoping to catch the eye of a friendly photographer who might record their presence for the folks back home. Other celebrities were to be seen, some pausing to sign autographs, others feigning a touch of deafness. But mainly there were new faces, faces that had never before been on the inside, faces that had always watched these ceremonies in the familiar surroundings of their living room.

They were there because they honestly felt they knew Jimmy Carter. They may have known him from the night he spoke at the Brotherhood Dinner at their hometown Baptist Church, the night they shared a table and a plate of buttered biscuits with him. They may have known him from that Sunday afternoon they had stood in line to tour the governor's mansion in Atlanta, the day they had shaken his hand and talked to Rosalynn about how Amy liked her new school. They may have known him only from the six o'clock news. They may have followed this man Carter over the dirt roads in backwoods Georgia, trying to get him elected governor. Later they may have braved the icy driveways of New Hampshire homes knocking on doors, asking the people to vote for their friend Jimmy.

Whatever the relationship, most of these people felt a kinship to this unlikely President. There was a feeling that he could easily be their neighbor, the kind of guy who'd lend you his hedge clippers, pick up your mail while you sneaked away for a quick vacation, feed the dog while you're away for the weekend, talk to you over the backyard fence. As the clock inched toward noon, these new faces who were now on the inside were thinking private thoughts. The occasion had the festive air of a football Saturday on a random campus. Yet, inside the minds of the Georgians, it was a solemn—almost reverent—affair. The combined choir of the Atlanta University Center was singing "The Impossible Dream." For Jimmy Carter's neighbors, the Impossible Dream was about to become reality.

  The hour was at hand, and out-loud whispering began through the crowd. "There's Mrs. Ford," someone said. "Oh, doesn't Rosalynn look pretty?" another woman exclaimed, her breath quickly turning into steam. As the Marine Band played "Ruffles and Flourishes," President Gerald Ford—soon to be just plain Jerry—arrived with a smiling Vice President Nelson Rockefeller. In a few moments their successors were on the podium, too.

Ford and Rockefeller hear cheers for one final time.

Chief Justice Warren Burger gives Jimmy Carter the familiar oath.

With Carter and Mondale in place, Bishop William Cannon of the United Methodist Church of Georgia gave the invocation.

"Save us a nation from the arrogant futility of trying to play God," the bishop prayed. He also asked that God give the new President, "like Solomon an understanding heart to govern our people rightly." As he finished his prayer, the white marine conductor stood at frozen attention, and the black Atlanta University choirmaster waited for his cue. It was a brief moment of symbolism on a day filled with symbolic moments. They were to join together in presenting the "Battle Hymn of the Republic." It was a moving moment as this predominantly black choir from Georgia sang this Northern fight song. The South was rejoining the Union. The oath to Vice President Mondale was administered by Speaker Tip O'Neill. And at 12:02—with the muffled sound of cannons firing in the background—the reunion of North and South became more than symbolic.

A Georgia farm boy was becoming President.

"I, Jimmy Carter, do solemnly swear that I will faithfully execute the

Office of President of the United States, and will to the best of my ability, preserve, protect, and defend the Constitution of the United States. So help me God."

Forty-one simple words. Familiar words. Words that a person of the nation's choosing repeats every four years, on this day, at this place. The scene has been repeated many times. But to many of the shivering people straining their eyes to see from the snowy, packed Capitol grounds, all of this ceremony took on new meaning. The feelings they felt were difficult to express in everyday words. The shivers had played octaves on their spine, but they weren't shivers from the frosty day. They came from somewhere inside.

"I finally believed it. I almost didn't take it seriously until he started the oath," said Doug Hall of Dublin, Georgia, his face pink from the brisk wind. Others from back home agreed. "It was sorta like dreaming something and then having the dream come true," explained Bobby Rowan of tiny Enigma, Georgia. "I wanted to cry," said Sanford Bishop of Columbus. Don Thompson of Macon said, "Thank God, it's over so that we can get the bad years behind us and get a new start." John Gunn of Pitts was a man of few words: "The South has risen again."

To this writer's wife Peggy, far away in what was called the "Preferred Standing Area," all that was happening on the steps of the Capitol was in miniature. She was huddled between the Carl Ungers (Billy Carter's token Polack) and others from prideful Plains who were straining to see the ceremony and shuffling their feet to ward off the cold. Hours later she was to read me her thoughts:

"...Why am I here and not in front of the TV where I could at least see and be warm? I thought....But as the first notes of the 'Battle Hymn of the Republic' were played, I felt my shoulders straighten and my head rise. I was really there in front of the Capitol, and two Presidents were there in front of me. History was being made....My eyes filled with tears. I no longer felt the cold. I didn't care whether I could see or had special passes to anything. I was not a nobody. I knew why I was there," Peggy Hyatt wrote in scribbled longhand. She was putting into words what those others who stood so far away were feeling. When the oath was repeated, they knew why they had come.

Shaking hands with Chief Justice Warren Burger, who had given him the oath; kissing a smiling Rosalynn; and shaking hands with Gerald Ford, President Jimmy Carter went to the microphone for his first address to the American people and to the world. His speech was to continue the spiritual attitudes of the morning, but before he moved fully into his 14 minutes of carefully prepared words, he paused to give thanks to Gerald Ford, the man who had stepped into the breach of Watergate.

"For myself and for our nation, I want to thank my predecessor for all

The old and the new: President Ford greets President Carter.

he has done to heal our land," he began. As his words still echoed, an obviously moved Ford accepted the applause, and a nervous Amy Carter moved down from her seat next to her grandmother to sit by her mother.

"In this outward and physical ceremony, we attest once again to the inner and spiritual strength of our nation. As my high school teacher, Miss Julia Coleman, used to say: 'We must adjust to changing times and still hold to unchanging principles,'" he continued.

"Here before me is the Bible used in the inauguration of our first President in 1789, and I have just taken the oath of office on the Bible my mother gave me just a few years ago, opened to a timeless admonition from the ancient prophet Micah: 'He hath showed thee, O man, what is good; and what doth the Lord require of thee, but to do justly, and to love mercy, and to walk humbly with thy God.'"

Carter's New Day was beginning with Old Testament instruction. Like the hymn-singing morning, the afternoon was taking on the simple Sunday-morning feeling of that Old Time Religion. This gave a certain style and tone to the day. Not that religion is exclusively Southern, but its way-down-deep-inside fervor for things that are holy is something that sets the South apart as a region. And, as a product of this South, it is also something that sets apart Jimmy Carter. As Southern poet James Dickey puts it, the difference between Southern religion and religion in other parts of the country is that Southern religion is "believed." On Inauguration Day, this sermon was again being preached. They believed.

Carter's text was not designed to provide a blueprint for a "New Frontier" or to outline a "Great Society." Rather, his words were extolling Americans to return again to old ideals.

"This inauguration ceremony marks a new beginning, a new dedication

Amy Carter has her hand shaken by a President.

within our government, and a new spirit among us all. A President may sense and proclaim that new spirit, but only a people can provide it. Two centuries ago our nation's birth was a milestone in the long quest for freedom, but the bold and brilliant dream which excited the founders of this nation still awaits its consummation. I have no new dream to set forth today, but rather urge a fresh faith in the old dream....

"You have given me a great responsibility—to stay close to you, to be worthy of you, and to exemplify what you are. Let us create together a new national spirit of unity and trust. Your strength can compensate for my weakness, and your wisdom can help to minimize my mistakes. Let us learn together and laugh together and work together and pray together, confident that in the end we will triumph together in the right. The American dream endures. We must once again have full faith in our country—and in one another. I believe America can be better. We can be even stronger than before," Carter said, in the rhetoric and style that had become so familiar in

Well-wishers gather around the new First Family after ceremony.

Betty Ford kisses Nelson Rockefeller good-bye on steps of Capitol.

just two short years.

He concluded with a list of pledges—a search for humane justice, a tearing down of racial and regional barriers, work for those able to perform, a strengthening of the family, a respect for the law and equal treatment under it, a government Americans can be proud of once again, and, finally, a lasting peace based not on weapons of war but on policies that reflect our most precious values.

"These," he said in closing, "are not just my goals, and they will not be my accomplishments, but the affirmation of our nation's continuing moral strength and our belief in an undiminished, ever-expanding American dream."

Following the closing prayer, his words duly recorded in the history books, Jimmy Carter began accepting handshakes from his family, old and new friends, and from those who had made up our government in the past and those who would be a part of it in the future. The white-haired Miss Lillian nearly stole the show on the crowded stand because everyone seemed to be interested in greeting the President's lively mother. Happy Rockefeller sought her out when the outgoing Vice President's wife first arrived. When the wind seemed to be picking up steam, Mrs. Rockefeller leaned over from her nearby seat, turned up Miss Lillian's coat collar, and patted her gently on her cheek. Many of the faces were recognizable. Many were not. The haunting thought was that one of those unknown faces might one day be the man of the hour just as Jimmy Carter—a nameless face in the crowd at Richard Nixon's inauguration four years before—was that January day.

As the new President left the ceremonial area and walked toward the

Capitol, a navy officer fell in step not far behind him. The erect officer was carrying the so-called "football," a black bag containing secret codes which—should Carter be forced to use them—might trigger the nation's military machinery. The navy aide had accepted the bag from the marines who had carried it for Ford. America's power had been officially passed on in this unseen ceremony.

While the flags were flying and the bands were playing in Washington, it was business as usual at Hugh Carter's Antique Store in Plains. Oh, Hugh wasn't there—he was seeing his cousin take the presidential oath and congratulating his son on his job as White House administrator—but 89-year-old Alton Carter was there. "I'm too old to get in those crowds," Jimmy's uncle said. "I'll visit him later, when it's quieter." Alton Carter stood ramrod straight in front of a TV set watching the ceremony. In the rear of the dusty store, a cavernous mixture of antiques, souvenirs, and cobwebs, about a dozen tourists paid no attention to the solemn ceremony being televised. They were hunting keepsakes.

One tourist, who had found himself a large brass bucket, a bag of peanuts, and a Jimmy Carter banner, thrust out a $50 bill and wondered aloud where he should pay for his treasures. "Man, they're inaugurating the President of the United States. Ain't nobody going to give you any change right now," a local man answered. The tourist, paying no mind to the advice,

Meanwhile, back in Plains, Uncle Alton Carter was watching on antique-store TV.

picked up three Carter postcards and moved on to a collection of buttons, gilt peanuts on chains, and goober tie tacks.

Watching the set, Alton Carter was at rapt attention. He smiled only twice—once when someone said his son Hugh had gotten a haircut and once when the very last syllable of the oath of office was said and their boy Jimmy was at last the President. The elder Carter grinned broadly, nodded to his wife, clapped his hands together, then returned his attention to what was being broadcast. Meanwhile, tourists kept on shopping.

In Washington, some were buying souvenirs, too, from the barking salesmen who walked the sidewalks along Pennsylvania Avenue. People were getting into position for the parade which was due to begin within an hour after the oath was history. At Carter's request, there were fewer official grandstands this day. There was ample space along the sidewalks for this parade, and people came early, hopeful for a glimpse of the 15,000 marching people, 54 bands, 31 floats, 17 mounted units, and—in the spirit of this day—even a helium-filled peanut to be carried by members of the "Peanut Brigade," that proud band of Georgians that had campaigned coast-to-coast for their old friend. The parade lineup was no different from past ones, but the results of this breezy, sunny day were to be quite different.

Once the signal was given to Grand Master Hubert Humphrey—the nattily dressed former presidential hopeful from Minnesota—that the time had come to begin the parade, it would not be long before the crowd along Pennsylvania Avenue and those watching around the world would see where the difference lay. The difference was Jimmy Carter.

"He's out of his car!" people were screaming. Television commentators could say it no better, for when Jimmy and Rosalynn left the warm and safe confines of their presidential limousine, everyone sat up and took notice. "Only a Southerner would do that," one fellow drawled, giving away his own background. It was a gentle touch that set a far different melody to this inauguration, coming only four years after armed military guards had lined the parade route while Richard Nixon rode the one and one-half miles from the Capitol to the White House reviewing stand. Even the uniforms could not keep the Nixons from being pelted with fruit near the Riggs National Bank, in sight of the White House.

The bareheaded Carter hand-in-hand with a smiling Rosalynn walking the broad and crowded avenue, waving and speaking to many of the 250,000 parade-watchers who climbed trees, shinnied up poles, and put their children on their shoulders for a glimpse of the strolling Carters signalled a new attitude, a new openness. Soon their sons were out of their cars joining Jimmy and Rosalynn. Jack Carter hoisted his bundled-up 17-month-old son Jason to his shoulder, where he stayed for most of the route. Nine-year-old Amy soon got into the act, skipping and hopping along the center-line, as relaxed as if she were taking a quiet walk to school. The only mishap of the 40-minute stroll came when brother Chip had to tie Amy's dangling shoelaces for her. Everyone waited until First Moppet Amy pronounced herself ready to resume. They were in no hurry, for the Carters seemed to be enjoying themselves as much as the delighted citizens who cheered and clapped when the First Family passed.

The following day a *Washington Post* editorial was to ask: "He walked? You're kidding. What, with his wife and family and all? The whole way? Great heavens, it must be all of two miles." And walk it he did. As he entered the White House that evening for the first time, the still-smiling President was to reveal that he had informed the Secret Service of his plans three weeks before—to their disdain, it would appear, although agents were to explain later that preparing for his walk was no different than protecting a President riding in an open car. All they asked was that the walk not be publicized. "They thought it would be all right, but if it got a lot of publicity it might not be so good," Carter said.

His unprecedented walk left a nation speechless. It epitomized his pledge of being a "people's President" and the call for his being a "people's inauguration." By coming out from behind the invisible wall that had been built between the presidency and the public, Jimmy Carter was again saying to all that he was "of the people." Others read more into his unannounced stroll. "They held hands all the way. Seeing them out there together, holding on to each other like they did will do so much for the institution of marriage," Charles Jones of Macon said. An emotional visitor from Michigan remarked, "Seeing him right out there where I could almost touch him made the trip worthwhile. I'll never forget it." Amy and Jason were noticed by many. "That should show the world that in America, we're still a nation of families," an Alabama woman said between the slits in her ski mask.

While the Carters were walking, Gerald and Betty Ford were flying to California, where the outgoing Chief Executive played in the Bing Crosby Golf Tournament the following day, teaming up with Arnold Palmer. The Fords, who had already packed and told their staffs good-bye, left the White House in a helicopter which took a sentimental turn over Capitol Hill before taking them to a waiting jet—now stripped of the Presidential Seal—at Andrews Air Force Base. January 20th belonged to Jimmy Carter. Overnight, after three decades in Washington as a public servant, Gerald Ford was suddenly a private citizen.

Behind the prominent foot soldiers, it was a predictable parade. Following the tempo of the Carters, whose walk set back the schedule hardly at all, the long line of marchers moved at a fast beat. Perhaps it was the nearly numb hands of the shivering drummers that put down the pace, but whatever it was, this was a parade without those unexplained moments when the marchers turn into a human accordion because of a roadblock. In contrast to the past, the military took a low profile. The last of the army horses has been put out to pasture, so there was no cavalry to lead the way, nor were there any tanks or cannons. Instead, high school bands from towns and villages across America were playing like—well—like every high school band you've ever heard. The first group of high school musicians to pass the reviewing stand was the blue-and-white-clad marchers from Americus, there at the invitation of their neighbor and fan, Jimmy Carter. This band had played for him at victory parties back in Plains, often tuning up in the wee hours. They had come by bus, slowed down by snow—not snow above the Mason-Dixon Line but snow 75 miles from Americus in Macon. When they broke into "Happy Days Are Here Again," Jimmy Carter's face showed his happiness. Near the end of the long trail of marchers came the "Peanut Brigade." They stopped in front of the man who once was their favorite candidate but who that day had become their favorite President. "Hi, Jimmy!" they yelled to him. By the time the end of the lineup came, winter had taken over from the now-departing sun. Appropriately, the final band was the Susitna Valley High School Marching Band. The cold didn't bother them. Why should it? When you've come South to Washington from Alaska, a January day feels like midsummer.

Inside the White House, work was moving as briskly as the marchers. As soon as the Fords departed, Mrs. Clarence Dodson moved in, directing other members of Georgia garden clubs who were to decorate the reception areas for the parties scheduled for Friday and Saturday. Mrs. Dodson, who lives only two blocks away from the Carters in Plains, not only had to coordinate the duties of the 14 other women who were to decorate but also had to worry about whether the four planeloads of flowers arrived intact. It was the first time non-professionals had been given this assignment, and the Georgia women were there at the invitation of one of their own—Rosalynn Carter. The new First Lady was a charter member of the Plains Garden Club.

Included among the decorators was Mrs. Virginia Callaway of Hamilton, who proudly took charge of the Red Room, wearing an apron that said "Over 40 But Feeling Foxy." Her son, Howard "Bo" Callaway, is a long-time competitor of Jimmy Carter, and in the early days of the campaign he was Gerald Ford's campaign director. Who did she vote for? Coyly she said, "I voted for both." After two hours of work, White House Curator Clemont Conger told them, "In 20 years here, I've never seen it better decorated."

When the chilled Carters came into the White House from the cold, there was time for hellos only briefly before most of the clan went exploring. Mrs. Lillian Carter and Mrs. Allie Smith, who were going to stay there that night, flipped a coin over which bedroom each would have. Miss Lillian won and chose the Queen's Room, Mrs. Smith taking the Lincoln Room.

("The bed slept good," Mrs. Smith was to say. "But in a place like this, they should be good.") It was a time of picture posing, private tours, things any tourist turned loose in the White House might do. The new President, in a private moment, got his first look at the Oval Office. Some of his aides noted that "his office as governor was larger," but the room obviously pleased Carter despite their assessment. The next few hours were family time. The Carters were together, right where they thought they would be from the beginning. More than a year before that day, Carter had told a touring reporter in Plains that he and Rosalynn had lived in a lot of places since they had married. "I only intend to move to one other place," Carter had smiled. He had now made that move.

Within a few hours those quiet moments would be forgotten. All over Washington, people were pressing their finery, shining their shoes, and getting every hair in place. Carter had dictated that the celebrations were to be "parties" and not "balls," but the preparations were the same. Georgians had brought along rented formal wear, and some wives had sat humped over sewing machines for last-minute hemmings right up to the hour of departure for Washington. "It was worth the whole trip to see Bud Duvall in his yellow tux," said Murray Smith of Plains, the First Lady's younger brother. Duvall is one of Billy Carter's Service Station Mafia, and like others who had journeyed there from Plains, old Bud had left behind his faded denims.

Six parties were to be held at various sites on Inauguration Night but demand was great, and a seventh was added at the stately Pension Building. The Jimmy Carters were to visit each before they returned for their first night at the White House. Entertainment was as varied as the Democratic Party itself. There were the electric country of the Marshall Tucker Band and the mellow melodies of Guy Lombardo. There were the soulful beat of Aretha Franklin and the dignified sound of Peter Duchin. There were the breezy up-and-away beat of The Fifth Dimension and the foot-stomping, beer-guzzling, 10-gallon sound of burly Charlie Daniels. It was to be a night when younger people would remark, "That couldn't be Guy Lombardo. He's dead." And a member of the older generation would agree with those who said, "Charlie Daniels' Band looks like a bunch of mangy cattle rustlers."

What the entertainers played mattered little because the elbow-to-ribs crowds at each of the seven sites were so intense that dancing anything other than the "bump" was impossible. The thickest mass of humanity was at the National Guard Armory, where the audience was primarily Georgian or members of the Carter staff. Here the coat-check line took an hour's wait and caused many to stand in line for their coats for two hours after the music had stopped and the floor had been turned into a mess of cracked plastic glasses and used flashbulbs. The $25-a-person price kept few away. Some were willing to swap two for one, offering a pair of tickets to one of

Carters like Jimmy's son Jeff were in demand at inaugural parties.

the other parties so they could get into the Armory, a sprawling barn of a place that was large enough to host the Beatles' first American invasion concert 12 years ago. But even John, Paul, George, and Ringo could have lost themselves in the inaugural crowd.

In the balcony people spotted members of the Carter Clan. Soon picture-takers were snapping pictures of the Carters taking pictures of them. Miss Lillian was there, and even boisterous Billy, wearing a brand-new tuxedo and escorting his smiling wife Sybil, now recovered from a virus that sadly had kept her away from the swearing-in. Jeff Carter was circulating through the crowd on the ballroom floor. "I didn't bring my camera tonight. I'm here to party," he said.

Soon the crowd became even worse as people began to anticipate the arrival of Vice President Walter Mondale. A human wall was formed down the center aisle, further bottle-necking anyone who might have wanted to circulate through the ballroom. But soon those who had formed the barrier were rewarded. With the Royal Canadians playing a marathon version of "Stars and Stripes Forever," the Mondales arrived, shaking hands and greeting those along the aisle.

When he finally made his way through the mass of tourists and press photographers, the Vice President took the microphone and said, "I'll tell you one thing—Washington is now Georgia Country." Pretty safe words, guaranteed to draw a cheer from that crowd. "I can't remember a day when I saw as many happy faces," Mondale said. And there were plenty of them smiling back at him from the Armory guests. He even took time to poke some fun at himself. "One man sent President Carter a letter the other day and said, 'If I had known that the first thing you'd do is send Mondale out of the country, I'd have voted for you,'" he joked, referring to the country-hopping diplomatic mission on which Carter had sent him. With Lombardo waving the baton to "Baby Face," Walter and Joan Mondale took a turn around the dance floor, to the delight of the picture-takers. But the dancers the crowd was waiting for still were to arrive.

The Carters were clearly the ones all came to see, although many Washington regulars, used to a society that never starts on time, missed seeing them. Love was sweeping Washington, and the love was for Jimmy and Rosalynn. Each of their party stops was almost a Xerox copy of the other. They danced to "Moon River" at the Sheraton-Park and the Mayflower, to "Moonlight Serenade" at the Shoreham, and to "Georgia on My Mind" at the Visitor's Center. Crowds were too thick for them to give it a twirl at either the Hilton or the Pension Building. Their last stop was to be with their old friends who were patiently watching the clock at the Armory. The President was giving in to his wife's stern plea and wearing a tuxedo. The First Lady, of course, was wearing that now-famous frock she had worn to her husband's gubernatorial inauguration seven years before. Amy? She was wearing a long dress and carrying along a book in case things got too boring.

It was past midnight when the Carters arrived at the Armory. Guy Lombardo was back on the bandstand, replacing Marshall Tucker. The crowd had its cameras poised, waiting. Secret Service agents were in place. The TV lights were warmed up. Many were waiting for the familiar sound of "Hail to the Chief" to herald the arrival of the President. Instead they heard the folk-rock beat of "Why Not the Best?" a Carter campaign song. It was another not-so-subtle hint that this was going to be a different kind of presidency. While Lombardo directed his orchestra, the Carters hugged and smiled their way toward the stage.

"Is anybody here from Georgia?" Carter wanted to know. The answer was predictable. "Right on," he said and "Thanks for getting me here." Appropriate words, for these were the people who had been beside him since the beginning...the beginning of his presidential quest, his gubernatorial

"Is anybody here from Georgia?" Carter asked partyers at Armory.

"We love all of you," Rosalynn Carter told friends at Armory party.

The Carters could have danced all night—and almost did.

drive, even his run for the Georgia senate. He was talking to those he knew best and those who felt they knew him best.

"This has been the greatest day in the life of the Carter family," he said in an understatement. Then he began to turn back the clock. "When I was inaugurated governor, I went to four balls. I had a date with the same woman, and she wore the same dress. How many like Rosalynn's old dress?" There was a roar of approval, then he spoke to those who would soon be returning to Georgia. "We'll stay here and take care of things. You're partners of mine. Together we'll reach greatness."

Checking with the waiting Lombardo, a legend with the baton, the President took his First Lady in his arms and they began to dance. "Red Roses for a Blue Lady" was the melody, but there were no blue ladies at the Armory that night, only smiles and tears, the kind of tears that come when happiness has crowded out the unhappy days and unhappy memories. They could have danced all night, but even Cinderella had to go home. And so did the Carters. To their new home on Pennsylvania Avenue.

Returning To Reality

The stiffly starched military aide was all spit and polish. "Tell the aide on your right your name, please," he would say on cue, working with the precision of a wound-up toy soldier that never seemed to run down. When he finished, the aide on the right would begin. "Your name, sir?" he would say.

As Murray Smith inched toward them, they began their act. Like the other 2,000 who had gone through the White House receiving line that day, Murray Smith followed orders. The final soldier turned to repeat the name.

"Murray...," but the aide never finished.

"Shoot, this is Rosalynn's brother," Jimmy Carter said, gripping his towering brother-in-law's hand firmly. He needed no prompting for Murray Smith, just as he hardly needed reminding who most of the folks were who had sampled the bland punch and store-bought cookies in the White House that Friday afternoon. You don't need an introduction to family, and many of the people who stood in the never-ending line that day were as much members of his family as anyone named Carter. These people had been there when he was smiling and when he was crying...when he had won and when he had lost...when he was known and when he was unknown...when he was just another face in the Democratic crowd and now, when he was President of the United States.

It was an eerie day. In one way they were saying hello, but in another they were saying good-bye. "Hello, we're glad you're here," but at the same time, "Good-bye," for at high noon the previous day Georgia had given up Jimmy Carter. He was no longer just a Georgian. Now he belonged to a nation. All this was reflected on the faces of many of those who filed through the White House that afternoon. When they looked at his face, they saw just plain Jimmy Carter. When they looked into his eyes, they saw the President.

These thoughts were going on inside many of their heads, but it was

Coretta Scott King had trouble getting into White House reception.

anything but a serious or morbid occasion. All of it took on the unthinkable mixture of stuffy protocol and front-porch friendliness. It was Amy Vanderbilt meeting Minnie Pearl. In the background was the tinkling cocktail-party piano bouncing off the historic old walls. Guarding every doorway was one of those by-the-number aides who offered formal but friendly assistance. The receiving line could have been composed of anyone, but this wasn't anyone. These weren't the type who came to offer a polite handshake and a crisp nod of the head. These were the people who had listened when Jimmy Carter told them he had a house picked out in Washington and that he wanted to move there. They listened, then they went to work to help him get that Pennsylvania Avenue house. Now that he was moved in, they wanted to share this moment with him. The line was emotion after emotion...kissing, hugging, crying.

For a day, love had taken over the White House.

Who were these people who had come all this way? They weren't just there to see the White House. Tourists buy tickets and see the public side of the President's home almost every day. They weren't just there to be seen, for many of the people who stood in that line are the kind who grow tired of the public spotlight, although they made up a minority. They weren't just there to collect autographs or gawk at the Beautiful People, for when Cher breezed into one of the reception rooms on the arm of husband Gregg Allman, no one seemed even to recognize her. These people were there that day for the same reason they had trudged through the New Hampshire snow just a year and two weeks before...because they cared about Jimmy Carter.

But who were they?

It must have been difficult for Sam Singer to talk to the *Washington Post* with his tongue so far into his cheek, but the Lumpkin, Georgia, peanut entrepreneur convinced one reporter that most of the folks who came were millionaires. "I'm a millionaire. That guy over there is a millionaire. They're all substantial people who've worked in the Peanut Brigade. They couldn't afford the trip otherwise," Singer said. What he said was partially correct. A lot of those who came were wealthy. But what about the Greensboro, Mississippi, couple who borrowed $500 to make the trip? What about the Howard Logans of Plains who got together enough money to bring their grandchildren? What about Capt. Lanny English of Plains who secured a special leave from the U.S. Air Force? What about young John and Sidney Gnann of Plains, who came to frolic through the White House living quarters with Amy while the grownups stood in line to speak to Amy's mother and father? No, these people were not all millionaires on a weekend lark, which Sam Singer knew before he began to put on the gullible reporter.

Singer himself is an interesting study. When he was born, Lillian Carter was the nurse. When Earl Carter decided to become serious about the peanut business in 1951, he bought his seeds from Singer's store in Lumpkin, 27 miles away from Plains. When Jimmy Carter ran for the Georgia Senate in 1962 against Homer Moore of Richland, Sam Singer was the incumbent's campaign manager. By the time the courts got through with that race and threw out the ballots cast by the dead folks in Georgetown, Carter ended up in the senate. Fifteen years later, Singer found himself accompanying his wife and mother to Manchester, New Hampshire, to campaign for Jimmy Carter. Ann Singer was there in the White House on Inauguration Day as one of the floral decorators. They stood in line to speak to the Carters, and afterwards Singer partially explained why he was there. "I'm on the board of Westville (a restored historic village in Lumpkin). After all Jimmy has done for Westville, I'd support him if he ran for Queen of England," he said. All who came had their reasons. This was his.

Who were these people?

Just regular folks. Sometime in the past, they had met Jimmy Carter or heard him speak. For reasons all their own, they had been impressed. It might have been two years before when he told audiences, "America deserves a government as good as its people." It might have been seven years before when he told Georgians, "The time has come to end discrimination." It might have been 10 years before when he had promised his faithful few followers that he would try again for governor in four more years. It might have been 15 years before when he emulated his late father and ran for that seat in the Georgia senate. They were druggists, tavern owners, ministers, realtors, farmers, grocers, standing in line with a governor, a lieutenant governor, a television star, and a rock music idol.

When they made their way through the line and spoke to Jimmy Carter, each brought his or her own personal message and reacted in ways as varied as the roads that had brought them there that afternoon.

"I said, 'Hi, Shug,' and Jimmy said, 'Hi, Beautiful,'" Sarah Turpin of Americus remarked, her eyes twinkling, and added with a quick laugh—"We both lied." Mrs. Merle Lefkoff, a political science professor from Atlanta, walked away from the line rubbing her cheek. "I've just been kissed by a President," Mrs. Lefkoff said, then repeated herself. "That doesn't happen every day." Twelve-year-old Lisa Moses of Albany wasn't sure what she said. "I was too nervous," she explained, something many of these old friends of Jimmy Carter admitted. "I called him Jimmy—is that proper?" C. L. Walters of Plains wondered after standing in line to see his former neighbor. Langdon Sheffield of Americus confessed to the same thing, explaining that "he's still Jimmy to me."

By the next day most who had attended the Carter housewarming were packing their memories in their suitcases and heading back to Georgia. For the first time in her history, Georgia had Washington on her mind. One of her sons was President. These other Georgians had been there to share in that moment. When a charter plane well-heeled with Georgia Democrats landed in Atlanta, there was a cheer. It sounded similar to a planeload of football fans coming home after seeing their team win a bowl game. That is just what Noll Van Cleave of Columbus, Georgia, called the experience. "It's obvious why we went," Van Cleave said. "If you were in college and your team went to the Sugar Bowl, you'd go, wouldn't you? When your neighbor is elected President, you go, too."

"See you again in four years," one confident woman told another at the luggage claim. But it wouldn't be the same in four years, even if they do meet again. These people from Georgia had shared in something they'd never experience again. John Pope of Americus felt this way when he walked into the Oval Office and was greeted by his friend Jimmy Carter. The emotion was overpowering, but Pope wondered if he would do it all again, thinking it might spoil the memories of 1976. Jimmy Carter is President, and Georgia will never be the same again. She's grown up through all of this. She has

Curator Clemont Conger welcomes Miss Lillian to the White House.

learned that she has no reason to feel left out and no reason to think she's at the bottom of anybody's list just because she's a Southern state. She can take pride in the fact that not only has she provided America its 39th President but that so many of her talented thinkers will be part of the administration that will lead the country into its third century.

Langdon Sheffield must have had these things on his mind as he struggled to get his bags into the lobby of the Sheraton-Park Hotel, minutes before a bus was due to take some of the Georgians to their plane.

"It's time," he said, "to return to reality."

If they ever can.

There's Even A Red Light

Town folk were bragging. Tourists were snapping. When Plains got its first traffic light, it was an occasion duly recorded. The light was to flash its red and green signal at the intersection where Bond Street crossed the railroad and bisected Church Street. There was even a box beneath the signal whose door would open automatically whenever a train approached, ordering cars that there were to be no turns. Plains had arrived. It already had a one-way street. Now it had a red light.

The signal gave its first stop-and-go orders only a day before Jimmy Carter was to make his first visit home since his inauguration. It had been only three weeks since he had thrown his suitbag over his shoulder, locked up his Woodland Avenue home, and headed for Washington. He had left home a neighbor. He was coming home a President. No one had figured the Carters would return so soon, but during that week the worst-kept secret around Sumter County was that the town's First Family was coming home. When the participants in his motorcade, with blue lights whirling, arrived on Friday evening and saw the light blink red, they may have thought someone had taken a wrong turn between there and Warner Robins, Georgia, where the President's massive "Doomsday" jet had landed. And the traffic light wasn't the only change in town.

There was talk about an amusement park being built on the outskirts of town. There was not one but two newspapers being published there. There was talk about a movie being filmed there with many of the town's leading citizens appearing in it, including 89-year-old Alton Carter and boisterous brother Billy Carter. Since his brother had left, Billy had hired himself an agent, and the First Brother was still a popular target for the tourists. His face now smiled on T-shirts extolling, "Billy Who 1984?" He was now appearing on many of the network talk shows, speaking in towns across the country, drinking beer at the Mardi Gras, riding with stock-car driver

Plains has arrived: traffic forced installation of a signal.

Richard Petty around the Daytona International Speedway oval, and being quoted in *Sports Illustrated*. He was due to open an art show in New Orleans, and his buddies joked about this appearance, saying that "the only art Billy appreciates is the girlie calendars on the station wall." But he postponed leaving on that trip long enough to visit with brother Jimmy, who early that Saturday morning took a stroll through town.

Around town were other changes. When Jimmy left for Washington, a lone van was hauling tourists to the sights and sounds of Plains. Now there were six vans—including two snakey trams that wound through the narrow streets—and even an old wagon, pulled by a pair of mules aptly named Fritz and Grits, although the city soon had them back in tne barn. There were new trinkets on sale in the busy shops and the promise of new souvenir shops to come in the form of zoning requests before the busy town council. There was a wax museum in the planning stage.

Some of the changes were not so obvious. A few years ago C. L. Walters decided to modernize the family grocery store. It was a proud moment when he was finished. "We bought all new metal shelves. I found room for the old counters in the storehouse out back. I never thought I'd need them again," he said. But he did. Today grocery items have been pushed to the rear of the Main Street store, making room for souvenirs up front. "It seemed to be appropriate to use the old counters," Walters explained. "Everyone is so

Trams take tourists on ride through the President's hometown.

caught up on nostalgia these days." Not everyone reacts the same way, however. Ernest Turner, who runs the dry goods store a few doors down the street from Walters, advertises that his store is just as it was in 1905. But that, of course, is a gimmick in itself, and tourists flock in there to see his counters piled high with bib overalls. Overnight, simple jars became treasures—if they were from Plains.

That's the way it was when Jimmy came home in February of 1977. Cars and campers with tags from around the country lined the street, looking for a spot to park. Assistant chief Kenneth Franks, a member of the town's newly expanded police force, was doing more than modeling his new blue uniform as he tried to keep traffic moving. More help was on the way, as soon as the recruit graduated from the police academy. "Hope he does well in traffic control," Franks smiled. Franks found that the 30-minute parking limits on Main Street were doing no good because tourists soon discovered that a parking ticket from Plains would be a souvenir not everyone could take home. It was the same with the town's phone book, which now was on

Crowds milled around outside during services at Plains Baptist Church.

Hands were extended to the church's most famous member.

sale at the souvenir counters, hopefully to keep people from snatching copies from the pay phones.

Those same tourists showed up at the Plains Baptist Church on Sunday morning, crowding against the ropes that were now permanent fixtures around the churchyard trees. The Carters noticed the waving crowd and after leaving the eleven o'clock services, they shook hands with many of them. Inside the church, other members stayed behind to install a new church rule that no one—newsperson or tourist—be allowed to bring a camera on the church property.

One week later—with the Carters back in Washington—a similar church conference engaged in a squabble with its minister, the Reverend Bruce Edwards, not in the beginning over Civil Rights, but over a debt. With a small number of members present, it appeared the minister would be fired, but finally they allowed him to resign his two-year-old pastorate. Three months earlier, the membership had voted 120 to 66 to allow blacks in its fellowship and 107 to 84 to retain Edwards. But in February 1977, the Carters had moved their membership to the First Baptist Church in Washington, and the old bitter feelings again erupted.

The Reverend Edwards was finally admitting publicly what he had expressed months before privately: "Our ministry here is over." So it was. "There was a lot of hostility and bitter feelings. I felt by resigning that maybe I could help the church heal its wounds, and all this bickering back and forth would stop," he said. State Sen. Hugh Carter, the President's cousin, spoke in Edwards' behalf. He was to call it a "dark day" in the church's history.

All of this makes you wonder what's ahead for this town that bore a President. Each time you go there you think things have peaked, that it couldn't get worse. But it usually does. There are new signs of change, and not always progressive change. There are new signs that an inborn greed is surfacing, that there's a new hand reaching out—palm up—looking for a dollar. The smiles on the faces don't seem to come as easily as they once did. As you see the tourists filing in for a first-hand look at the town, you only wish they could have seen it the way it once was.

Take the little shop that is now selling old beer cans salvaged from Billy's service station...Who knows, maybe Billy himself popped its top. The going rate is a quarter a can, and you choose your brand. One naive customer asked the cashier about a Budweiser can she had selected, wondering if Billy ever drank that brand. "Yeah, he'll drink a Bud," the guy said, realizing that this souvenir-seeking tourist must have slept through those TV news reports showing the First Brother with a death grip on a can of Pabst Blue Ribbon. This is living proof that trash makes cash around Plains.

Between 2,000 and 5,000 tourists a day file through the tiny town,

Traffic backed up for miles during President's visit back home.

fighting for a parking place, hoping to run into Miss Lillian on the street, or planning to hoist a cold one with Billy in the back room of the station. Neither is likely to happen. Miss Lillian makes few public outings close to home. A sign on her front lawn says "No Admittance," although many tourists pay no attention to it and knock on her door anyway. She's most upset about the controversy at her church but also complains about the commercial invasion of her once-quiet home. "I don't think Jimmy intended for it to be this way," she says. But it is.

Billy is disgruntled, too, so much so that he packed up his family and moved them to Draineville, a community so small that it isn't on any maps, 19 miles away from the maddening crowds of Plains. "We've had as many as 30 tour buses a day pull up in the driveway," Sybil Carter explained. "They turn around, and a lot of the tourists get out and come to the door, knocking and wanting Billy to come out and pose for pictures or sign autographs." But it is not the imposition on them that sent Billy and Sybil packing. They were concerned mainly for their children. Mandy, their youngest daughter, is only 10, and Earl is still in diapers. The daily invasion of visitors hardly allows their parents to rest peacefully. "Nothing has happened to them yet, but you never know these days," a worried Billy explained.

To escape the visitors in the summer of '77 and to wait for their new home to be ready, Billy and Sybil planned to find themselves a quiet Florida hideaway, although he threw out the first ball for the Oakland Athletics' home opener and was due to make numerous other personal appearances around the country. His favorite speech topic? "What a President Can Do to His Home Town."

However, neither Billy nor the other folks in Plains have completely given up. The Plains Civic Improvement, Incorporated, is said to be a brain child of the President himself. Billy serves as its president, but Mrs. Maxine Reese is the on-the-job foreman. Money from souvenir sales at the old depot goes into the fund, and donations are forthcoming from other sources. Their goal is to put as much money as possible into maintaining the town. "We're not sure yet what we'll do," Mrs. Reese says, but their ultimate plan is to create a Carter Library that would house the President's private papers and other historic material. For now, their money is tied up in souvenirs and other stock for the shop.

On the surface the town has turned into a Tourist Trap. Items that would never sell on a discount-store shelf in any other town sell easily here. All they need is a Plains price tag. The town has come up with far more uses for the peanut than George Washington Carver ever dreamed of—even peanut butter ice cream. "Those Plains folks are tore up," believes Mayor Johnny Sheffield of neighboring Americus. "Their little town is gone. It's just pitiful, except for those folks who own the buildings along Main Street or a couple of hundred acres nearby." Where it will end, no one can be sure. But every time a frequent visitor thinks to himself that it couldn't get worse, it somehow does

This is not a plea for a return to the not-so-distant past when Main Street in Plains was unpaved and peanut bins sat peacefully alongside the railroad tracks. Nor is it implying that the town could have avoided everything that has happened to it. Much of this is a result of inborn American curiosity of the presidency. This is only to suggest that there was beauty to that former way of life, a tranquility that those of us who fight traffic, curse traffic lights, argue over parking places, and keep a too-fast pace would welcome. Plains had this tranquility—had it and lost it.

Langdon Sheffield was talking about it being "a time to return to reality." The question around there was not whether it was time for Plains to return to reality, but whether reality could ever return to Plains.

A QUICK GLANCE AT THE CARTERS OF PLAINS

James Earl Carter, Jr.

Born: October 1, 1924, in Plains, Georgia.

Parents: James Earl Carter, Sr., (1894-1953) and Bessie Lillian Gordy (1898—).

Uncle: Alton "Uncle Buddy" Carter (1889—) of Plains, brother of James Earl Carter, Sr., and father of Hugh Carter of Plains.

Sisters: Gloria Carter (Mrs. Walter) Spann of Plains; Ruth Carter (Mrs. Robert) Stapleton of Fayetteville, North Carolina.

Brother: William Alton (Billy) Carter of Plains.

Education: Attended Plains School, elementary through high school, graduating in 1941. Attended Georgia Southwestern College, 1941-1942. Attended Georgia Institute of Technology, 1942-1943. Attended United States Naval Academy, 1943-1946, graduating 59th in the Class of 1946.

Married: Rosalynn Smith of Plains, July 7, 1946, in Plains Methodist Church. Daughter of the late Edgar (1896-1940) and Allie Murray Smith (1905—).

Children: John William (Jack) Carter, born July 3, 1947. A graduate of Georgia Institute of Technology. Married Juliette Langford of Calhoun, Georgia, in 1971. Has one son, Jason. A lawyer and agri-businessman in Calhoun.

James Earl (Chip) Carter, III, born April 12, 1950. Attended Georgia State University and Georgia Southwestern College. Married Caron Griffin of Hawkinsville, Georgia, in 1973. One son, James Earl, IV. Lives with parents in Washington. Works for Democratic National Committee.

Donnel Jeffrey (Jeff) Carter, born August 18, 1952. Attended Georgia State University and will attend George Washington University. Married Annette Davis of Arlington, Georgia, in 1975.

Amy Lynn Carter, born October 19, 1967. Attends public school in Washington.

Military: United States Navy, 1946-1953. Specialized in nuclear submarines. Resigned upon death of father to take over family business in Plains.

Business: Owner of Carter Warehouse, a peanut warehouse in Plains.

Religion: Baptist. (A member of First Baptist Church of Washington. Previously he was a deacon and Sunday School teacher at Plains Baptist Church.)

Political: Member of Sumter County School Board and Sumter County Library Board.

Elected to Georgia State Senate in 1962. Elected by his colleagues as one of the outstanding members of his freshman class in the senate.

Ran for governor of Georgia in 1966. Finished third in Democratic Primary behind eventual winner Lester Maddox and former Gov. Ellis Arnall.

Elected governor of Georgia in 1970, defeating former Gov. Carl Sanders in Democratic runoff, then Republican Hal Suit in the general election. (Georgia law at that time prohibited a governor from succeeding himself.)

Announced as a candidate for the Democratic nomination for President in January 1975, just days after leaving office as governor of Georgia.

Nominated for President at the Democratic National Convention in New York in July 1976. He was chosen on the first ballot. The party selected Sen. Walter Mondale of Minnesota as its vice-presidential nominee.

Elected President of the United States on November 2, 1976, defeating Republican incumbent Gerald Ford of Michigan.

Inaugurated as the 39th President of the United States on January 20, 1977.